SURVIVING
MYSELF

HOW AN EATING DISORDER, A CAR CRASH AND A STROKE
TAUGHT ME TO LOVE MY LIFE, AND FINALLY LIVE IT

DINA PESTONJI

WITH ERIN McCANN

Tellwell Talent
www.tellwell.ca

ISBN
978-1-77370-840-9 (Hardcover)
978-1-77370-839-3 (Paperback)
978-1-77370-841-6 (eBook)

*To the three pieces of my heart - mummy, daddy and Yassy.
I am so grateful for your unwavering support, love and
always finding the "bright side" in any situation we face.*

*Erin McCann - Your patience and steadfast encouragement
in helping me to dig up memories I had suppressed and
share this story has changed my life for the better. Thank
you for helping me to understand the healing powers of
vulnerability and what love of myself really means.*

TABLE OF CONTENTS

PART ONE

HUNGRY

GRADE 10.
AGE 15.
WEIGHT: 107 LBS.

I LOCK THE BATHROOM DOOR, slowly and quietly turning the latch so as not to wake my parents. To my left I have an eight-inch steel chef's knife that I took from my mom's drawer of kitchen utensils. To my right I have a bright pink dollar store razor. Come hell or high water, one of them will kill me and set me free today.

There is so much noise in my head. Loud, vicious voices shouting at me constantly, calling me fat, telling me how pathetic and worthless I am. They tell me to eat, then not to eat. They call me ugly and make fun of my lumpy, acne covered face. I picture them as pointy-toothed devils, hissing at me and taunting me with their endless criticism and sinister laughter. I feel outnumbered and overpowered; there's no chance I can beat these awful bullies and why should I even try? They're right. All I really want is for them to be quiet. I crave silence. If I kill myself, my mind will be clear and I'll finally be at peace. The sound of nothingness is the sweetest dream imaginable.

When I get to heaven, I will be able to eat anything I want in total silence. No judgment, no voices telling me I'm a disgusting pig. My mouth waters as I imagine my first meal in heaven: crispy fried chicken and buttery garlic scones oozing with cheddar cheese, followed by warm fudgy brownies, topped with vanilla bean ice cream and smothered in rich, luxurious chocolate sauce. I will be able to eat everything I desire and never gain an ounce. I will be beautiful, like the supermodels I see on magazine covers and idolize so much. Once I cross over, the chubby Indian girl with acne I see in the mirror will magically transform into Cindy Crawford.

Over the past year, I have desperately wanted to die. I've fantasized about the various ways I can commit suicide. The thought of blood and gore sickens me but despite this, I long to have a gun so I can shoot myself in the head. A small discreet single-shot black pistol, three-inch barrel, and .25 caliber ammunition. All I need to do is point the gun at myself and pull the trigger. So simple! My life would be over in less than a millisecond. The gun scenario is my favourite.

There's just one problem—I don't have a gun. I don't know anyone with a gun, and I'm pretty sure no one will sell me a gun, being only 15 years old. I also have no idea where these "gun stores" are even located, and I know that in Canada the gun laws are very strict, so "death by handgun" is probably not in the cards for me.

Despite this wrinkle in my plan, I can't stop fantasizing about shooting myself. While watching the nightly news with dad last month, I heard about a shooting of a young innocent boy and wished it was me instead. Maybe if I put myself in a bad seedy neighborhood where violence and shootings are the norm, I'll get lucky!

There's also a bridge that I've heard about, called the "Bloor Viaduct." Apparently people jump off this bridge all the time. I have no idea where the Bloor Viaduct is, since I pretty much live my life within a few square miles of our North York home. My parents drive me a few blocks to my school every day and back again and that's about it. But perhaps I could find this bridge, jump and plunge to my death ...

For the bridge scenario, I have planned out the whole day: it will be perfect. First, I'll eat a huge burger on a toasted brioche bun with melted cheese, sautéed onions and bacon, the whole thing slathered with mayonnaise. The grease will drip from my lips onto my chin but I won't care. It's my last meal on earth! Who the heck cares if the sauce gets all over my face—it tastes divine. On the side, I'll have seasoned, double-coated crispy French fries AND onion rings with ketchup. For dessert, a huge slice of decadent creamy cheesecake with a thick graham cracker crust, topped with raspberry sauce. And the kicker? I'll drink a whole litre of Coca-Cola!

Then, I'll call a cab because a cab driver will know where the Bloor Viaduct is, of course, and they will drive me to the bridge. I think about standing on the ledge, my eyes closed as the wind whips at my face. I take a huge leap into the air and the wind caresses me as I plunge 131 feet into the Don River. I'll hit the icy waters below and die on impact. Worst-case scenario, I'll drown. Either way, in just a minute or two, I'll be in heaven.

I could also overdose on pills. I'm already secretly taking a mix of pills to help me lose weight, or suppress my appetite. The red oval-shaped ones are for weight loss. The bright blue pills you take with water 30 minutes before a meal and they help reduce your fat intake. I also use these long circular blue and yellow pills that magically keep me from getting hungry. And then there is a whitish pill that I think contains extra Ephedrine to help to keep me energized and lose even more weight. I've already ended up in the hospital once after taking my usual cocktail of pills. I fainted and had a very irregular heart rate. I do the math: if that amount of medication got me into the emergency room, I'm 99% certain that if I took ten times the amount, it would kill me. Probably ...

But I want a foolproof plan. I need to know, without a doubt, that if I do this, I will die.

I've heard about Dr. Jack Kevorkian, the American euthanasia activist. "Dr. Death" is my hero! I dream of being one of his patients. The thought of lying in a hospital bed with a specially mixed cocktail of drugs flowing from my IV into my arm, peacefully falling asleep forever ... perfection! This would actually be the best way to die, I think—peaceful and painless, with Dr. Kevorkian holding my hand as I gently pass on to the afterlife. Unfortunately, I know that I have to be terminally ill, brain dead, acutely disabled and in pain in order to get on Dr. Death's waiting list of patients, so that won't work either.

So instead, here I am. On the cold, tiled floor of my bathroom in my PJs, staring at this kitchen knife and this cheap razor. My only options. Which one will I use? Both instruments are one inch away from my face. I'm scared, but this has to be the day I go to heaven. I know that in heaven, I will fit in. I will never feel like an outcast or that I don't belong. My mind will be at peace. I will finally, finally, be happy.

1

1993.
GRADE 4.
AGE 10.

"GOOD MORNING, DINA! GUESS WHAT day it is? It's … Submarine Day!"

It's 7:02 a.m. and the day is off to a great start. Ken, one of the daycare staff, always tells me what I'm dying to know—what's on the menu for lunch that day. Is it Sweet and Sour Meatball Day? Or perhaps Fish Cake Day? My mind is always thinking of the tasty possibilities that await me at lunchtime.

Every day at 7 a.m., Dad drops us off at the Shaughnessy daycare where I spend mornings before the bell rings. The daycare centre is on the first floor of my school, Shaughnessy Public, along with the kindergarten and grade one students. The grade 2–6 classrooms are located on the second floor. I feel a little old for daycare at this point, but my parents insist on it. At the same time, I feel a little out of place with the older students on the second floor. I feel different, like I don't fit in. The girls in my class are all starting to wear makeup and dress in the latest "girlie" fashions, whereas I prefer sweats and comfy clothes. Compared to them, I am definitely more of a "tomboy" type. I relate to the boys way more than the girls, but for the most part, boys want nothing to do with me either.

It's only 7:03 a.m. and I'm dreaming of the noon hour. I can't wait for that soft white submarine bun slathered in mayonnaise, topped with salami, slices of turkey and chicken breast, Swiss and cheddar cheese, lettuce, tomatoes and sweet pickles. All those layers of tasty, colourful goodness! My tummy rumbles.

On the second floor, lunch is more of a "social" time. Everyone chatting constantly about the latest TV show or video game or classroom gossip. Eating is almost an afterthought. But I'm hungry! I'd rather enjoy my food than talk! I can't help but feel like everyone is watching me eat and thinking I'm weird because I don't talk like them, or dress like them, or act like them. We're not even allowed to watch TV or play video games at home so I rarely have anything to talk about. So, every day for lunch, I go back to the daycare program to help the staff serve lunch to the kindergartners. It's the perfect solution! I'm doing a good deed by helping the staff with the children, and I get to eat the delicious meals they prepare for the kids without feeling awkward.

It's now 7:10 and I've got to distract myself from thoughts of lunch or I'll never make it through the morning! Soon a few other kids will arrive at daycare, including Kris and Jay, who love to hog the Nintendo machine, not to mention the comfy beanbag chairs. The rule is that the winner stays on and plays the next person, but if I don't get the controller first, the boys always find some excuse to not let me play! It's mainly because I'm a girl and am so much better at it than they are. It bothers me a little how they always exclude me—what's the problem anyway? I just want to play. Does it matter that I'm a girl? I quickly scramble to claim the green bean bag and Nintendo controller. I'm ready for these boys.

My little sister Yas and I have begged and pleaded with Mom to buy us a Nintendo set but she refuses. She tells us that in India, they never had a TV set and that is the way we will grow up, too. She says that because they didn't have a TV, it allowed them to socialize, read books and play outside in the fresh air. She will never "plonk us in front of the TV set," she tells us.

"Baccha, bahar jai nay ramo. Under gehayrma TV nay Nintendo ma aaproo mun jaasti nehee khilay." (My children, no Nintendo

or TV. You must be outside, fresh air, play and read! Enrich your minds. None of this TV nonsense.)

As much as we try to explain to our parents that we live in Canada, not India, and that we *should* have Nintendo and get to watch TV, our feeble pleas never amount to anything. At daycare, though, I can be like the other kids and play all the video games I like. I feel a bit rebellious, "tasting the forbidden fruit" so to speak, which is probably the reason I love playing so much.

The bell rings and I begrudgingly make the trek from first floor daycare up to my Grade 4 classroom. "Four hours until lunch," I tell myself. It can't come quickly enough.

2

1994.
FIRST DAY OF GRADE 5.
AGE 10.

SO EXCITING! I FEEL LIKE Grade 5 is a fresh start for me. I'll finally fit in and everything will fall into place. I see my name tag on the desk and eagerly sit down. Each desk has two people, so it looks like I will have a partner in this class! I'm dying to know who my buddy for the year will be ...

My new teacher, Mrs. Parker, is standing at the back of the room observing each student come in and take their seats. She is tall, thin and has a very formal, businesslike manner. She doesn't seem like my previous teachers, who were always very warm and friendly. She doesn't smile very much. Suddenly I feel very uneasy.

It's my first time being put in a "split grade" class, with half of the students in Grade 5 and half in Grade 6. I've never really talked or interacted with any of the older kids at school, and I feel very self-conscious being among them. I've known everyone in my class since junior kindergarten, and now, here I am facing a whole new group of classmates. Now I'm actually nervous about who my desk mate will be. What if they hate me and I'm stuck with them for the whole year? It starts to hit me that this split class thing might not be so fun. Things are different now, and I'm about to learn just *how* different they are ...

When I see Nancy and "The Fantastic Four" for the first time, time seems to stop. Nancy is a grade sixer, and as she breezes into the classroom–followed by her posse of three: Amber, Haley and Suzy—the mood in the room changes and the din of loud conversations gets quieter. They seem more mature, and more important, than everyone else in the class. Like royalty entering their court.

I immediately notice Nancy's bust. Her boobs are huge! She is wearing a thin, maroon-coloured cotton top that buttons up to the neck, but she has left the top buttons undone so you can see her giant, exploding cleavage. I've seen this kind of look in magazines, but this is the first time I've seen a young person emulating it. I'm awestruck. I can't look away!

I take a moment to look down at my own cleavage. It's like looking at two sad little anthills. Even if I were to tape my minuscule boobs together and wear the tightest bra I could find, I could never have that kind of cleavage! And if I were to wear a revealing shirt like Nancy's, I'm quite sure my dad would have a heart attack if he saw me. Or, he'd take one look at me and tell me to march right back upstairs to get a "proper" top. In India, revealing clothing is definitely frowned upon, especially for a ten-year-old.

"Attar ghari uper jai ne kaapra badlo ... Ai ghanu nagu-ugharu che!" (March yourself right back to your room and change into a proper clothing. What is this revealing outfit? Nonsense!)

Nancy's waist-length brown hair is blown out and (like almost everything about her) is also huge. It looks like she has used hairspray and a crimping iron, or braided her hair overnight to make it voluminous. I always wear a plain, demure ponytail, which my mom insists on to "keep my hair out of my pretty face."

Her eyes are painted with a thick layer of sky-blue eyeshadow and her lips are coated with shiny gloss. I've never worn makeup and am not even sure what to call it at this point, but I'm amazed by her artistry.

Next to her, I feel like an insecure, invisible little dwarf.

I notice her walking towards me and feel an excited panic wash over my body. Is she looking at me? Does she want to be my friend? Why is she walking over to me? Ugh. Just be cool, Dina! Be cool!

My jaw almost drops to the floor when she takes a seat next to me. My desk mate for the year is Nancy? The most popular girl in school is *my* desk mate? I'm nervous to even make eye contact with her but now my mind can't stop racing: Maybe we can be friends? I wonder if she'll like me. What does she think of me? Is she noticing what I'm wearing? I happen to glance downward and am embarrassed by my childish sneakers. I secretly check out Nancy's shoes, which are, of course, the latest fashion: shiny leather with a small heel ...

FULL. STOP. I can't quite believe or understand what I'm looking at. Forget the shoes ... her legs! HOLY. SHIT. She has NO hair on her legs? I have so much black hair on my legs you can barely make out skin under there. I quickly try to hide them under my desk so no one will see how beastly I am. Note to self: Must ask mom about body hair removal. I've completely zoned out of class and all I can think about is the hideous hair on my legs. I want to be hairless and smooth! Just like Nancy.

I'm overwhelmed and confused by this new feeling of inadequacy. EVERYTHING is wrong with me! Up until now, I've always felt comfortable with the way I dress, the way I look. I've never really thought about any of those things to be honest. Now, I can't help but feel painfully different. I'm too plain, too boyish, too hairy and to top it all off, I'm brown, and all of the popular girls are white. I think about trying to pull off Nancy's look and maybe joining her posse but I know I would look ridiculously out of place. Still, a part of me desperately wishes I could do it. For the first time, I think about what others see when they look at me—and I don't like it.

3

SEPTEMBER 1994.
GRADE 5.
AGE 10

FOR THE PAST THREE WEEKS since school started, every one of my classmates has been vying for the Fantastic Four's approval. We all want to be on their team when we break out for class activities. We all want to work on group projects with them. We all want to hang out with them at recess, and lunch, and before and after school. I even feel the teacher likes them better and it makes me crazy! These girls can do no wrong it seems.

I have to get in with this group. I want to be the most popular girl ... desperately. I want to be noticed by everyone, including the boys that hang on to Nancy's every word. I want to be the one everyone else wants to emulate.

From this point on, the only thing that matters in my life, the only thing I want, is to be one of these girls. Nothing less than a complete and total transformation will do.

I watch them from across the schoolyard and wonder if one day, they will ask me to spend recess with them. I realize I need a plan. Step one: I will make myself over to look like them.

I tell my mom I want to shave my legs, wear makeup and have bangs just like Nancy. Mom says no and that I must be comfortable with myself. Blah, blah, blah ... I don't hear a word she says. What a load of crap! I want to be popular; *that's* what will make me "comfortable!"

"Jaanu, jay che te che." (Sweetheart, be comfortable with who you are.)

It frustrates me that my Mom won't just let me do what I want. All of the Fantastic Four have parents who let them do whatever *they* want! I'm envious of them. They seem more like cool "friends" than strict parents. Nancy and Amber always have the best lunches, with lots of junk food—chips and chocolate and soda pop. They wear fashionable clothing and set the trends in hairstyles and makeup, so obviously their parents let them shop on their own. My parents still make me go to daycare every day! It's becoming unbearable. Why can't my parents be more like the other parents? Why do they have to be such annoying authority figures who won't let me watch TV, or play video games, or eat junk food, or wear makeup? I mean, what *can* I do for heaven's sake?

Mom is a dead end so I'll have to find another way to get in with the Fantastic Four. I come up with a secret plan: I will forge a note from the other "cool" girls that says I should be a part of their clique and hide it in Nancy's desk for her to discover. She'll read it, and boom! I'll be IN. Foolproof.

One day after school, I check the hallways to make sure that everyone, including the teachers, has left for the day. I sneak out of daycare and go upstairs to my classroom. The janitor is cleaning another classroom so I covertly dash inside and carry out my plan.

"Nancy, we all agree, Dina should be part of our group—Signed: The Gang."

I gingerly place the note in Nancy's desk knowing she will find it the next day. I'm just a day away from being popular! The Fabulous Four will soon be the "Fantastic Five."

The next day, I watch as Nancy finds the note and nervously await her reaction.

"Who wrote this?" she asks out loud. So loud that the *entire* class and teacher can hear. Oh, SHIT! I am mortified. This is not how things had played out in my mind. She was supposed

to read it quietly, tell me I'm awesome and that I must be part of their group, and badda boom, all of a sudden, I'd be popular too.

I feel my face getting hot and red and I have to think fast.

"Uh, yeah, seriously guys? Who on earth wrote this?" I ask in a bold, confident tone that somehow manages to mask all my nerves and fool the class. I can hear Nancy muttering that she thinks it's another one of the popular girls and I play along. Better that Suzy or Haley be humiliated than me! The teacher tells us all to quiet down as we must get back to the lesson plan for the day.

I wipe my sweaty palms on my pants and breathe a sigh of relief, making a mental note to do better next time. If I really want to be like one of these girls I can't be making stupid rookie mistakes like this.

4
OCTOBER 1994

A MONTH INTO GRADE 5 already and much to my dismay, I'm still the same loner tomboy I was when school started. Despite my constant longing, I can't seem to change myself enough. I hate what I see in the mirror, and rather than focusing on school, or making other friends, or really anything positive, I fixate on every ugly detail of my face and body. My mom says I have "big beautiful eyes," but I know she just says nice things to me because she knows I'm awkward-looking, and she's only trying to make me feel better. If she really wanted to help, she'd help me change! I think less and less about doing well in school and instead spend my time plotting ways I can escape my parents' controlling gaze and become a "cool girl." They're always watching me, though, so it's hard. I start thinking about ways I can do this in secret: How can I change myself gradually enough so that they don't notice?

At school, I'm still looking for my way in with the Fantastic Four. After the whole "secret note" disaster I've been a little gun-shy, but I've been rebuilding my courage and am ready to try a new strategy: get in with Nancy's younger *sister.*

Amber is one year younger than Nancy, and her familial connection makes her automatically popular by association. She and Nancy are almost exactly alike except Amber has blond hair and is three inches shorter. Amazingly, Amber also has huge boobs. What dumb luck this girl has!

Amber has a coat cubby right next to mine, and I've been waiting patiently for the right moment to make my move and "break the ice" with her. Today is the day.

The recess bell rings and we all run frantically out of the classroom to gather our coats and snacks from our cubbies. I reach my cubby and Amber is already there. My heart is racing.

"Hey. I'm Dina. I sit next to your sister I think," I say casually.

"Cool," she says. "I'm Amber."

"Cool."

I feel my palms getting sweaty again, and the silence after our brief exchange is excruciating. I have to think fast! Don't screw this up, Dina!

I notice Amber retrieving her snacks from her cubby and am impressed with her haul: BBQ Bugles corn chips, Gushers and Shark Bites gummies. My snacks by comparison, Ritz crackers and cheese with apple slices, seem completely lame!

"Oooh! I love Ritz! Can we trade?" she asks me.

Is this really happening? For some reason, this girl wants to trade her delicious junk food snacks for my boring "healthy" snacks. In this moment, I could not feel luckier. Not only am I getting the better end of the trade deal, I've found my "in."

"Sure," I tell her. "I get them all the time. We can trade whenever you want."

We exchange our snacks and make our way down the hallway to the outdoor playground. Amber opens the door and I see Nancy, Haley and Suzy on the other side of it. I feel the door whoosh behind her and as it closes, I see my window of opportunity close as well. How could I be so stupid to think that maybe this girl would let me in? Why would she ever want to be friends with a weird loser like me?

I disappointedly make my way outside, prepared to spend recess alone like I normally would, when I notice Amber turning back toward me.

"Where did you go? You should come hang out with us."

Oh. My. GOD. What is happening here? Am I actually spending recess with the cool kids? A second ago I was convinced I would spend Grade 5 as a social leper, and now here I am. I am hanging out with the Fantastic Four. Breathe, Dina. Be cool. Be COOL.

I spend the rest of recess playing with my new friends and dreaming about my new future self. I will be perfect. I will be popular. I will be so much better than the girl I am right now. I feel relieved and hopeful, knowing that I'm headed in the right direction at last.

5

NOVEMBER 1994

I SPEND AS MUCH TIME as I possibly can with the Fantastic Four. The two Persian twin girls I used to hang out with when school started sometimes wave to me at recess, but it would be counterproductive to play with them now. They don't exist in my new world. All I can see, or make time for, is being in this new clique. Nothing, and no one else matters.

I always try to get paired with one of them for class projects, I try to be on their team if I can in gym class, and I spend every recess with them. After school, they all hang out and walk home together—alone. This is another huge obstacle: I'm still in daycare, and not allowed to leave the property until my parents come and pick me up at 5:30 p.m.

What the hell is up with *that?* Daycare is for babies. I feel completely embarrassed by the fact that my parents insist on keeping me in daycare and picking me up every day. "Why are you going to the first floor, Dina?" Nancy asks me one day. I can tell she thinks it's completely uncool and I worry that the Fantastic Four will ditch me because I'm immature. Thankfully I can use my little sister Yas as an excuse. "My little sister is in daycare. We go home together most of the time. UGH. So lame, right?"

They all nod in agreement. I've thankfully dodged that bullet for now, but I've got to get out of daycare somehow! Whenever I plead with my parents to let me walk home alone with my friends they shut me down. "You are staying in daycare, Dina. No ifs, ands, or buts." They refuse to give me any free time, instead signing me up for tons of extracurricular activities that

I hate. While the other girls get to hang out at the park and eat McDonalds and just chill, I'm always having to do something. "You can't just be idle, Dina," my mom tells me on numerous occasions.

Screw my parents. I now hate everything about them. They force me go to daycare. They want to have home-cooked meals as a family EVERY single day. They insist on "family" time and are always trying to get me to "talk" and share stories about my day. They won't let me change my hair, or shop on my own, or do anything cool. I want nothing to do with them, or Yas. The thought of having to explain my embarrassing Indian family to my new friends makes me nauseous. I can't let anyone see how very different we are. It would jeopardize my newfound standing in the popular crowd. Outside of home, I pretend my family doesn't exist.

I feel trapped by them, by their rules and their strange customs that are so completely unlike my friends' *normal* parents. I have to escape. If I don't, nothing will change. I'll keep seeing that same stupid loser in the mirror and I *have* to get free of her.

I decide to run away. Just for a couple of hours. I know that this will be just enough time to hang out with my friends, but not so much that my parents will ground me forever. I can handle the punishment and the trade-off will be so worth it!

On this particular day, I don't have any extracurricular activities, so that leaves me with plenty of time to run away and be with my friends. I can't wait to just be "idle" and do nothing! I know that Nancy and the gang usually hang out in front of their houses or at Havenbrook Park, both of which are just a few minutes away from my house. After dinner, I tell my parents I'm going to catch up on homework in my room (they love hearing that kind of thing). Instead, with my heart pounding through my chest, I quietly sneak out the back door and gun it down the street and around the corner. Only when I am fully out of sight of my house do I stop to take a much needed breath. Holy crap!

I'm free! I keep running until I reach Havenbrook, where I see all my cool friends hanging out. Maybe I'll tell them my awesome story about running away and defying my parents. That will make me sound so badass!

We sit in the park talking, eating fries out of a bag and drinking Coca-Cola. My parents would never let me do this! It's the best feeling ever. I get to be a different "Dina" here. A rebellious and carefree, junk-food eating cool girl who sometimes even swears. The costume of this new "Dina" is intoxicating.

After half an hour in the park, I've completely and blissfully forgotten about my family entirely. Here, I'm just one of the girls, and I imagine my parents are just like Nancy's. They let me hang out as long as I want and won't be angry when I get home in an hour or two. And when I do get home, they'll tell me to just eat whatever I want from the fridge, and won't force me to sit down with them and eat curry or rice or any other "different" foods. I'll just grab a pizza pocket from the freezer and head up to my room (where I'll have my own TV) and watch whatever I want. Heaven!

"Dina ... ? DINA!"

Like an alarm clock waking me from a sweet dream, I hear my name being called out in an all too familiar accent.

I turn and see my mom leaning out of her car window with a perplexed, and angry expression on her face. I. Am. Mortified.

I calmly and casually tell my friends "I've gotta go," as if it's nothing. I can't let anyone see that I'm a nerdy little baby whose parents follow her everywhere and don't let her do anything!

Once I've shut the car door behind me, my parents unload. Thank goodness it's cold out and they've rolled up the windows because they are LOUD and it would be horrifying if my friends heard any of this.

"Tu kehah uti ? Apoonay ghani fikar lagi ... Pachu koi divas em na karti." (Where have you BEEN? You didn't tell us where you were going? We've been worried sick! Why would you not tell us?

We thought something happened to you? Can you please never, NEVER do this again? Please, *please* promise us?)

I know they are concerned and a part of me feels bad, but at the same time, I can't process or understand their worry. If it weren't for them, I would still be chilling in the park with my friends! They are ruining my life! They are the reason I am unpopular, and different, and for that, I resent them.

I mutter "Yeah, yeah, never again" just to shut them up. I just don't care what they want or think. They don't understand: I *hate* my life. I wish they would just leave me alone already.

6
MARCH 1995.
MIDDLE OF GRADE 5.
AGE 11.

I GUESS YOU COULD SAY I'm officially in with the "in crowd." I've worked so hard to be a part of this group, and to be popular … so, why do I still feel so unhappy? I act like them, talk like them and now dress like them, but deep down I know it's not me. I can't help but feel like I don't belong. I try to walk the walk and talk the talk, and I seem to have the Fantastic Four convinced, but I know I'm different. That awkward brown tomboy in the mirror just won't leave me be! Being different feels lonely. Painfully so. There's no one else like me at school, and I wonder why that is. Why am I like this? What can I do to just *be* the same, *truly* the same, as everyone else? I feel cursed.

Soon, I really am "cursed"! In early March, I get a brand-new "friend," one that I despise. It's my period. According to my mom, I now get to "look forward" to seeing this new "friend" every single month.

"Are you KIDDING me? I don't want this new friend. It's painful and I want no part of it! Make it go away."

I'm apparently going through this "lovely miracle called puberty." Ewwwww—so gross! It's way too early for me to be a "woman." Every time mom brings up this vile word, "puberty," I cover my ears while she blabs on and on.

I'm the only girl in my class who has gotten her period. Great. One more thing that makes me different when all I want to do is blend in. Now I've got to use bulky maxi pads, which make trips to the washroom a nightmare (How do you conceal a giant maxi pad? EVERYONE knows what you are doing ... embarrassing!). Gym class is even worse (it is *impossible* to move wearing those giant things between your legs).

My new monthly "friend" also seems to have sparked puberty, and I grow a foot almost overnight. I've always had an awkwardly lanky body—now I'm lanky and tall, the worst combination! I feel like an ogre compared to everyone else at school.

As if that weren't enough, my body clearly has it out for me because it has also decided to suddenly sprout lumpy, little ant-hill-sized boobs. I look like a freak in gym class with these two things bouncing around underneath my T-shirt! Even though the popular girls that I now hang out with have boobs, theirs are somehow more "mature," and attractive. Mine look like half-deflated balloons.

To top it all off, my Indian heritage has taken puberty to a whole other level of embarrassing. I've always been hairy. Now, I'm like a wildebeest. Is there a full moon out? Because I'm officially hairier than a werewolf! Did I mention I've also developed a "unibrow?" Oh, yes. My eyebrow looks like an out-of-control caterpillar in the middle of my face, with my "sideburns" catching up quickly. Was this my body's way of offsetting all of the awkward new female developments I'm seeing? Lucky me. I now have hairy, man-ish features to balance out my bee-sting boobs.

I'm not ready for all of these changes. The mirror has never been my friend, but now it's an outright *enemy.* My reflection is becoming more and more hideous with each passing day. I want it all to STOP. Thinking about how other people see me makes me anxious and on edge almost all of the time. They must think I am a total *freak.* I just want to hide, but I can't. Everyone sees me because I'm different. I just want to disappear!

How is it fair, or right, that my body is growing up, but I'm still forced to go to daycare? My parents wake me up, drive me to school, tell me exactly what time they will pick me up, when dinner will be, drive me to all my sports practices and events—they even tell me when bedtime is each evening! I'm not a kid, but I'm not quite a teenager. I'm somewhere painfully in between, with no control over my life, or my body. Goddammit! Is there anything about myself that I *can* control?

For a start, covering the mirror seems like a good, temporary solution to my self-loathing. I leaf through one of my many fashion magazines and come across a picture of the supermodel Cindy Crawford. She's gorgeous. Very fit and attractive and feminine. She seems so completely confident in herself. Not surprising, since she's basically a perfect specimen! I tear her picture from the magazine and tape it strategically onto my mirror. Now I will see her beautiful image every day and be inspired to work harder.

You can do this, Dina! Just stay focused, and you will figure out a way ...

7

APRIL 1995.
MIDDLE OF GRADE 5.
AGE 11.

I HEAR MY MOM CALLING me to come down for dinner. The last thing I want to do is eat, and the thought of eating with my annoying, control-freak parents is like pure torture. I hate my body, and I hate being told what and when to eat. Naturally, this makes my parents enemy number one, since they always make us eat together as a family.

"Be sure to wash your hands, Dina!" my mom yells out. Seriously? Does she think I'm still in kindergarten? I ignore her calls and pray that she gives up and leaves me alone.

"Haat dhoi ne khava bes." (Wash your hands before we sit down to dinner, please.)

Nope, not so lucky. I can hear her making her way upstairs and lament the fact that I have no lock on my door.

"Jaanu, can you not hear me? I have made your favourite meat-and-cheese lasagna. And there is soft garlic bread and a fresh salad. Come, Jaanu, let's all have a nice dinner together."

"Avi ne khava chaal. Tahru favourite bhonu banaviu mei." (Come, come! I've made your favourite dinner.)

Her sudden kindness makes me that much more irritated. Making me a meal I used to like won't make things better between us. I want control of my life, not lasagna!

"Dina ... let's go," she tells me in a firm tone, making it clear that dinner and family time is not a choice, it's a requirement. I begrudgingly roll out of bed and head downstairs, completely avoiding any eye contact with her. I may have to obey her rules but I sure as hell won't pretend to like them, or her for that matter.

I barely look at anyone as I sit down at the table. If I do, I might blow. Lately, every interaction with my family seems strained, and ends in some kind of shouting match. Even Yas looks nervous, like she's waiting for the other shoe to drop and the yelling to begin.

Mom serves me a heaping plate of lasagna and puts two slices of garlic bread on the side. I can feel everyone's eyes on me, waiting for me to submit to the meal so that things can go back to "normal" with us all. It smells divine. The waft of parmesan and tomato immediately makes my mouth water uncontrollably.

I want to eat. I want that lasagna so badly, I can barely contain the impulse to just shove the whole plate of food into my mouth all at once. I know that my eating it would be a relief for everyone at the table, not just me. In our family, to eat is to show appreciation for one another. When we share a meal, we are sharing love. I know if I eat, my parents will be so happy and relieved, because it will mean that I'm still the "same old Dina." That things can go back to the way there were. A part of me wants that, too. Which is exactly why I can't give in to it. I have to keep reminding myself, "You want to be different, Dina! They just want things to stay the same! What's more important? Your life or this lasagna?"

"Dina, it will get cold. I made this especially for you," my mother pleads.

As I stare at my plate and gently prod it with my fork, I make a monumental discovery that changes everything.

"No."

As I hear myself say the word, I feel a rush of adrenalin that scares away the hunger pains, the confusion, the anger—everything. I feel strong and more alive. This thing I've discovered I can do, this word I can say, "NO," is the key to my independence!

It all becomes clear. If I want my life to be my own, "no" is the way I can make that happen. I will NOT eat! I get up from the dining table, march up the stairs and slam my door. I know

Mom and Dad are staring at me with their mouths open in shock and disgust, and I feel stronger than ever. I'm fucking hungry and mad but it doesn't matter. What matters is I'm in control. I've gotten my revenge against my parents and shown them once and for all: I control ME ... like it or not.

"No" quickly becomes my favourite word. It's so much more than a word! It's my manifesto. I put it into practice on a daily basis: How many things can I say "no" to? What are the ways I can say "no" without always saying the word?

Mom picks me up from school every day at 5:30 p.m.—but I just won't be there. I'll go to Nancy's house instead without telling anyone.

When my dad tells me to wake up in the morning, I'll say, "No, I'm not going to go to school today." What is he really going to do? Fight me? Not likely.

If my math teacher gives us a problem-solving assignment, I'll just decide I'm not going to complete it. I don't care if my grades suffer—no one controls me but me! From now on, I'm going to do whatever I want.

I can even tell my body "no!" It may be changing without my consent, but I *do* have power over it, because I can say "no!" I can control what I eat. Mom made dinner again yesterday but I refused again to eat it. "I'm just not hungry. I ate earlier." I know it drives her crazy that I'm not eating her food. My stomach was grumbling loudly at lunch today but I didn't give in. I'm stronger. My body may want to grow, but I can stop it if I want to!

"No. No. No!"

I love saying the word. Every time I say it, I feel better. It's the solution I've been waiting for!

8

JUNE 1995.
AGE 11.

"DINA, GO CLEAN UP THE mess on the dining table. NOW please," Mom says.

"NO. FUCK OFF!"

The second these two words come out of my mouth, I freeze. I have never said a swear word out loud to my parents. Swearing is "vulgar" language and is *not* tolerated in our household.

I want to run into my room but my legs are frozen. I've never felt this scared. The look of shock and dismay on my mother's face pierces right through me like an icy dagger. I know she's beyond fed up with me and before I have a chance to say anything else, she slaps me right across the face.

"Don't you EVER speak to your mother that way!" Dad yells out from across the room.

I am in shock. My cheek is hot and stinging and I feel so many things in this moment—shame, embarrassment, hurt, regret—that I don't quite know what to do next. So, of course, I fight back.

"THANK YOU for hitting me! I'm going to call the cops and tell them that you beat me! They'll take me away from you! I'll never have to see you EVER, EVER again."

My mom seems strangely calm. In a condescending voice, she then coolly asks, "Shall I dial 9-1-1 for you?"

Ummm … WHAT? I try to stay confident but I'm utterly perplexed. I wasn't expecting this response but I'll just have to go with it.

"Yeah, sure! Dial 9-1-1 and tell them what a horrible person you are!"

To my surprise, she calls my bluff and does indeed call the police. Five minutes pass and I see the red and blue lights of a squad car flicker through the window. I immediately wonder what the neighbours are thinking. My life is like some TV melodrama! Two large cops in blue uniforms come into the house and ask what's happening. My parents invite me to tell the police my story.

After I finish the elaborate, rather embellished version of my ordeal, the two policemen proceed to lecture me: I should not swear at my parents and there are insufficient grounds for them to remove me from my family and I should be grateful to have loving parents who set boundaries and I will value that someday blah, blah, blaaaaah ... They will not take me away. WTF? These darn cops have some nerve.

Why can't things EVER go my way? I have the worst luck!

I run up the stairs and into my room but keep the door slightly ajar to hear what my parents are saying to the police. It seems they need to vent to the cops as to just how much of a rotten child I am. Hearing them talk about "how difficult" I am, and how they "can't handle" me is more hurtful than I expected. I know I'm troublesome and I'm certainly no fan of myself, but the fact that my own parents despise me this much, too? I must be even more worthless than I thought. I'm no good to anyone.

I've had enough. I close the door to languish in my anger and sadness. I'm hungry but it feels good to go to bed that way. I know my mother wouldn't like it, so it's my little revenge for the day.

9

JUNE 1995.
END OF GRADE 5.
AGE 11.

I OVERHEAR MOM AND DAD contemplating if they should send me to boarding school. I don't really understand what boarding school even means. Are these schools in Toronto? Does it mean I'll have to go to another city? Will I live at this school? Does it mean I'll never see my parents?

Maybe they want to give me away or give me up for adoption. I don't really blame them. I'm such a pain in the ass. They have Yas. Maybe one good child is enough.

They don't like the people I've chosen to spend time with, the popular girls. Mom says these girls are "latchkey children," "disobedient," and have carefree parents who are more interested in "being their friend" versus "parenting their children properly."

Dad says I have become very defiant, mad, and an "unruly child." They are not happy with the company I keep these days.

Listening to them, I can barely contain myself! I want to run out of my room and scream at them. "You don't like my friends? You think I'm a bad kid? Too frickin' bad! I'll do whatever the hell I want!"

"It's a good thing school will be done in a few days. She'll be at summer camp and at least she will be away from those girls." I hear my Mom say.

UH, EXCUSE ME? I have gone to summer camp every year, but this year—no WAY. I want to stay and be with my new friends this summer! They have already talked about how they will go to the mall every day, and hang out at the park. THAT is what I want to do. I open the door of my room to yell out one decisive, final protest.

"I am NOT going to camp this year. NOT. GOING." I slam the door shut. No one comes upstairs so I interpret that as success. They aren't going to fight me anymore. Perfect!

• • •

"OPEN the door, Dina … NOW," my father says sternly through the bathroom door.

"NO! I will not!"

It turns out that my parents are indeed sending me to overnight summer camp, and we are leaving today, like it or not.

FAT chance! I will not go. I have locked the door and I will stay in here for as long as I have to!

I now hear two other voices. Aunty Dhun and Uncle Farokh are now here. My parents called in backup? NOT FAIR. I hear them discussing what to do with my parents.

The only word I pick up on is "locksmith." Man, now I'm doomed. I stand my ground but after one hour, I'm tired and they are all wearing me down.

Huffing and puffing, I open the door. I tell them I will do absolutely nothing at camp. I will not have fun. I will not eat. I will just hate them even more. They just wasted their money—dumb move, parents.

Just as I feel I was gaining some control, they completely strip me of it. I hate them!

My parents grab me by the wrist and literally buckle me in Aunty Dhun's SUV. Apparently I need four escorts to ensure I don't escape.

We reach Camp Pine Crest which is in Muskoka. I am fuming and completely ignore my family. I refuse to even say goodbye. They tell me they will be back in two weeks to see me for one day before my next camp session starts. I'm informed that this will be my home for this summer: four two-week camp sessions.

Even between camp sessions, we will stay in a hotel for the night and I will not be getting anywhere close to my house and the Fantastic Four.

10

JULY 1995.
SUMMER CAMP.
AGE 11.

ON THE VERY FIRST DAY of camp, I make it clear that I am *not* interested in participating in anything, with anyone, in any way. I have to show my family that sending me away was a terrible mistake. My suffering is the only way to teach them a lesson. I refuse to leave the cabin and stay in my bed the whole day. I'm starving but I won't eat. I'm bored to tears and everyone seems to be having a grand ol' time, but I will not move, not talk, and not enjoy *anything.*

"Do you want to come eat some supper, Dina?" my counsellor gently asks me as everyone prepares to head to the dining hall. "Our camp chef is amazing, and I think he's making hamburgers tonight!"

"I'm not feeling well. Thanks," I tell her. It takes all my strength to tell this little lie. The thought of a juicy hamburger sends sweet shivers through my body. She gives up, tells me she will bring back some broth for me, and leaves with the others.

The cabin is eerily quiet without the din of laughter and chatter to fill it. I feel more alone than ever. This charade is exhausting on every level. Hungry and disappointed, I cry into my pillow and fall asleep.

• • •

My passive rebellion doesn't last very long. After a week at Camp Pine Crest, I've reluctantly ended my hunger strike and started to take part in the daily activities. When you share a cabin with seven other campers and a camp counsellor, it's pretty much impossible to avoid people! I make friends with a couple of the other girls and soon, we're thick as thieves. The memory of Nancy and the Fantastic Four starts to fade, and I'm feeling better about myself. I decide it's best for me to temporarily abandon my manifesto of "No!" and embrace camp life. Coincidentally, I make this decision when our counsellor announces that we'll be making s'mores at the campfire one night ...

The time passes quickly, and before I know it, two weeks have passed and my parents come to collect me for the break. Miraculously, I find myself excited to see them. I've missed them, and although I hate to admit it, I've had a great time at Camp Pine Crest.

I see my mom at the car and sprint to her so quickly I'm sure I've broken some kind of Olympic record.

"Mummy!" I yell out as I launch myself into her arms. I've been craving her hugs. It's strange to think how angry I was at her just a couple of weeks ago. Dad joins in and we all hug for a good long minute.

"Let's go, *Jaanu.* We'll have some lunch and talk about some things," Mom tells me.

To my great delight, we go to Webers, a legendary burger place on the way to Muskoka. There is always a mile-long lineup of cottagers waiting to order their delicious flame grilled burgers, so we often drive past, not wanting to wait in line for so long. "Next time," my dad always says. But today, we're finally going!

I sink my teeth into the mile-high burger with complete abandon. Mom and Dad are smiling.

"Dina, we want to talk to you about school next year," my mom tells me. I'm too engrossed in my burger to protest and decide I'll just hear them out. "We talked about boarding school for you, but maybe, if you are willing, there is another school in North York you can go to. Shaughnessy isn't good for you anymore, it's time for a change. What do you think of this?"

I gulp down the last of my burger, and for an instant, I think about telling them to "fuck off" again, but something has changed. I'm not as angry with them, and I appreciate that they are asking me for my perspective. I take a moment to process and weigh my options before answering.

"I don't want to be far from home. I can try a new school, yes."

Yas and I will be going to Seneca Hill Public School in North York, just north of Peanut Plaza. Mom and Dad explain that this new school has a very good reputation, and that they think the kids at Shaughnessy are a bad influence on both of us.

It makes me sad to think I will be away from my new friends, and what's more, I'll lose my hard-won popular status and have to start all over again. At the same time, I've always felt like such an outsider at Shaughnessy, always fighting so hard to find my place there and feel "normal." Maybe this new school will be different. The prospect of "fitting in" and feeling "normal" sounds good. What's more, no one will know me at this new school, so technically, I can be whoever I want! I will make myself into a whole new "Dina" before September! Everyone will love her and she'll be popular and cool *and* a good student, too. Suddenly, Seneca Hill sounds like the greatest thing ever, and I can't wait for school to start.

Mom always reminds me: *"Dina, tara dosto thee tu judee hoi tau kai nehee."* (Dina, it's okay to be different than all your classmates. It's okay.)

We leave Webers and head back to town. I daydream about my new life at my new school for the whole ride home.

11

OCTOBER 1995.
GRADE 6.
AGE 11.

IT'S BEEN ONE MONTH SINCE I started at Seneca Hill and I've done my best to adjust to my new school. At Seneca, the classes are split into the "Gifted" or "Regular" curriculum. I've been put into the "Regular" classes, which stings a little. I like to think of myself as more advanced and mature, so why am I not in the smarter classes? Apparently I missed the testing last year, which is why I wasn't accepted into the program. I explain this to everyone but I suspect they think I'm making up some kind of excuse and secretly think I'm dumb. It's starting to take a toll on my self-confidence.

I figure if I can't be "Gifted" academically, I'll become a sports star. I'm much taller than everyone else, so I decide to join the basketball team and track and field. I begin to excel and make friends on the teams, but instead of making things easier for me, being "different" in this way backfires. The girls in my "non-gifted" class are obsessed with girlie things like clothes and makeup, so they can't quite wrap their heads around me. They call me a "tomboy" since I dress in sports clothes and spend most of my time hanging out with the boys. "You're so weird, Dina! You're basically a guy," one of them tells me in class one day.

I try to ignore her and brush it off, but it bothers me. Mom tells me "it's okay" that I'm "different" than the other girls, but I know all the other girls think I'm weird. Why is this happening to me all over again? Is there *no one else* like me anywhere? What is *wrong* with me?

I still have eight more months of Grade 6, so I'll have to just suck it up for now.

12

MAY 1996.
GRADE 6.
AGE 12.

"CHAAL JULDI, APRAY AUNTY DHUN na ghare jayah." (Children, get ready quickly. We are going to Aunty Dhun's house.)

Hooray! We never need a reason for going to Aunty Dhun and Uncle Farokh's house—we *love* it there! My aunt from my dad's side of the family is a very highly respected pathologist, also known as Dr. Noria. She is also a remarkable businesswoman and super glamourous. Yas and I admire her greatly and are in awe of how fabulous and successful she is. Uncle Farokh is super tall and is a very sweet and patient person. He has jewellery companies in both Canada and India, so you could say he and Aunty are quite "well off."

They live in a huge, opulent mansion near Bayview Village mall, not far from us, but it is definitely a more affluent neighbourhood than ours. All of the houses in their area are massive and unique, with immaculately manicured lawns, gorgeous fountains, colourful flowers and rose gardens and long cobblestone driveways. Yassy and I always laugh because there is a bus route on that street; however, no one that lives there takes public transportation—they all have cars, multiple cars! And some even have drivers! The only people you see in those buses are the nannies and maids and the gardeners who keep all of those lush green lawns alive.

When we pull up into the driveway, I notice Dad look at Mom and take her hand in the front seat. I whisper to Yas, "Daddy looks a little tense, eh?" She shrugs it off and launches out the car like a rocket once she catches a glimpse of our favourite auntie and uncle.

Aunty Dhun and Uncle Farokh greet us with huge, warm bear hugs. When we all get into the house, Aunty Dhun shows us an exciting new addition to the house—a new elevator. WHAT? I can barely comprehend this: a house that has an elevator *and* THREE floors? Nuts! Playtime starts as me, Yas, and our cousins Sab and Zubin (who we all call "Zubby-Do") and Liam and Raja, their majestic dogs, all take turns running up and down the stairs to meet each other at the different elevator stops.

"Okay kids, settle down. Come downstairs for a bit. We are having a family talk," Aunty tells us.

We go into the grand living room, which is more like a ball-room, and see all of the adults sitting solemnly in a row on the couch. This is very different from our usual visits, which are typically filled with laughter, food, and more food.

"Kids," my mom begins, "I have learned from my doctor that I may have cancer. We will need to do further tests and your aunty will be helping us through this, but we wanted everyone to know."

Cancer? I am 12 years old and Yas is 10, so neither of us really understands what cancer is or what it means. It can't be that bad because Mom and Dad seem pretty cool and collected about this news. No tears or sadness, so maybe this cancer thing isn't too bad after all? We learn that the cancer is in her breasts and that Aunty D has swiftly arranged for mom to have a biopsy the next day.

At dinner, mom and dad explain that the "biopsy" will determine if the "lump" in her breast is indeed cancerous and if it is spreading. Mom goes on to tell us that if the tests do confirm the cancer, she will have a mastectomy.

"If they are putting me under, get it all done and cut them off! Boom! No muss, no fuss," she half jokes.

They have to remove her breasts? This sounds terrifying to me, but again, she is so calm and collected. I was under the impression cancer was a death sentence but I guess I am wrong.

A few days later, Mom and Dad sit us down and tell us the news: the biopsy did, in fact, show cancer cells and Mom will be having a mastectomy.

The thought of my mom being sick makes me feel unbearably guilty. I think of how awful I've been to her in the last year. And now she is the one suffering? I am the worst child ever. The fear of losing her now is a crushing weight on me, but I hide it because I know she needs me to be strong.

The whole thing happens so quickly. Mom goes to the hospital for her surgery and Dad tells us she will be spending a week there in recovery. It's strange to think I won't be seeing her every day, that she won't be picking me up and dropping me off every day, or urging me to come join the family for dinner, or helping me put my hair up … There are so many things she does for me every day! Every night, Yas and I cuddle up with her to read a book, one of us nuzzled up on each side of her. The thought of not having her to snuggle with before bed terrifies me.

Dad takes us to the hospital so we can see her after she's had the mastectomy. Everything went well and he tells us the doctor confirmed the surgery was a "success." Yas and I hold hands as we arrive; her hand grips mine so tightly I think she might crush it. She's not the only one freaking out! I'm trying to be "the strong older sister" for her, but, truthfully, I'm completely unnerved by the weird smells and sounds of the hospital. Everything is one colour there: green. Why on earth would they choose this sickly colour for all of the walls and uniforms and patient gowns? It creeps me out and makes me feel nauseous as soon as we enter.

We head up to the fourth floor recovery where Mom is being kept. We enter her room, and when I first catch a glimpse of her lying in her bed, I let out an audible gasp. She looks so different! I'm used to seeing her up and about, full of energy, always dressed in vibrant colours. She looks so frail and tiny in her bed, wearing a pale green hospital gown that seems to suck the colour from her face and turn her skin green as well. There's an IV attached to her arm and strange tubes everywhere. I wonder how I will be able to even touch her without getting tangled up in everything.

As soon as she sees Yas and me, she smiles and tells us to come over. We hesitate—how do we do this exactly? Is there a protocol for hugs? What if we hurt her? I look up to Dad nervously and he promptly takes each of our hands and leads us to her bed.

"It's okay, girls. I've missed you both so much. Come and give me a hug!"

She opens her arms and I almost pounce on her before thinking better of it. I awkwardly lean in and embrace her, careful not to disturb any of the medical apparatuses. I notice there is a tube with yellow, brownish liquid in it coming out from her gown and am startled.

"It's okay, *Jaanu*. It's a drain, the doctors put this there after my surgery, but it will come off soon."

I do my best to smile, to let her know I'm okay and can handle seeing her like this, but all I want to do is get out of there! After Yas takes her turn hugging, we all sit together around Mom's bed, and she explains everything about her mastectomy, and what the future will hold.

"I am still the same. I just have a little less boobie!" she jokes. "And to be honest, there wasn't much there in the first place, so it's nothing any of us will miss."

Despite my best effort, I start to tear up a little. Will hugs always feel weird now? Hugging Mom has always been soft and cozy and comforting. Now I think of touching her lopsided, hard chest, and it scares and upsets me. She sees my getting emotional and, as is typical in our family, tells me to shut it down. Getting emotional is not something we do.

"No messy tears, Dina! I am fine. This is nothing for me—you will see. I'm ready to get up out of here and get on with things!"

She explains that although her body is different, she is okay with it. Apparently, the doctors can do other surgeries and "reconstruct" her missing boob, but she won't be doing that. "One surgery is enough!" she tells us. She will be in the hospital a few more days, and then she can come home, where she will have to rest for a while before she can go back to work. The doctors will be monitoring her to make sure the cancer stays away, but they think that the surgery "got all of it" and that she will not have to go through any radiation or chemotherapy, which she explains is very lucky.

We hug her goodbye and head home. Dad assures us in the car that we will be coming back to see her the next day, but I'm not looking forward to it. I want to see her, but the whole experience of the hospital has thrown me.

A week passes, and Mom returns home. Finally! A week without her has been a challenge, to say the least. Dad has done his best to make up for her absence, but let's be honest—it's not quite the same! The three of us jump into action to ensure Mom can rest properly. We do the dishes, laundry, lift all the pots and any other heavy things. Yassy still needs a step stool to even reach the kitchen counter but we all make sure Mom gets to rest and not worry. She's always taking care of us so it's our turn now.

I'm over the moon when she tells Yas and me to join her before bedtime one night for our regular reading session. As we snuggle up next to her, I notice her chest, and the flat spot where her breast used to be. As always, she knows exactly what I'm thinking, and smiles warmly to reassure me.

"Would you like to see?" she asks.

Yas and I look to one another cautiously, and nod yes. She lifts her pajama top and reveals the scar where her breast used to be. It's huge! We're both quite afraid to touch her because we don't want to hurt her, but she explains to us that we won't. I nervously run my fingers over the red, bumpy skin and she doesn't even flinch.

For a moment, I am almost grateful for the cancer, since it has made me love her even more. I feel closer to her now, and want to be strong for her and take care of her. My own troubles seem unimportant now, and in a way, it's been a relief to have all of this cancer business to take my mind off of school, and friends, and fitting in.

13

JUNE 1996.
END OF GRADE 6.
AGE 12.

GRADE SIX DIDN'T REALLY TURN out to be the magical year of "reinvention" I had hoped for. I'm definitely changing—but not at all in the way I had hoped. I looked in the mirror today and noticed that what started as a single bump on my face earlier this week has now multiplied to form a lumpy red cluster in the middle of my forehead. These little bumps are very noticeable so I immediately set about doing my research to figure out what the heck is going on!

I hate to pester my mom about anything, it seems stupid to be bugging her about my own problems when she is still recovering from her surgery, but I've reached a breaking point.

"Mom! What is going on with my face? It's so ugly!" I exclaim to her through tears.

She tells me it's acne and that it's just another normal part of puberty (Again, HATE that word!). She tells me not to worry, and to just be diligent about washing my face (especially after playing sports and sweating) and to keep my hair off of my face. Okay ... so, wash my face and keep my hair back? I do those things anyway! These seem like stupid suggestions but I should leave her alone now.

Every day there's another bump. I scrub my face even more vigorously, which only makes my skin red and raw and shiny. Mom advises me not to touch my face because that will only make things worse but it's becoming impossible to avoid the impulse to scratch these ugly things off. They just keep coming! I wish and pray for this acne to please STOP appearing … please! It's now spread to my cheeks and chin, and has become angrier—red and sore and the bumps are getting bigger. I read in *Seventeen* magazine that hairspray can cause acne, especially on the forehead, but I'm confused because my hair is always pulled back like my mom told me, and I don't use hairspray anyway. So incredibly frustrating!

I can't take it anymore and one night, after scrubbing my face with a rough loofah sponge, I lock the bathroom door and set to work. I squeeze one of the bigger lumps between my fingers until it bleeds. To my dismay, the lump doesn't empty out and flatten but becomes even bigger and forms a scab.

The next day at school, I can feel everyone's eyes like laser beams on my forehead. None of the other girls in my class have acne and they are totally freaked out by my scabby face. I wear my hair down for the day despite my mother's warnings, trying to hide my face at least partially.

Enough is enough! Mom has always discouraged me from wearing makeup and for the most part, I'm not really into wearing it, but I can't keep going to school looking like this! I beg her to take me to Shoppers Drug Mart to buy some concealer so I don't have to endure any more strange looks than I already do.

Mom sympathizes and understands how much this is bothering me, so she agrees to go see the doctor next week.

The doctor recommends washing my skin with Neutrogena, and applying a benzoyl peroxide lotion that I dab on my face at night. We also get a strawberry-cucumber peel-away mask at Shoppers Drug Mart as well as a tube of Clearasil "Rapid Action Treatment," just in case a pesky bugger comes up that the benzoyl peroxide can't take care of and eliminate. I cross my fingers and hope one of these treatments works. As if I don't already have enough to deal with. I look at the picture of Cindy Crawford taped to the mirror and pray to her like some kind of beauty god:

"Please, please take away my ugly acne and give me clear, beautiful skin like Cindy before school starts. I'll do anything. Please!"

14

SEPTEMBER 3, 1996.
GRADE 7.
AGE 12.

TODAY IS A BIG DAY. I'm starting junior high at a brand-new school, and Mom is going back to work after spending all summer "resting." Watching her "rest" and "recover" from breast cancer, you'd never know she had been through such an ordeal! I've seen her struggle with the odd physical task here and there—wincing slightly as she reaches for dishes on the higher shelves, or being a little winded after longer walks—but mostly, she seems completely normal. I've read in a magazine that breast cancer is a death sentence for women, which confuses me. My mom hasn't let it get in the way of anything!

Her strength is at once remarkable, and overwhelming. I know it's a big deal that she's going back to work, but all I can think about today is what everyone at school will think of my lumpy, pimple-covered face. Last night, I cried myself to sleep thinking of all of the weird, judging looks I would get from the kids at school. It's like a vicious circle: I cry because I'm terrified, and then I get angry at myself for crying like a little baby about something so small, and then I can't stop crying because I feel like a total fool. If mom is able to stare down a death sentence and make cancer look like nothing more than a mild irritation, what kind of wimp does that make me for crying over my acne?

"No messy tears, Dina," I remember her say as I ready myself for another first day at school.

My new school—Zion Heights Junior High—is not too far from home, but far enough that Mom and Dad still insist on driving me there and picking me up. I tried to convince them to let me take the bus but that got me absolutely nowhere. I don't push it. When I think of what could have been—having no mom at all to drop me off at school, I feel grateful that she can, and is.

I arrive and make my way to my Grade 7 classroom. A million nervous thoughts buzz noisily in my head: Is my outfit stylish? Does my hair look cute? Who will I sit beside? Who are all the new boys? Who will be my partner in science class? Will anyone want to sit with me at lunch? Does everyone buy their lunch or will I be the only dork whose mom makes my lunch? Will other people have to wait after the bell rings for their parents to pick them up?

And of course, I can't stop thinking about my face. I have blackheads, whiteheads, pimples and red blotchy skin. I know I'm not supposed to pick at them or try to squeeze them but last night in a fit of tears and rage, I went to town. The result? Angry looking bumps and scabs. I look around the room at the other girls and all I can see around me is perfection. Perfectly clear, lily-white skin, perfect hair, perfect bodies ... I keep my head down and try to think of a way to get through another year of being the weird looking girl on the outside looking in.

NO. I tell myself. I will NOT go through this again! No more messy tears. I will find a way to get clear skin, and that is THAT. It becomes my new mission in life.

I survive the day (mostly keeping to myself) and as soon as we're home, I tell my mom we need to go back to the doctor to get things under control. I have read about a drug called Accutane, which sounds like the perfect solution. All I have to do is pop a few pills each day and in six months, my skin will be acne-free. What a dream!

"I want Accutane, Mom," I decisively tell her. It's not up for debate!

We go to the dermatologist again later that week where he explains to me that, unfortunately, Accutane is not something they like to prescribe until every other option has been exhausted.

"Dina, we'll start you on orals (Clindamycin) and give you a stronger topical cream (Retin-A) that you will apply every morning and night before bed."

"But what about Accutane?" I plead. "It seems like that is the only permanent solution. Why can't I take that?"

He begins to go through all of the reasons why I can't or shouldn't be on Accutane and rattles off a list of side effects: joint pain, back pain, dizziness, drowsiness, irritability, dryness of the lips, mouth, nose and skin, cracking or peeling skin, itching, rash, yellowing of your fingernails or toenails … I tune it all out: the only thing I can hear is that Accutane gets rid of acne. Forever. He does also mention that some patients have to go on the medication two or three times, but I just shrug that off too. I won't be one of those people! It will work for me the first time.

I leave his office frustrated and disappointed. It seems like this dermatologist is just beating around the bush with these weaker medications. I feel like crying but suck it up and take comfort in the fact that in a couple of weeks, I will be seeing my family doctor. Maybe *she* will listen to me.

15

OCTOBER 1996.
GRADE 7.
AGE 12.

MIRACULOUSLY, I MAKE A FRIEND at school. Her name is Harper and she is a spunky, hilarious redhead who makes me laugh so hard I sometimes almost pee my pants! We become inseparable. She explains to me that she is going to start gymnastics. Naturally, I have to do this as well! Anything Harper does, I do. I explain to my mom that I want to be a gymnast. My mom and dad have no problem keeping me occupied with extracurricular activities, so thankfully, they agree! Normally you have to start the program in September or January but Harper's mom pulls a few strings so we will both be starting gymnastics this month.

Harper's older sister Lori competed professionally and won some actual competitions, so Harper knows all the ins and outs of the sport. I'm pretty clueless so I'm very happy she is there to explain everything to me. We are actually going to the same club Lori used to train at! The thought of training with the "pros" and getting to see how they do things is exhilarating.

Our parents make arrangements to take turns driving us out to the club in Richmond Hill. We will be training two days a week, on Sundays and after school on Wednesdays. Harper lives very close to school, so we will be going to her house after school on Wednesdays and her mom or dad will drive us from there. At last—I can escape the dreaded pickup by my parents at least one day a week! We get to kill a little time at her house as well, playing and goofing around for an hour before we go to gymnastics.

Harper takes me to her room and shows me our "training" bodysuit and our "competition" bodysuit. They competition one, especially, looks pretty skimpy, and frankly, it makes me a little nervous to think of showing that much skin. Everyone will see my body? Yuck. She is so nonchalant about it! I decide that if she can do it, I can too. She also tells me that you have to always start your floor routine with perfectly pointed toes and that you must address the judges at the beginning and end of a performance. I watch her as she acts out this greeting for the judges. Her back is perfectly arched and she seems so confident—I hope I can be as good as her one day.

We eagerly pile into Harper's dad's car to head to our very first training session. Harper's younger sister Mia sits in the back seat with me. She is the same age as Yas, and will also be coming to train with us. I have to admit that I'm relieved Mia is there. Harper is such an expert on gymnastics and has already been training for a year, not to mention the fact that she is naturally talented. Mia is new to gymnastics like me, so at least there is one person at the club who is a beginner too.

Once we arrive at the club, we get changed and hit the floor! As we walk into the gymnasium for the first time my jaw pretty much drops. The head coach is there training with the elite athletes. These girls are SO fit and SO incredibly beautiful. They seem to defy the laws of gravity as they jump and flip their way across the narrow beams and leap, feather-like, between the uneven bars.

The head coach's name is Petra. She sounds like a drill sergeant and doesn't look like she possesses a single motherly trait. She is a very strict and harsh woman, definitely lacking any sense of warmth. Picture Cruella De Vil from the movie *101 Dalmatians*. I find her choice of footwear amusing. Pointy stilettos seem odd in a gym, but apparently she produces world class athletes, so who am I to judge?

Mia and I glance at each other and I'm pretty positive we are both thinking the same thing, "Yikes! I am SO glad she's not our coach!"

Harper glances over to see Mia and me taking in all the surroundings and whispers to us, "That's Petra. She was just talking to that girl's mother saying she couldn't work with her anymore. She's too 'big' now. Dina, puberty kills a gymnast. She hates older girls—they don't perform well. She wants short, thin, young girls to mould into elite gymnasts."

I gulp down a nervous gasp as panic and desperation set in. I am already 5'5 *and* I already have boobs! Is it terrible that in this moment, I wish for a mastectomy? Last year mom had a mastectomy and she got to remove one boob, which equals three pounds of fat. She got thinner and flatter overnight! Breast cancer suddenly seems appealing.

We begin by running around a track, which I am good at! Some of the other girls get tired but I can run for a long time without getting winded. I decide that I am sporty enough since I can handle this part of the training, which naturally means I am going to pick up on gymnastics very quickly and be a champion like Nadia Comăneci or Shannon Miller or Mary Lou Retton!

We then start drills of jumps, cartwheels and flips—and my Olympic dream quickly fades as I comically attempt to keep up. I'm taller than everyone else there and my lanky limbs can't seem to agree on anything. I feel a bit like Bambi when he first tries to stand up on the ice pond. Harper flips and twirls gracefully across the floor while I struggle to keep from falling all over myself. Every time I try to flip, my arms or legs get in my way. I suddenly understand why Petra only likes small, thin, young girls.

I don't want to be a failure before I even begin. I *have* to be good at this. I am so tired of always being the odd one out. I have to make this work somehow. I'm running out of options!

It's been a while since I used my favourite word, and I suddenly remember its power: "No." Of course! That's it! When everything seemed completely out of my control, "no" was there to give me back a sense of power. I remember how good it felt to say "no," the loud voice of hunger coming from my belly. That's how I can conquer my awkward body once again. I will eat EVEN less, become the thinnest girl at gymnastics, become flat chested again and all of this will also halt the growing process so I won't get taller.

A new-found reserve of strength and focus swells up in me, and I hit the gym floor again more determined than ever.

16

NOVEMBER 1996.
GRADE 7.
AGE 12.

IT'S BEEN A COUPLE OF weeks since I started gymnastics, and although it's given me a new-found sense of belonging, it's also made me notice new, ugly things about my body. I can barely do anything or go anywhere without noticing how unfit I am to be a gymnast. Too tall, too fat, too much boob, and then there is the fact that I'm Indian. Have you ever heard of an East Indian gymnast? Exactly! All the world champions, and most of the girls at my gymnastics club are white. I have to do everything I can to fight these odds stacked against me, and it's hard.

I still take part in a few other extracurricular activities—piano lessons, karate, and swimming—but all I think about is how I can be better at gymnastics, like Harper. At swimming practice this week, as I headed from the change room to the pool, I caught a glimpse of myself in my bathing suit in the mirror and paused to look.

My legs are too chubby, my inner thighs touch, I've got child-bearing hips, my butt sags and my chest sticks out. On top of all this, despite the fact that my family doctor put me on a birth control pill months ago to "regulate my hormones" and get rid of my acne—it's gotten worse. I thought my mirror at home was bad—but this one takes the cake. Who is that troll staring back at me? As other people walk by, I feel them staring at me, noticing my jiggly thunder thighs and pizza face.

I make a mad dash to my locker and put my T-shirt on and wrap my towel around my lower body to cover up. Instantly, I feel better. Phew! Now nobody will be able to see me.

As soon as my swim instructor says it's time to get into the water, I take off my T-shirt and jump right in the pool as fast as I can. I make a bit of a comical *splash* as I hit the water hard and everyone laughs, as though I was making a joke. I play along. Anything to help distract people from looking at my body is a good thing.

I wave and smile to my dad who is watching my swim practice from the gallery above the pool. He is always smiling and rooting for us. I can tell he is so proud, and he loves this Saturday ritual we have, coming to the pool and often going for a treat somewhere afterward—ice cream or pizza. He's the one who first put Yas and me in the pool at barely a year old to learn how to swim. I'd rather quit altogether and focus on gymnastics, but seeing him waving down makes me feel a little guilty. I guess I can suffer through it for his sake.

17

DECEMBER 1996.
GRADE 7.
AGE 13.

IT WAS AT HARPER'S HOUSE that I clearly remember first discovering a scale. It was a plain black-and-white square thing tucked in a corner of her upstairs bathroom, with a thin black pointer that went from zero to three hundred pounds. Three *hundred* pounds? I shudder to think of how utterly disgusting it would be to be so fat! Is it even possible for a person to be *that* heavy?

I jump on it to see my weight, having absolutely no idea what it might be. I know for sure I'm nowhere near three hundred, though! The little pointer dances about a bit before it settles on a number: 120 pounds. Is that good or bad? I really have no idea what 120 really means. But I do know I don't like how I look when I'm in a bathing suit, so I'm guessing 120 is way too much.

I've never weighed myself at home so I'm not even sure we own a scale, but now I want one. I want to be able to monitor myself and watch the number on the scale go down, because that would mean success! Before this moment, the idea of weighing myself never even occurred to me. I'd never heard of Mom weighing herself or speaking of her weight. Until now, the only time I got on a scale was at the doctor's office when I got my yearly checkup.

After gymnastics practice that evening, I casually ask Mom (very casually) if we have a scale. Mom yells to Daddy, *"Soli, apree paasay 'vehjun noo scale' chekay?"* (*Soli*, do we have a weighing scale in the house?)

We do have one! My dad used it once to see if there was enough fuel in the propane tank for the barbecue, but apart from that, it had no use in our household.

"Where is it?" I ask (again, *very* casually).

"Oh ... I'm not even sure, *Jaanu*. I think hiding in the spare room somewhere. We have no use for it. Why do you want to know?

I have to think quickly. What possible reason could I give that won't sound suspicious? I don't want her to bug me any more than she already does about not eating enough and being too skinny.

"Oh ... We're learning about measurements in math class. I just wanted to know if we have it in case I need it for homework."

I've gotten pretty good at coming up with excuses like this. She pays no mind and I head to the spare room to find my new best friend—the scale.

I start to weigh myself each morning. Just to be informed and set goals for myself. Soon, I want to be even *more* informed. So, I weigh myself before each meal, so I can figure out how much to eat (or not eat). Then, I start weighing myself before *and* after every meal, so I can also know how much fat I have to burn off after eating.

I then start to weigh myself before and after each workout using the scale at the gym. I've been a member of the YMCA for many years and probably walked past the weigh scale a million times but only recently noticed it. Now I weigh myself about eight times a day. It seems perfectly normal and harmless; I just want to be informed. "Knowledge is key," my mom always says.

Each time I weigh myself, I hear one of two voices in my head. They are like coaches, alternatively cheering me on or scolding me to do better next time. I hear these voices so frequently (and so clearly) that I've given them names. I always hope I will hear "Sweet Sally." She is a kind woman who greets me warmly, and is always positive and encouraging. I imagine she looks like Kate Moss, super thin and beautiful and ultra-cool. She is always smiling coyly and greets me with a wink of approval, like we are part of some top secret club. "Way to go Dina! Nice one!" When I hear Sweet Sally, I get off the scale feeling strong, powerful and accomplished.

At other times, I encounter "Stern Sammy." I hate those days. He sounds, and looks, like the Joker in Batman. He barks orders loudly at me and tells me how fat I am, how ugly I am getting, how no one likes a fat girl, that I have to stop eating so much, and that I need to work out more. "Get with the program, *Diiiiinnaaaaaaa,*" he teases. He tells me I will never be a good gymnast, and mocks me for trying. When I hear Stern Sammy, I get off the scale feeling sad, incredibly mad at myself, worthless and so frustrated that I almost always have tears in my eyes.

As I gingerly step on the scale this morning, I am *so* anxious. I pray that it's Sweet Sally who will visit me today. I hope Sally tells me I weigh 118 pounds. I just know I'll be happy at 118!

121 pounds.

I practically leap off the scale. Stern Sammy is *not* going to be pleased ...

18

JANUARY 1997.
GRADE 7.
AGE 13.
WEIGHT: 120 LBS.

I GET HOME FROM GYMNASTICS practice and Mom gives me a great big hug!

"Welcome home, *Jaanu!* Guess what we're having for dinner? Lasagna with lots of meat sauce, a big salad with fresh juicy tomatoes … and honey garlic bread! Let's all sit down after you change."

Normally Mom serves me as we all sit down to dinner, but today I casually ask to serve myself. Normally I have at least two large helpings of lasagna and a minimum of three slices of garlic bread, but today I have 1.5 helpings of lasagna and two pieces of garlic bread. It's not that much less but I'm curious to see what happens. I think Sweet Sally will be proud of me. I really hope I don't have to deal with Stern Sammy at my next weigh-in.

I have never thought about what I eat in terms of quantity, calories, or nutritional content. When I started refusing meals back in grade 5, it was less about avoiding calories and more about defying my parents' expectations of me. I have always eaten whatever I like until I'm full. Simple as that. Mom's food is delicious and it's something I look forward to every single day. Food is happiness to me.

I love the mornings when Mom is off from work because that means it's Pancake Day and Yas and I make smiley face pancakes with blueberries and chocolate chips topped with lots of butter and maple syrup. Or the dinners when Daddy makes homemade burgers on the barbecue and I pile the burger a mile high with cheese, tomatoes and pickles and it topples over right after my first bite. Not to mention the seasoned McCain curly fries that Yassy and I dip in mayonnaise and ketchup!

After Saturday swim practice, Daddy takes me and Yas to Bayview Village and we get a chocolate cupcake that has a HUGE muffin top with tons of icing! We also get our favourite "cheese knot bread" that is so fresh and delicious. When we get home, Daddy makes sausages and eggs and we lather slices of the cheese knot bread with butter and guava jam. And, of course, freshly squeezed orange juice, and Mom cuts up a fruit bowl with whatever fruits are in season ...

"Stop salivating, Dina!" I hear Stern Sammy yell at me. "Do you think your pal Cindy Crawford pigs out like that every Saturday?" Stern Sammy has a cruel sidekick, "Temptation Teresa." It kills me as one yells at me and the other shows me EVERY morsel of food that I cannot eat. It's as if she presents each of these forbidden foods on a silver glowing platter just to see how much I can take. It's so intoxicating and I find myself drooling as she shows me everything I cannot have.

I realize I am almost *always* thinking about food! This has to *stop, or* I will never see the number on the scale go down like I want it to. I read an article in my *Seventeen* magazine about the supermodel Niki Taylor, and how she maintains her "rocking bod." Apparently, if I start paying more attention to my "calorie and fat intake," and also practice "portion control," I will look more like her. The more magazines I look at, the more I notice that every month there are always different diets promising various ways to help you get to "a thinner, happier you." The Protein Power Plan, The Juice Fast, The 7 Days to Lose 7 Pounds Diet, and so many more.

Normally I skip that section in magazines, but I start to read it more intently. Come to think of it, *most* of the pages in all of the magazines are devoted to the topics of dieting, and fitness, and how to be thin, so it *must* be important.

I wonder why I've never heard Mom or Aunty Dhun or really any of my aunties talk about what diets they are on. I ask her one day, "Mom, how do you keep your figure?"

She looks curiously at me as if I've just spoken to her in Swahili. "Keep my figure? I don't worry about that, Dina. Who cares about my shape as long as I am healthy and strong? Why are you asking about this?"

I shrug it off like it's no big deal. But it is! I need help here, Mom! When I go to Harper's house, her mom and older sisters are always talking about their diet of the week or month. I was hoping that my own mother could give me some insight into a subject that is clearly very important (See *Seventeen* magazine!), but I suppose that's asking too much. I guess I'll just have to pay greater attention to Harper and her mom and sisters when they are discussing their dieting habits next time I am there.

I guess Mom doesn't know Stern Sammy, Temptation Teresa and Sweet Sally. It's so odd to me because they are always in my head. I don't really remember what it's like to NOT have these voices yelling at me. Man, Mom is lucky!

19

APRIL 1997.
GRADE 7.
AGE 13.
WEIGHT: 117 LBS.

AS THE WEEKS AND MONTHS go on, I get savvier at restricting food. I get such a high when I think of how skilled I am becoming. I've never done drugs but I wonder if the people who do drugs get the same feeling of exhilaration that I get from not eating.

I have a long list of excuses as to why I don't eat. Why I can't eat lunch at school, why I will only eat baby carrots at gymnastics practice, why I will not eat dinner when I am at home ...

For all the crap Temptation Teresa hurls at me, I've got "Cautionary Claude" yelling at her that I'm NOT allowed to mess up my good streak. He warns her that I cannot, cannot, cannot eat even one bite of the ooey-gooey wonderful brownie. Cautionary Claude has my back and doesn't want me to fail. Sweet Sally also chimes in and reminds me that I'll hear her gentle congratulatory voice only if I weigh less. It's often hard to know which devil to listen to as they ALL speak at once.

At school, I cleverly ask my teachers for extra help at lunch time. This way, when I walk into the cafeteria and join my friends, it's easy to say that I had to eat earlier, while Mr. Johnson helped me with the geography assignment I was having trouble with.

My gymnastics coach, Sue, asks me why I only eat a few baby carrots during our breaks, but I've got her fooled too. I vividly describe to her the large dinner of oven-roasted barbecue chicken, sour cream mashed potatoes and a large salad with avocados that I had before practice. I tell her that Mom always has a snack of fruits, a cookie and milk ready for me when I get home from practice, so it's not possible to be any more full than I already am!

I make sure that it looks like I eat the lunch Mom packs for me every day so as not to arouse suspicion. I usually throw away the sandwich and give my snacks away to my friends. I always make a point of leaving a few little scraps behind in my lunch bag—like cheese and cracker bits or a half-eaten cookie—so Mom thinks that I have eaten mostly everything. It's these little details that make the story convincing.

I invent elaborate stories that Natalie and I swapped snacks— she wanted my Fruit Roll-Ups and I wanted her Dunkaroos, so we switched. I tell Mom that the cream cheese sandwich she made me was so tasty and Hanna, Nat and Mary who I sat with that day were so jealous. They all wish that my mom had made them such a fantastic lunch.

Avoiding dinner at home is easiest on gymnastics days. Whenever I get home from practice, I just tell Mom about the amazing (imaginary) ham-and-cheese sandwich on whole wheat toast that I ate during the break, along with the vegetables and dip I had. Again—the details make it sing! "It was a red pepper hummus dip! And Sue brought us homemade cookies too and so I ate the oatmeal raisin cookie AND a chocolate chunk cookie. I'm SO full mom, there is no way I could possibly eat any more. Sue worked us so hard! I'm exhausted … I just want to go to bed." It always works. I think I would make a great food critic since I have such amazing powers of description when it comes to things I am not actually eating.

As I invent my lies each day, Stern Sammy has a cunning smile on his face. He's never nice to me but I live for his evil smile. It makes me feel like I'm making progress versus having him yell at me. I must keep him happy.

The lying can get tricky, though, and I do slip up. Sometimes I can't keep track of the different lies I've told to which person, so I have to invent more lies to make the original lie somewhat believable. There are times that I slip up because I lose my adrenalin high and crash. Hard. At these times, I am so exhausted (and hungry) that the slightest provocation causes me to snap at my parents, or be rude to my sister, or burst into inexplicable tears. It's careless. I know if I want to avoid being found out, I have to keep my emotions in check.

Lately, I feel like my parents are beginning to suspect something is up with me. They comment often on how thin I'm getting, and when they notice something suspicious, they don't let it go.

"Tu behoo putlee chay, Dina." (You're so thin, Dina.)

Yesterday I told Mom that I absolutely loved the tuna and mayonnaise sandwich she made me and it was so thoughtful to add celery and mustard! She told me we didn't have celery in the house that day, so I had to think fast and quickly correct myself with another lie. "Oops ... my mistake. As I was eating my delicious sandwich, Harper had given me some of her celery sticks so I was eating both at the same time." Honest mistake—at least, I hope that's what she thought.

"What the hell is wrong with you, fatty? Didn't I WARN you? Don't make me yell at you again when you step on the scale tonight," Stern Sammy says.

I really don't like lying to my parents but I can't tell them the truth. I am in control at last and I like being thin. I feel successful. I'm better at front handsprings now in gymnastics and with each passing day, I get closer to looking like my new idol, Kate Moss.

Overall, I'd say I'm pretty good at having everyone believe that I eat, despite the fact that I am getting noticeably thinner by the day. Whenever it comes up, I say that I am just "lucky" and have a very fast metabolism, not to mention the killer workouts I get at gymnastics twice a week.

Last Saturday was a bit tough. Dad was just about to get in the car to take Yas and me to our weekly swim lessons. He called me into the living room, sat me down, and hugged me. "*Beta,* why are you so thin. Why do you not eat?" He was crying and held me close, forcing me to look him in the eyes. "*Jaanu,* Mummy and me came to Canada to give you both a life that we could never dream of in India. Why, *Beta?* Why are you doing this? Is this something you are learning in school? To be so skinny? All these sick models? Why? Please tell me, *Beta* ... please. How can Mummy and I help you?"

I didn't know what to say. I hated to see my dad so scared and upset. Had I really lost that much weight? The thought made me happy, and frightened in the same moment. Looking at my dad, I realized that he came from a place where refusing food was an unknown concept. Food meant love, happiness and family. Seeing me turn it down all the time must be so utterly confusing to him. He was equating my new eating habits with something I learned from growing up in North America. The place where stick-thin models are revered, the place where plastic surgery is the norm, the place where unrealistic body expectations run rampant, where youth is idolized and where you are taught that one must strive to always be "perfect." Where Dad is from in India, these notions are unheard of.

Daddy grew up in Hyderabad and is the youngest of seven children. His family is quite wealthy in India and he was expected to join the family business once he was finished his engineering studies. He never wanted to be part of the business or stay in India despite the fact that he would have been set for life. He felt that India was corrupt and wanted to move to either Canada or the US and make it on his own.

His parents sent him to St. Patrick's in Secunderabad, a private boarding school where they sent all of their children to be "properly educated." Dad knew if he studied and did well, he could go to university for engineering and then move away to create the life he envisioned. He likes to mention that the food at St. Patrick's was absolutely horrible and that his sister and saviour, Aunty

Dhun, brought him good food like lamb biryani and chicken korma every Saturday.

Daddy got top marks in high school and in engineering and moved to Toronto (since Aunty Dhun had moved to Toronto after medical school). Like most immigrants, he had to recertify himself so his engineering degree was recognized in Canada.

He had many setbacks, including the fact that companies in Toronto wanted engineers with Canadian experience and he had to literally go door to door with his resumé and beg for work. He started at the very bottom and eventually, after an extreme amount of persistence and determination, got the job he worked so hard to get as an engineer at Ontario Hydro in Pickering.

Mom grew up in Bombay (now Mumbai) and had also gone to boarding school. She was taught by British nuns and has a very strong grasp of the English language. Even though my grandparents had put Mom on the most expensive meal plan at the school, there was never enough food. Mom was tall, thin and always wanted more food. If someone didn't finish their meal, Mom happily ate it!

Mom has always had a very confident sense of self and a healthy body image. Being thin was never something that crossed her mind. Her biggest worry was if a boy would ask her to dance at school functions as she was always taller than the boys.

Mom loved breaks in school sessions because she got to go home and get proper filling meals. She says that in Indian culture, when you're happy, you eat, when you are sad, you eat and when you're done eating, you talk about the next meal! Life is centred around food.

In India, the concept of refusing food is ludicrous. There, having "heft" or weight is a sign of wealth and prosperity. The more food you are able to buy, the more money you have. The thin, emaciated look that girls in North America see in all our fashion magazines would be condemned in India. I can see my parents are trying to understand me, why I don't eat, why my walls are plastered with pictures of stick thin lily-white super-models, why I'm so moody. I feel badly that they are struggling with this new me but what can I do about it?

Seeing my dad cry definitely makes me question my choices. This is the sweet man who gets up every Saturday morning to teach us math so that we can gain confidence and excel in class. This is the man who taught me to ride my first bicycle and practised with me until I was ready to take off my training wheels. This is the man who is home for dinner every single evening. This is the man who did my hair every single morning if Mom had left for work—he is a better hairstylist than any of the other moms! This is the man who only wants to make sure his girls are happy and smiling. This is the family man who is completely present—every single day. He is here for Mummy, Yas and me no matter what. Daddy always shows me with his actions that there is no place he would rather be than with us.

I'm letting this incredible person down. But I can't eat. I've worked too hard.

"I'm sorry, Daddy. I've just been feeling pressure at school. It can be hard. I'm okay, I promise. I've been stressed but I will take better care of myself. Can we go to swimming now? I don't want to be late."

I hug him hastily (somewhat aware of how he's assessing my weight every time we embrace) and quickly scamper off. Before I've left the room completely, though, I turn back and smile at him assuredly—hoping to convince him that everything is indeed "okay." I can feel him watching me as I head towards the front door, so I amp up my chipper performance.

"Let's go, Yas! Time for swimming!"

20

JUNE 1997.
GRADE 7.
AGE 13.
WEIGHT: 115 LBS.

MY FAMILY DOCTOR PUT ME on a birth control pill to "regulate my hormones" and clear up my acne. I'm convinced it's caused me to gain weight. On top of this (as if that weren't bad enough), my skin is not perfect. Let me be more specific: it is FAR, FAR away from being even remotely bearable. Mom has told me, albeit very empathetically, that it can take a while to see results because "everyone's body is different" and my body had to get used to it. Blah, blah, blah.

Every single day I look in the mirror and pray that my face will be clear, and every day I get more and more discouraged.

When I walk into the gym I feel like people are pointing and laughing. Yesterday the gentleman who scans my gym card didn't even say hello. He must not say hi to people with acne. I was waiting for a leg machine and asked the guy how many sets he had left and he didn't answer me. People don't acknowledge me because I don't have nice skin.

"No one likes you because you're ugly! Pimples are NOT attractive! Can't you have clear skin like everyone else," "Acne Adam" says.

"Exactly—that one fry you had yesterday full of oil and the one Lindt chocolate you stuffed in your mouth last week didn't help you," Stern Sammy chimes in. It's as if every voice in my head is teaming up, ready to bulldoze me over, ALL the effing time!

The more discouraged I am, the more desperate I get. I've now tried topical treatments, oral treatments, birth control pills, first separately and gradually combining them. I hear things like "eating chocolate and fried foods cause acne." Naturally, I don't touch those foods! Do carrots and celery cause acne? Because they are one of the few things I do eat consistently, and as far as I know they are both "skin saving" foods! At least according to all of my fitness and fashion magazines.

I've tried every home remedy possible: applying apple cider vinegar to kill the bacteria on my face, dabbing toothpaste on pimples before bed, pouring boiling water into a bowl and covering my head with a towel so the steam can unclogs my pores, peel-away masks, Bioré strips, homemade egg-white masks, dabbing tea-tree oil on the pimples to absorb excess oil, using aloe vera gel to sooth my skin, dabbing lemon juice for its "exfoliant" properties as well as ability to reduce redness, making my own sugar-scrub mask. I am beyond exhausted and feel helpless. NOTHING has worked. All I want is clear skin.

"Try harder, Dina ... Get clear skin, otherwise you'll always be an ugly child no one likes." Acne Adam makes me so frustrated and want to cry. I'm trying as hard as I can! Don't you know that!

I spoke with one girl at the gym last week and she swears by her naturopathic doctor, and so I implore my mom to set up an appointment with this miracle worker next week.

I meet Candice, the naturopath. She's a short woman, 5'3 max, can't be more than 25 years old, fit but by no means skinny. She's definitely not perfect but the main thing I notice right away is that she has clear, glowing skin. She must know what she's doing! She is very soft-spoken and tentative with me. I have to resist the urge to say, "Let's skip this two-hour session, okay, lady? Tell me the pills to take so I can be on my way."

The session starts and the sheer volume of her questions is already driving me nuts, but I try to stay calm.

"Tell me about your family."

"What do you eat? Spices you use? How much water do you drink? Alcohol? Caffeinated beverages? Do you eat fried food?"

"Tell me about your stress? What causes it? Are there any particular days of the week or in the month where you feel particularly stressed?"

"Where on your face do you feel you breakout the most? Which type of pimples and the location on your face? Do you get breakouts on your back or chest?"

AHHHHHHHHHHH! I start plotting my escape plan from "Candice," who I now see will only torment me with intrusive questions and hocus pocus. I dig my fingernails into my palm painfully in order to settle myself. Stay calm, I tell myself. Don't be rude. She's only trying to help you. But seriously, woman: get to the POINT! I'll buy the damn pills—just give me a list. Holy crap, we're only halfway through this darn intro session and I'm ready to jump out of the nearest window.

Candice finally tells me her recommendations after nearly an hour of questions. She begins reciting an exhaustive list of vitamins, minerals, and natural remedies I have to take that I can barely wrap my head around. I ask her to write it all out because my head is spinning.

There's omega-3 that I'll be taking twice a day to reduce inflammation. Then Vitamin A to shrink my pores, probiotics to cleanse my colon, Vitamin D to control inflammation, zinc and milk thistle to detoxify my liver and too many others.

I also have to have one cup of water right when I wake up with three drops of lemon juice in order to detoxify my system.

I'm also supposed to take 15 minutes each morning and before I go to bed to meditate so I can "be stress free." Just thinking about this plan is causing me about a million times MORE stress!

It all sounds like a bunch of baloney but I'm desperate to have clear skin and so I go along with it all. Truthfully, I feel like she's talking out of her ass, but I listen anyway. Might as well give it a try.

A week goes by of taking what seems like my weight in vitamins and supplements. One evening, I start violently throwing up and it doesn't stop. I spend over an hour lurched over the toilet vomiting. I can't even keep down water. Water! Mom and Dad are getting worried. They don't like that I've been taking so many pills, and think I should be getting vitamins and minerals through food and not supplements.

Mom gives me a few plastic bags and sits with me in the back seat as dad drives us to North York General Hospital just a few minutes away from home. I throw up in the car, then again as we walk into the ER, and another two times once we are inside.

The triage nurse sees me throwing up and admits me within 15 minutes. The doctor comes and assesses me. My parents have brought along the 15 different pills bottles I take on a daily basis and show them to the doctor.

I'm so exhausted from throwing up that I can barely lift my head off the gurney. I'm crouched in a little ball and praying to God I don't throw up again. The doctor looks at me and says in the most condescending, matter-of-fact tone, "There is real medication that real doctors can prescribe to clear your skin ..."

If I had the slightest ounce of energy, I would have sucker-punched this dumb doctor, tried to wring his neck and yelled at him, "DON'T YOU THINK I'VE TRIED EVERYTHING? I'M DESPERATE, YOU JACKASS!"

Instead, I doze off as they hook me up to an IV. "Get up, you wimp! Find something to make your red, scar-filled blotchy face clear up." Acne Adam never fails to find a moment to kick me when I'm down.

"No more pills, Dina," my mom tells me when we get home later that night. Seems it was all a case of dehydration along with a negative reaction to something I was taking.

"I'm going on Accutane then, Mom. You need to explain to the doctors that nothing else is working."

21

OCTOBER 1997.
GRADE 8.
AGE 13.
WEIGHT: 114 LBS.

LAST WEEK IN GYMNASTICS, HARPER said pretty bluntly to me, "Umm ... Can you, like, just get over this non-eating thing?" How can I expect my parents to understand what I am going through if my best friend, someone my own age who grew up in Toronto, doesn't even understand it?

No one gets me and I feel like I'm all alone. I can't count on anyone. Just me, all by myself. The whole point of gymnastics was to feel like I was part of something, with people "like" me. I see now that is not the case, at all. I'm definitely not good at the sport like Harper. Today, the head coach Petra (a.k.a. Cruella de Vil) gave me heck for not sticking my landings, and my front handspring is not as tight as it should be and I need to strengthen my arms for the uneven bars. "Work harder, Dina," she tells me. I see Harper looking over at me from the other side of the gym and it sinks in: there is "that" side of the gym—for the talented girls and real athletes, and there is "this" side of the gym—for the klutzy girls like me. I feel like Harper is a million miles away, and gymnastics suddenly feels like the loneliest place on earth.

"What is wrong with you, Dina? Why are you so uncoordinated and such a sad excuse for a gymnast? I'm embarrassed to even look at you," "Exercise Eddie" hisses. "If you exercised more, practised your routines more, maybe you wouldn't suck as much!"

So, I've got Petra in real life and Exercise Eddie in my head. Clearly I'm not good enough and need to step up my exercises.

It's my mom's turn to pick us up that night and I guess she notices that I'm particularly sullen during the car ride home. "Is everything okay, Dina?" she asks me. I nod dismissively and turn to look out the window.

We arrive home and I head up to my room as usual. A few minutes later, my mom taps gently on the door.

"*Jaanu.* You seem so sad. What is wrong? Tell me and I can help?"

I begrudgingly explain to her that I'm feeling lonely, that Harper and I aren't as close, that I feel isolated from her in gym because I'm not as gifted.

"It would just be nice to have a real pal, you know, Mummy?"

She nods kindly and gently tucks a lock of my stray hair behind my ear. "It will be okay. Don't worry so much."

The next morning over breakfast, my mom gives me some unexpected news. "Dina, we will visit a kennel later this week. Are you ready to take care of a pet?"

What? I shriek with glee. I've been begging, *begging,* to get a dog for months! Harper has a dog, a Border collie named Loki. He is great to cuddle with and is very smart, always entertaining us with his tricks. Whenever my parents have pressed me to explain my erratic behaviour, I've told them if I had a dog like Loki, I would be happy! Day in and day out. The only thing that will make me happy is if we get a dog.

It seems my sad and lonely routine has finally convinced them! We are getting a *dog.* We drive to the kennel out in the country later that week, and the moment I see her, I am in love. She is a Cavalier King Charles Spaniel and is the runt of the litter. I identify with her right away. The breeder can't keep her because she is the "runt," doesn't have the right markings, size, weight and all the other "perfections" necessary to be a show dog. She is about 25 pounds, white with brown-reddish dots across her body and looks like a chocolate cookie, and I name her "Cookie." She has beautiful big brown eyes that look at me with so much warmth.

The breeder's loss is my gain. Cookie is perfect to me. She has this ability to know exactly what I need. When I have a yelling match with my parents for refusing to eat at dinner, she is always right behind me as I storm up the stairs and into my room. When I get home from school, she knows that I am more than likely exhausted but have to keep up a good front with my parents so they will think I ate lunch that day.

She always greets me, her tail wagging so hard that she sometimes slips on the floors. But it is her way of telling me, "I'll help you this evening. You can count on me to make you smile no matter how sad you are. I'll give you the energy you need this evening. You are never alone—I'm always here with you."

Cookie helps ease my mind at night. She sleeps in my bed and I have found that I am able to get to sleep easier because she helps me fight the devils in my head that usually are at their strongest at night.

She also helps me justify to my parents as to why, in addition to sports and the gym, I am taking Cookie on so many walks a day. I have to keep moving and burn more calories each day to keep my weight down. Cookie has a tiny bladder, just like me, so it is only fair I take her on many walks. This isn't so I can get exercise—my walks are for Cookie.

I feel that Cookie loves me regardless of how I look. She doesn't care that I have so many pimples and red blotches all over my face. She is not concerned about the dimples on my thunder thighs. She doesn't notice the fact that I am too tall. She just loves me—regardless of my imperfections, flaws and all. She is the only one that I can look at in the eye without lowering my eyes in shame. Cookie does not bombard me with questions about what I ate for lunch and tell me I need to eat more. She is just happy to be with me. She doesn't control me or try to change me.

I used to feel like I was alone in the world and that no one understood me. But not anymore. I now have Cookie.

22

JANUARY 1998.
GRADE 8.
AGE 14.
WEIGHT: 113 LBS.

IT'S A FRIGID DAY OUTSIDE so I'm not surprised to see the cafeteria so full. Harper, Denise and Alexia are at a table already so I sit down, ready to hear the latest gossip on whether Mark, the hunky soccer player from Brebeuf, kissed Melody, a girl in my class that I don't really know too well.

As I try to pay attention to the hot-off-the-press gossip, I can't help but notice some food sitting on the table. One lonely Oreo inside a plastic bag, one snack-size Wunderbar and a banana. This is too tempting. I have no idea where it came from, it could have been sitting there all day and be crawling with germs. Nothing alleviates temptation than the thought of a germ-infested Oreo … except when you're me, and starving. Denise spots me staring and says, "D, I couldn't eat them and the banana. All yours." DAMN! No, no, no!

"Dina, that perfectly ripe banana will feel like heaven. So sweet …" Temptation Teresa says.

"Don't give in, Dina," Cautionary Claude warns. "You don't want to ruin your good streak."

Why, why, why could she not have just finished her Oreos? And who on earth STILL has Halloween snack candy?

Okay, Dina, stop looking at the food and focus on the conversation at hand. Focus … FOCUS! Oh, but they look so good. I can almost taste them. NO! I can't eat it. I CANNOT ruin the great streak I am on. The top and bottom chocolate wafers of the Oreo look like arms, reaching out and beckoning me to eat them. The white layer of icing in between looks like the white pillowy clouds of heaven. Oh, how I wish I was in heaven. I'd devour you in a second! Oh the joy of eating the entire box! If only there was a world where Oreos have no calories!

"Mathematician Matty" pops into my head and crunches the numbers as Stern Sammy hurls more insults.

Alas, I do not live in this no-calorie world, so I set about doing my food accounting. One Oreo has 45 calories. One snack-size Wunderbar contains 60 calories. That banana I know will be 105 calories. That is a total of 210 calories, which is absurd! What if I just eat the Oreo? Then I can add an extra 10 minutes on the elliptical tonight to take off those 45 calories and actually burn more, another 56 more so I'd be in negative territory!

But I want to taste the ooey gooey caramel inside the Wunderbar! If I got a knife and cut it perfectly in half, then it would just be 30 calories. Maybe I could have half the Oreo and half the Wunderbar, which would give me 53 calories and I'd make up for it by doing 15 extra minutes on the Elliptical ...

Exercise Eddie and Mathematician Matty are talking amongst themselves trying to figure out the best option while Acne Adam is huffing and puffing at the idea of having chocolate and Stern Sammy is giving me an evil glare for even contemplating having one teeny tiny bite of SOMETHING!

"D, did you know that? She totally actually said THOSE words ... Can you believe it?" *Fuck! Don't these girls realize I have like 10 voices in my head? I can't keep track of their stupid girly conversations AND listen to ALL these voices at the same time! URGH!*

I realize I haven't been listening to a word of the conversation but say, "I know, eh! Totally nuts ..."

My mind turns back to the dilemma at hand. There are so many options. I could cut them in half or thirds or quarters and eat a small segment of each. Then I would work out to burn double the amount of calories. But what if I eat one and then mess up and eat it all. I can't do that! I WON'T. I've got to get outta here.

Cautionary Claude gives me a high-five. Phew!

23

JUNE 1998.
GRADE 8.
AGE 14.
WEIGHT: 112 LBS.

MY PARENTS HAVE MANY PARTIES—SUMMER and fall parties are their favourite because my dad loves to barbecue and the warm months allow for everyone to be outdoors in the garden. My parents adore gardening as well.

As you walk out of the solarium and into the backyard, to the left is my dad's rose garden. He has at least 10 varieties and they are his pride and joy. My favourite is the "Knock Out" rose because its stunning dark pink colour is breathtaking. Mom's favourite is a rose called "All the Rage." It's quite unique because the buds start out as a shade of coral and open to apricot-pink flowers with a yellow sunshine-coloured centre. Then, as the bloom ages, they turn pink. It's quite the sight to see!

Daddy is very fond of his "Sunrise Sunset" roses, which are fuchsia-pink! Yassy loves them all and always feel like the belle of the ball when Dad presents her with her "special bouquet." It is very cute!

Along the two other edges of the garden, my parents plant other flowers, bushes and my favourite, the mock orange tree. The smell that it gives at night is wonderful!

Even though I do really like our garden and used to enjoy the parties, I hate them now because there is always SO much food, meaning SO much temptation. I try to hide out in my room so

I don't have to look at all the delicious dishes and smell the aroma that wafts throughout the house.

As I hear the doorbell ring, I get more anxious. I know that sooner or later, my dad will tell me in a stern voice to get downstairs. My dad is a very gentle man so I know when he tells me something in a louder or harsher tone, he means business.

As I feared, dad knocks loudly and tells me I must come downstairs and say hello to all my uncles and aunties. In our culture, we always have to greet our elders no matter what. It is very rude if we do not say hello to each person. So I put on some clothes (which are always dark and baggy) and reluctantly go into the garden.

As I greet each aunty and uncle, I can feel the sets of disapproving eyes on me.

"*Shahnaz—Kaytli putlee che!*" (She is so thin!)

"*Soli—Khavaraych ke?*" (Do you feed her?)

"*Beta, come, tahra daddy nee tandoori marghi kha.*" (Darling, have some of your daddy's tandoori chicken—literally shoving it in my face.)

I know my parents are furious and embarrassed, but more than anything, sad that I don't eat. So I chime in, "Uncle, I play many sports and have a fast metabolism. I eat a lot of Mummy's delicious food." I continue talking in order to convince them that my parents feed me and that I am not too thin.

Stern Sammy laughs. "Dina—you are fat! Don't let these people tell you you're thin. You have a ways to go, thunder thighs!"

In my family and culture, food plays a large role. There are always copious amounts of many different dishes to satisfy everyone. Indians are incredibly hospitable and every celebration is centred around food. The emaciated look is not at all welcome and Indians will continuously tell you to eat more and more if you look even slightly thin.

The amount a person eats indicates how much a guest enjoyed the hosts cooking. It is actually very insulting to the host if one doesn't take a second helping. It just dawns on me: I must be insulting Mummy every night by not eating.

So as not to get any more aunties and uncles to question my eating habits and thin body, I quickly give everyone a hug and kiss and say I need to do my math and chemistry homework. This way, the aunties will at least see that my parents have instilled the value of education in me and that I am an academically inclined girl—even if they think I am too thin.

24

SEPTEMBER 1998.
GRADE 9.
AGE 14.
WEIGHT: 111 LBS.

REGARDLESS OF WHAT MY PARENTS say, I eat well. For breakfast, my dad makes me Carnation drinks; chocolate is my favourite. While I only take a few sips and throw the rest down the drain when he's not looking, I'm fine. I don't *need* to have the entire glass. My body functions perfectly well on three sips of milk.

At lunch, I make sure to include fruits and have a variety. Mom packs me way too many items. If she gives me grapes, I will eat 10 and give the rest away. Or, if my fruit is an apple, I will take 12 small bites and throw the rest away. I wish she could see that I am eating AND I have a varied diet! Frustrating!

I also have a mix of dishes I will eat at dinner. I have a routine favourite: I chop up five stalks of celery into one millimeter cubes. I only eat from one blue-and-white bowl because I know that this particular bowl is equivalent to 1.5 cups, so I know exactly how many calories I am eating. I fill the bowl with celery up to the brim! Next I add copious amounts of salt and pepper. To finish it off, I put one Kraft Fat-Free Singles cheddar cheese slice on top and put it in the microwave for 36 seconds.

I've got the okay from Mathematician Matty. Temptation Teresa tells me how much better my dinner would be if I added some bacon, parmesan cheese and a huge serving of Mummy's amazing rice on top. Cautionary Claude is beating her down for this meal. One point to me for this meal! I'm getting better at kicking Teresa's ass!

I eat it with a small fork, eating each cube of celery separately.

There are times when Mom gets mad I am not eating tacos or meat sauce for dinner like my family, so I decided to start making it myself. Mom, Dad and Yas can have their version and I can have my own. I ask her to get me extra lean ground beef and I prepare it in the following way:

I put the meat in a pot on the stove. I watch it all the time and scoop out any fat. I do this for at least an hour till the meat is very brown, almost burnt. That way I know the fat is all out. But to just ensure that there is no fat that perhaps I cannot see, I take the pot and put all the meat in a strainer. Then I rinse the meat under hot water and use a wooden spoon to press the meat against the strainer to eliminate any last particles of fat.

Then, using a measuring cup, I take a half cup of meat and place it into a small glass bowl that perfectly fits my half cup of meat so it, too, is topped to the brim.

I have already told Mom that spices hurt my tummy so all Indian food is out. I also "don't care for" any sauces, gravy, condiments, or toppings that other people enjoy putting on food. I eat "clean" and only like salt and pepper.

So, people can say whatever they want. I eat! I am completely fine and like MY style of eating. It works for me and that's all that matters.

25

DECEMBER 1998.
GRADE 9.
AGE 15.
WEIGHT: 110 LBS.

FINALLY! MOM HAS MADE AN appointment with the dermatologist for me. She has seen what a toll this horrible acne has taken on my confidence. I cry whenever I pass by a mirror or see my reflection in a window. I complain constantly about how I'm the ugliest girl in junior high. She knows I have exhausted every possibility and that the birth control pill is not working. She confidently tells the doctor that she believes I should be on Accutane and that I should not be experiencing SO much pain and hardship. It's a huge relief to have her fighting this battle for me. I'm not as strong as her, and I know if I were the one pleading my case, I'd be leaving—again—with no Accutane.

The dermatologist agrees! I'm going to start Accutane next week. I could not be more excited. Once again, he lists off all of the side effects. I smile and nod obediently but I could care less about side effects! They are a small price to pay for clear, gloriously clear, healthy-looking skin.

I feel like I've waited forever for this moment. Mom sees the tears of happiness in my eyes and wraps her arm around me as the dermatologist continues telling me about the side effects.

I will be going on a six month course of Accutane. The medication apparently makes you very sensitive to sunlight and the doctor never likes to start treatment in the summertime. If I had to wait any longer, I honestly think I would lose it.

We leave the dermatologist's office with a prescription—hallelujah! I ask my mom if I can look at the precious piece of paper and hold it close as we drive straight to the pharmacy. I must be noticeably happy because my mom remarks, "It's nice to see you smile, *Jaanu*." Of course I'm smiling! I've suffered with this revolting acne face for far too long. In six months, I will have clear skin and I know that at least a few of the voices in my head will be quieted as a result.

We get home and I feel like a kid at Christmas, eager to rip open this delightful package and start the treatment. I can't wait! It has to be now! I take the little pharmacy bag to the bathroom and unwrap it. There is a large booklet of instructions and despite my inclination to just pop the bottle and get going, I figure I should probably read through it.

I quickly scan through a list of side effects, all things that the dermatologist went through when we were in the office. Not important. I toss it aside and grab the bottle itself to read the directions.

"Take twice daily, with meals."

Oh. Shit. This is going to be tricky. I knew it was too good to be true! No matter—I can do this. I'll have to find a way to mentally tolerate eating two meals—it's only for six months, right?

I catch a glimpse of myself in the mirror—revolting. It gives me the motivation I need to do things properly. If I have to eat two meals, I will. I pop my first pill and head downstairs to make myself this first meal: three stalks of celery, half a slice of processed cheese, and a diet Coke.

26

APRIL 1999.
GRADE 9.
AGE 15.
WEIGHT: 109 LBS.

MY PARENTS ARE HAVING GUESTS over for dinner tonight. That means lots of food. Lots and lots of fragrant, glorious, fatty food. In order to avoid the temptation, I stay out at the library and study. But inevitably, the library closes, and so I take the longest possible route home that I can think of to avoid home for as long as possible.

I start to get anxious as I picture all of the dishes that will be on the table. Flaky delicious samosas, *bhel puri*, chicken *vindaloo*, *rogan josh, tawa paneer masala, dal makhani*, peas *pilau, raita*, warm naan, lamb *biryani*, and so many desserts....*gulab jamun, kaju katli, kulfi, rasmalai, kasha halva* and caramel custard.

As I near my house, I feel my heart pounding as the panic sets in. What am I going to do in this situation? I've been having a good week!

"Dina, just have one small piece of naan," I hear one of the voices in my head tell me. "That can be your reward." Clearly, this is one of the kind voices. I can handle this one. But I know if one of them shows up to the party, the others are sure to follow.

"Don't do it fatty. Naan? That is pure carbs! Disgusting." Stern Sammy has arrived. Great. My heart starts pounding even harder and I feel my chest tightening.

"Come on Dina, eat the piece of bread"

"Fatty, you don't deserve to eat."

"That piece of bread has 69 calories, one gram of fat, 12 grams of carbohydrates, four grams of protein ..."

"DON'T eat! You are doing so well! Don't ruin it!"

"The less you eat, the stronger you are."

While the voices in my head continue hurling pieces of advice and yelling at me, I side with Voice A, the nice one. Just a small piece of naan. I would do it and then go work out to get rid of the calories I had just ingested.

I greet all the guests in my house and then sheepishly lower my eyes and grab a piece of naan. The instant the piece of bread hits my lips—I know I've lost. My willpower vanishes and in mere seconds, I scarf down anything I can get my hands on. I am not even tasting the food. I'm barely chewing anything. I just keep eating, and eating, and eating.

The surprising thing is that I completely don't care who is around or if anyone is watching. It's like I'm possessed. Normally, I am very cognizant of my surroundings and only eat in private. I am so embarrassed to eat like this and I always make sure no one is around when I binge and make sure to clean up any evidence. But this time, I can't stop. After a few minutes, I feel defeated, horrible, and sick. I *have* to get rid of this food.

I decide I will throw up. That is the only way to rid myself of all this fat and calories. I have never induced vomit on my own before so I'll have to learn how to do it. Seems like a brilliant plan, though! I can stick my finger down my throat and all the disgusting calories and food will vanish as I flush it away. I feel proud and congratulate myself! Stern Sammy will be pleased because in just a few minutes, the naan and any memory of it will disappear.

I run to the downstairs washroom to start my mission. As I stick my finger down my throat, I start gagging. But nothing is coming out. Oh, no! Oh, no! This food has to leave my body. It HAS TO! I'm so frustrated that tears are streaming down my face. Why isn't this working? This food has to be eliminated.

I grab a toothbrush—maybe it will be able to reach farther down my throat. I can barely breathe and am now sobbing uncontrollably, gagging and coughing as I jab the toothbrush violently into my mouth.

My throat stings and aches from the toothbrush. I cram it down there again and again and still, nothing comes up. The muscles of my neck and back are sore from heaving; I can't take this much longer. Finally, I feel the food coming up from my esophagus and into my mouth. I can taste the spices again as they burn my mouth a second time. As the food comes up, I suddenly realize what I am doing. It's like my mind was "shut off" for a time and, now, it has suddenly turned back on. I cannot believe what I am doing! It's as if I have stepped outside my body and watched myself trying to carry out this unthinkable plan. Other people savour and enjoy food, yet I feel compelled to keep jabbing that toothbrush down my throat till every morsel of food is gone? *What* am I doing?

My dad must have heard me because he knocks on the bathroom door (which I locked of course) and nervously asked me, "*Beta,* are you okay. Can I help? Do you want Mummy?" I take a deep breath and say in a happy, perky tone, "I'm good, Daddy!"

I am clearly not very skilled at how to throw up properly because my parents are wondering why I am still in the bathroom. It's been over 20 minutes. Note to self: You MUST learn and do better next time. Actually, scratch that. Not eating is WAY, WAY easier. I'm never, EVER, going to allow myself to eat like that again. Throwing up is hard. Just not eating is much easier.

"Stupid girl—you can't even throw up right!"

Stern Sammy quickly chimes in with his evaluation of my attempt at bulimia.

Sammy haunts me almost daily when I step on the scale. Even if I am the same weight, he'll yell at me, "You NEED to be smaller, fatty! Why isn't the scale number dropping? What's wrong with you?"

Then there is Temptation Teresa. I despise her. She always manages to point out the fudgy brownies, warm biscuits lathered in butter, the blueberry pie that I'm dying to eat. Whether I'm in the cafeteria, walking by the café in the gym, at home or trying to fall asleep, she finds a way to imprint these images of food in my mind. I battle her all the time as she ridicules me, "Come on, Dina. Take a bite of the cookie, just one bite. You know you want that chocolate cookie. Can't you just taste it?"

Cautionary Claude always has a rebuttal or argument for Teresa. "Dina can't eat the cookie. Her entire day will be RUINED! Dina, don't eat it. If you take one bite, one SINGLE bite of the brownie, you have messed up everything today! Don't eat it. Don't fail. One bite and you WILL fail."

Mathematician Matty has numbers running through my mind at every point of the day. I look at Harper's lunch and he manages to run through the calories of the sandwich, fries, bag of chips and Diet Coke. When I walk down the hall, he'll tell me how many more calories I'd burn if I hopped the stairs two at a time. Matty gives me numbers regardless of whether I want them on not. He is a complete nuisance!

Exercise Eddie yells at me daily. He never gives me any praise no matter how much exercise I've done. I should always do more. "You call that a sit-up? Do another 15 more to flatten your fat belly! You've cycled for only half an hour. WHY haven't you done another 15 minutes more? Do you think your ugly thunder thighs will disappear on their own? Why has it taken you three minutes to walk up the stairs? You could have done that three times over and burned more calories. Why are you sitting in a chair doing NOTHING? Start those butt clenches immediately, fatty!"

Acne Adam does two things. First he tells me how ugly I am by pointing out every single pimple, blackhead or whitehead on my face. Second, he somehow manages to point out every single person that has better skin than I do and reinforces his point—I'm an ugly, acne-filled mess.

"OCD Owen" always manages to scare me that "something bad will happen." He put the fear of God in me and tells me that if, when I walk into a room, I don't turn the light switch on and off five times, "something horrible will happen to me." He never gives me details as to what will happen but it scares me enough that I do EXACTLY what he tells me to do.

He yells "NEVER step foot on the cracks on sidewalks." Or that I have to run up the staircase two steps at a time. Or that when I go out of the house, I have to check all the appliances around the house precisely three times, starting at the top of the house and working my way downstairs. And that I have to lock the front door four times to ensure it is actually done.

Or that I must wash my hands with soap, first lathering the soap, then scrubbing the tops of my hands, then my palms, then scrubbing each of my ten fingernails, then under each fingertip, and that I must do this six times.

I cannot escape these devils. Even when I am trying my best to fall asleep, Sammy reiterates how I've failed at my last daily scale check-in. At the same time, Teresa reminds me of the smell and how delicious that blueberry muffin would have been. Claude yells at me that I am not allowed to give into temptation. Matty informs me that if I had eaten that amazing looking blueberry muffin at Tim Hortons, I would have ingested 340 calories, 11 grams of fat, 57 carbohydrates, and 25 grams of sugar. Eddie questions me, "Would you have run for one hour to burn that off, fatty?"

On top of that Eddie barks, "WHY are you lying down? That doesn't burn calories. Do leg lifts NOW," and at the same time, Owen asks, "Did you turn the lights on and off five times BEFORE you got into bed?"

The devils persist, each one talking over the next. Talk about a lack of being polite. I want to yell: *"Didn't your mom tell you to wait your turn in a conversation?"* Guess not! These inconsiderate devils! They are with me every hour of every day. I am never ever able to escape. I want to kill myself to get a moment of quiet. They tease me and taunt me every single day.

I never feel at peace. I wish I could just slice my head open, scoop up these devils and close my brain back up. Oh how I long for quiet. Silence. Pure bliss.

27

SEPTEMBER 1999.
GRADE 10.
AGE 15.
WEIGHT: 105 LBS.

IT'S GETTING MORE AND MORE difficult to justify my diet to everyone. I am running low on excuses and I can only take Cookie on so many walks. I see a pained look in my parents' eyes every time I explain to them why I'm not eating dinner or why my lunch was left untouched. I need a new, believable lie to tell them that will buy me a little more good faith. I feel like a genius when I come up with the solution: I'm going to become a vegetarian!

I confidently walk up to the table in the sunroom where my parents and sister are having lunch and declare, "I'm a vegetarian!" It's the perfect excuse! I have effectively eliminated a HUGE number of questions I always get at meals. Now, I'm not eating lamb *biryani* because "I'm vegetarian." No, Mummy, I can't eat your meatloaf because "I don't eat meat."

Dad looks bewildered and says to Mom, *"Su? Havay ay gosh nuthi khati?"* (What? She's vegetarian now? So no meat?)

I feel like superwoman! Or a Power Ranger. I shot, fired and those guns of success went back into their holsters. I'm on fire!

Next up, I need to find plausible reasons as to why I don't consume dairy, bread, rice, pasta, fruits or pretty much everything in between. Maybe I can fake some kind of allergy? I've heard of a thing called "lactose intolerance," which basically means you can't stomach and kind of dairy. Maybe if I begin to feign slight indigestion whenever I drink milk or eat cheese, I can convince everyone I'm developing this condition.

I smile to myself as I pick through the plain, undressed lettuce leaves on my plate while my parents and sister eat their lunch. I look up and notice Mom's furrowed brow. Her face is tense and full of worry—I can tell she's not entirely buying this new vegetarian act. I think quickly.

"Mom, are these potatoes meat-free? I'm so hungry! But I don't want to eat any of the curry since there is lamb in it ..."

Her brow smooths somewhat and I take this as a sign that she is now convinced my vegetarianism is authentic. She serves me a heap of potatoes, which I strategically move around my plate (without eating) until the three of them are finished. I covertly scoop the potatoes into the garbage when everyone has left the room.

Stern Sammy shows his evil grin. I'm doing great!

28

DECEMBER 1999.
GRADE 10.
AGE 16.
WEIGHT: 102 LBS.

I'M SITTING UPRIGHT ON AN exam table in Aunty Katy's office. It's not a large room by any means—perhaps 10x5 feet, if even. One wall is pink, which makes the room less dull and sterile-feeling. She takes my temperature, blood pressure and looks into my mouth and ears.

Aunty Katy, also known as Dr. Driver, is looking at me quite intently. Like all of my family, she is also from India and immigrated to Canada. She is a very good family friend in addition to being my pediatrician.

Mom is here, too. She booked the appointment despite the fact that nothing is wrong with me, which I told her, many times! I can feel they're getting ready to attack me—hoping to shake some "sense" into me and get me to eat. Aunty Katy can see I'm getting a tad nervous and claustrophobic in the tiny room with both of them hovering over me.

Mathmatician Matty chimes in, "D, don't listen to whatever numbers they say. I've done all the calculations. You're good to go!" Stern Sammy will never overtly praise me but he flashes an evil grin, which motivates me to ignore all the nonsense I know will be laid out by Mom and Aunty Katy.

"Don't you believe a word they say! You need MORE exercise, tubby!" Exercise Eddie yells. It jolts me. Okay ... ignore everything you hear. You are NOT too thin. You must lose more weight.

We move into her large office where I now feel I can breathe. I plonk myself down in one of the two vintage club chairs. They are Italian brown distressed leather with small gold stitching on the outer part of the arm rests. These chairs exude "wealth" to me. I imagine being super rich, with my own mansion and a private plane.

My mind wanders further. I'm now on my jet plane, on my way to heaven. I've started having these kinds of fantasies more often lately. Wouldn't it be nice to lie perched on a fluffy cloud, without having to worry about calorie counting or acne or having to come up with new lies to tell everyone? Just me, looking down on earth from above. Alone and peaceful, no cruel voices in my head shouting at me, no mirrors to reflect my ugly body and strange face, no one looking at me and noticing my many flaws.

God welcomes me with open arm and says, "Dina, my child. We have been expecting you." There is no judgment or disapproving looks, just a calm voice and a loving embrace.

My fantasy is rudely interrupted.

"Dina, I have reviewed your tests and you have a very high level of ketones in your urine. Do you know what that means?"

I shrug my shoulders to indicate that no, I have no clue what "ketones" means. What I really want to do is tell her is, "I don't give a shit, and I don't care about what these tests tell you!" I'd leave immediately if I had the choice but I clearly do not—Mom is standing authoritatively behind me, like a wall preventing me from escaping.

"Dina, when a person has ketones in the urine, this means that the body is eating itself to survive. Your body is burning fat for energy because there is not enough fuel, meaning food, to use for energy."

"Ane samaj parach ke? Ketlu serious che?" says Mom to Aunty Katy. (Is she understanding us? And how serious this is?) I know they mean business when they speak in Gujarati.

"Dina, this is very dangerous. When was the last time you got your period?" Aunty Katy asks.

I open my mouth to answer but when I actually stop to think about it—I honestly don't know. I can't remember the last time I had a period. Amazing! Perhaps six months ago? Longer even? It dawns on me for the first time: my plan has worked. I have succeeded. I have reversed puberty! I can't let them see that I know this or that I'm blown, so I just shrug my shoulders.

"Dina, your liver enzymes are elevated. Mummy tells me you are intolerant of the cold and always wearing multiple layers even when indoors. Your blood pressure is extremely low and you are showing signs of osteoporosis."

I know I'm supposed to care and be scared, but I'm not and I don't. I feel cool as a cucumber. I actually feel powerful and completely in control. Is it odd that I feel like I'm on a high?

"I'm a vegetarian now, Aunty Katy. Maybe that's the reason." That should buy me some time I think, as I silently chuckle inside at my own cleverness.

My mind wanders again and goes back to God and his warm embrace. I'm now in heaven. I wonder what I will have to eat. In Heaven, I can eat to my heart's content. I have a pristine view of heaven and I feel like an angel, but funnily enough, I also feel like Homer Simpson, salivating at the thought of food! Rather contradictory images but, hey, it's my heaven—I can think whatever I want to!

And yet again, I'm brought back down to dreaded earth.

"Dina, if you don't change your way, you will not be able to bear children."

It takes SO much restraint to not just laugh out loud in their faces! I will never have kids. I have NO desire to have any rug rats. I hate kids. Ewww! The thought of those messy, demanding little people makes me want to hurl. I almost drift back to my dreams: What will be my very first meal? But Aunty Katy continues on ...

"Dina, you will end up in the hospital if you don't start eating more. Can you at least agree to go to therapy and get some counselling? We can arrange it so you can have individual therapy in addition to family counselling. Will you please at least do that?"

I look at Mom and then back to Aunty Katy. I feel horrible that I don't care. The pleading look in their eyes forces me to shift my gaze away. Mom's eyes look like they are tearing up and I'm scared. I really don't want her to cry. I quietly mutter "Yes" in answer to their question. The look in Mom's eyes changes from tragic and tear-filled to hopeful and twinkly, so I feel better.

It sinks in. CRAP. What have I agreed to? How often will I have to endure these counselling sessions? I'm sure the therapist will be a condescending jerk. I'm such an idiot for saying yes! The thought of talking about eating is excruciating! All I want to do right now is run away and keep running. I feel trapped by all of these adults, who want to force me to talk, force me to eat. All of the control I've worked so hard to get over these last couple of years is slipping away from me so quickly! My heart starts to race; I feel desperate and panicked. I want to cry.

At least for the rest of the day, Mom will be happy and smiling. Me? I'm terrified. I can feel all of the nasty voices collecting themselves in my head, ready to pounce on me when I get home. "What have you *done*, Dina? Don't listen to them! Do you *want* to become fat and ugly? You're pathetic ..."

The whole car ride home I am on the verge of tears. I can feel everything falling apart around me. I hate being so helpless! Everyone wants to control me—make me talk, make me eat. I have to find a way out of this. I'm so tired of fighting—my parents, my body, my mind. I just wish for a moment that I could take a break from "me" and feel free.

I think again of that fluffy cloud up in heaven. So quiet. So peaceful. So easy.

29

APRIL 2000.
GRADE 10.
AGE 16.
WEIGHT: 100 LBS.

I'M NOT SURE WHEN THE first time I thought about suicide was exactly, but I do remember the first time I got close to actually going through with it. Those daydreams of heaven, with that cozy cloud, became more and more frequent. The voices in my head were becoming increasingly nasty and *loud*, to the point where I couldn't hear anything else. Imaging being trapped in a room full of screaming infants all day long! Only these infants tell you what a piece of garbage you are—constantly.

I begin plotting out ways I could quiet the voices and make my fluffy white-cloud life as an angel a reality. Before I know it, I'm on the floor of my bathroom holding a pink dollar store razor and a kitchen knife.

I try to cut myself with the razor and realize that yes, I am bleeding but it's not going to be nearly enough to kill me. It will have to be the knife.

I eye the *huge* kitchen knife, as well as myself in front of the mirror. Where on my body do I plunge this knife so that it actually kills me? I've heard the term "jugular vein," and IF I plunge the knife in the exact spot, I will bleed to death. I really should have asked either Aunty Dhun or Sabrena more about this as they are doctors and would know this information! URGH. So dumb!

I'm sure I can stab my heart—that should kill me. I also think if I sever my wrist, I would bleed out, but as big as this knife is, I don't think it will do the trick as effectively as a dagger to my heart.

Okay, my mind is set: knife to the heart it is! I pick up the knife, turn it around so that both my hands are firmly grasped on the handle and the knife is facing me. The tip of the knife is barely three inches from my heart. All I have to do is create some momentum and plunge.

I CAN'T! Why is the knife stopping? WHY can't I push the knife into my heart? I feel this huge force surrounding my body such that I can't get past the barrier. PLUNGE! PLUNGE!

I am so close to heaven, why can't I go through with this? It's what I've been dreaming about! My hands let go of the knife and I fall to the floor, crying hysterically. I'm on the bathroom floor in shock that I could not properly kill myself, as well as in disbelief as to what I have tried to do. I have a new hatred for myself in addition to being ashamed of my actions.

I clean up the bathroom and quietly go to my room, shut the door and turn off the lights. I pray I'll be able to sleep but I know the devils will have a field day with me tonight.

30

OCTOBER 2000.
GRADE 11.
AGE 16.
WEIGHT: 99 LBS.

I'VE BEEN DREADING THIS DAY since I stupidly agreed to it—family therapy with a psychiatrist. I'm wearing dark blue jeans that are about fives sizes too large, a loose black T-shirt and a grey knit sweater that I love. It feels hand-knit and is comforting, even though I bought it at the store.

I'm silent on the drive over to therapy. We all sit in the waiting room and this super tall man who must be six feet tall asks us to enter the room. First off, WHAT? My therapist is a man? Seriously, dumbest idea ever! I couldn't have gotten a girl therapist? Men are so easy going, laid-back and worst of all, can eat whatever they want. There is no way in hell he's going to understand what I'm going through. Second, he is white! Oh yeah, I can see him being able to relate to me perfectly. FAT chance! And thirdly, he's about 50 years old. Are you actually kidding me? Somehow this 50-year-old white man is going to have some insight as to what is going on in my head.

URGH! I can't believe I have to sit in this room with this quack for the next hour. He has a large room with multiple options for sitting in a round circle. My parents take the couch across from me, the therapist is to my right and Yas is to my left.

"Good afternoon, Dina. I'm Dr. Saunders and I'm very pleased to meet you and your family. So tell me, what brings you to therapy today?"

This dude is joking, right? Does he not know? I was FORCED to come here. I'm not explaining it to you, dummy!

I know I decided to do this because Mom was so upset when we last saw Aunty Katy but I feel extremely defensive and can't help myself.

I just shrug my shoulders as my answer to his first question.

"What do you think the reason is that you are here? What would you like to discuss today?"

He asks similar questions and can tell he's getting nowhere with me. I haven't said a single word. So he proceeds to ask Mom, Dad and Yas the questions he asked me. I tune out and have my hands across my chest. Partly because I'm mad but also because I'm cold.

After an hour the session is done. As we walk out of the room, Mom puts her arm around me, which I find rather surprising. I thought she'd be mad at me. She just says, "I'm proud of you for agreeing to go to therapy. Maybe you can say just a few sentences next week if you're comfortable."

While I have no clue how I will feel next week, I nod my head yes so Mom feels better.

31

FEBRUARY 2001.
GRADE 11.
AGE 17.
WEIGHT: 97 LBS.

"DINA! DINA! ARE YOU HEARING me? You are going to have a heart attack if you don't change your ways ... RIGHT NOW! Dina!" A tall, older male doctor is desperately trying to figure out if I understand him. I'm trying to be alert and act like I'm listening as well as not faint in the process.

Aunty Katy, Mom, Dad and Yas are in the ER room as well. I'm sitting on a hospital gurney but I feel like the room is spinning.

Aunty Katy, in a very stern voice says, "Dina, listen up! You have two choices. You either drink these two drinks OR you are getting a nasogastric tube and you WILL be fed that way. It's your choice."

She must know exactly what I will ask as she adds, "You cannot go to the bathroom to drink it. You WILL do it in front of me."

My mind is a mess. How can I allow them to feed me through a tube? I cannot. I will NOT allow them to take control. How can I drink these vile meal replacement substitutes with SO many calories? Tears of frustration roll down my face.

Dina, you have one minute to choose or you will get the tube!

My family and Aunty Katy are so far past sympathy, empathy, compassion and trying to reason with me. They are COMPLETELY fed up with me. I can hear it in their angry voices and see the harsh look of madness on their faces.

I can see the older doctor prepping the nasogastric tube and start bawling. I point to the drinks and agree to have one. They don't waste any time and put the drink in a plastic cup filled with ice. I take a sip and cannot believe I've lost. I feel so ashamed and defeated.

I'm sobbing as I try to take sips of the drink. I feel like I am going to throw up, mainly because I have not consumed more than 100 calories in a day and my body isn't quite sure how to respond. My stomach is gurgling and they can see I'm trying to keep it down. I'm gagging and so they agree I will finish this drink, and in one hour when I get home, I will drink the second can.

It is restated to make it crystal clear: "Dina, you will drink the second can with Mom and Dad watching. If you do not, they will dial 9-1-1 and you will return here and get a nasogastric tube and I will admit you to stay here. Do you understand me?"

32

MAY 2001.
GRADE 11.
AGE 17.
WEIGHT: 93 LBS.

MOM AND I WALK IN the house after running errands. Since it is tea time, she asks me, ever so calmly if I will have a cup of tea with her. To her surprise, I lower my eyes and nod my head.

"Dina, can I make *duthni* chai (milk tea)?" She says it slowly as to not scare me since milk has calories. I shake my head no. She gently asks ... half milk? I nod my head yes and although she knows she is pushing her luck, she asks, "May I please add one spoon of sugar? It will increase your energy, *Beta* ..." I agree.

I slump into a love seat in the living room. This is the ugliest love seat but incredibly comfortable. It is a dull orange, brown and yellow colour (whoever thought those colours belonged together is beyond me).

Mom straddles one of the armrests of the love seat so she can be beside me while watching my tea boil.

"It's okay, *Jaanu*. We'll have a small cup of tea. It's mostly water. Don't worry."

I turn to face the back of the love seat and am curled up so I can rest my head on my mom's leg. I cling on to her with all my might.

As I smell the tea's wonderful aroma, I am scared that I am allowing myself to have calories but at the same time, for some unexplainable reason, I feel safe with Mummy.

"*Jaanu*, are you happy?"

Instead of my usual reply of, "Sure, I'm happy. Nothing is wrong. I'm great," I actually hear those three small words. I hear her this time! They register in my brain.

I am silent and start sobbing. I clutch her leg even tighter. For the first time in 10 years, I realize that my mom is not the enemy. She isn't the horrible woman that wants to make me fat.

I lift my head and look into her eyes. I look deep into her kind eyes and finally, finally see her love, the genuine motherly concern that's been there all along. I also see the hope in her eyes. She knows in that moment that I finally hear her.

I can't say the word no—"No I'm not happy"—but I shake my head from left to right. She can tell she is getting through to me. She quickly moves to where I am on the loveseat and she indicates for me to come sit on her lap. She hugs me and holds me tight. She whispers to me while rocking me in her arms, "*Jaanu,* you will get better. We will do it slowly together."

I know I am at rock bottom. How on earth can I banish the demons in my head? How will I ever be a healthy person? A happy person? A fun person? I feel like it is an impossible feat—I mean, I am already so messed up.

I am not quite sure if I'll ever be a normal girl but I am relieved that I am going to try. I am not alone anymore but instead have someone by my side that will help me.

After I stop sobbing, Mom asks if she can also make me *machan* and cheese (toast, butter, and cheese). The look of fear in my eyes is evident so she gently says, "Only one piece of toast—nothing else. You will get more energy." I agree.

I want to be happy and I have to start somewhere.

33

JUNE 2001.
GRADE 11.
AGE 17.
WEIGHT: 93 LBS.

MOM AND I GET IN the car. Today is the first day of the North York General Hospital Eating Disorder Program.

Mom called Aunty Katy the minute we got off the couch to tell her that I do want to try and get better. I guess doctors work fast because I got into the program right away, which is surprising.

I nervously sit in the car as Mom buys a ticket for parking. My shoulders are hunched over and I am quiet. Mom opens the passenger side door and helps me out of the car. As we walk past the sterile-feeling ER department, we make our way to the elevator and up the floors to get to the Eating Disorder Room.

Mom can see how nervous I am and holds my hand. Walking into this room means changing everything I've known and become accustomed to over the years. I only realized last week that I had a serious problem but I'm not sure if I can change and become healthy. I'm used to hearing the voices and commandments of the devils that haunt me every day. How will they know to leave?

I'm used to seeing every single rib when I take off my shirt. What if I don't see them anymore if I gain weight? Whenever I sit down, my butt hurts because it's all bone. What if one day I sit down and there is no pain? It will mean I've gained weight. How will I know the difference between a normal weight and if I'm fat?

I've been told that I look like a skeleton, but when I look in the mirror I see a very fat woman. When will I see what other people see? I'm scared because I feel my eyes are deceiving me.

I don't know who to trust: Myself or everyone else? I don't know if I should continue to listen to the devils in my head or my doctors and parents.

I'm used to exercising at the gym for at least two hours a day, most often two times a day and then doing my extra-curricular sports. I've been told that I exercise excessively but what else do I do with myself? I always have to keep moving to burn calories. I don't know how to just sit and relax.

How will I ever sit down and actually enjoy eating like a normal person? To sit down and savour a meal is a dream but I haven't done that in years. When I look at any food, all I see is calories and the amount of exercise I need to do to burn off those calories. I don't understand how people enjoy food. I don't know if I will ever be like them.

What if I gain weight and have to buy new clothes? I want to stay thin. I'm in control. But if I step into this room, I've lost control. I don't know if I am okay accepting that. I don't know if I can change and if that change will be a good thing.

I also think I'm too far in; there are too many things that I would need to change in order to be a normal healthy girl. It feels like way too much work. I'm exhausted even thinking about it. There is an episode of *Friends* where Rachel says, "I really thought I hit rock bottom. But today, it's like there's rock bottom, then 50 feet of crap, then me."

That is how I feel. I'm in a huge hole filled with darkness. I don't know if I'll ever be able to climb out of that hole and see sunshine and be happy. It feels discouraging at how far deep I am.

Mom can tell there must be a million things on my mind and hugs me tight. She can tell I'm too nervous to say anything. She just looks at me and smiles. It's as if she's telling me, "*Jaanu,* I am proud of you."

We walk in the room and take our seats. As I look around, I see about 10 girls there; most have their mom with them but there are also a few with their dad or both parents. I am shocked. I am not envious of these girls but I ACTUALLY see that these girls are very sick.

Maybe this is what my family sees when they look at me. All I see is very frail, emaciated young girls. I feel very sad for them. Mom, who is already holding my hand, leans in and whispers to me, "*Jaanu,* we will get better. I promise you."

In that moment, I know I have a long journey ahead of me, but for the first time, I WANT to get better. I make up my mind that I WILL find a way to be healthy: physically, mentally and emotionally.

October 1983: "Agani" or baby shower for me

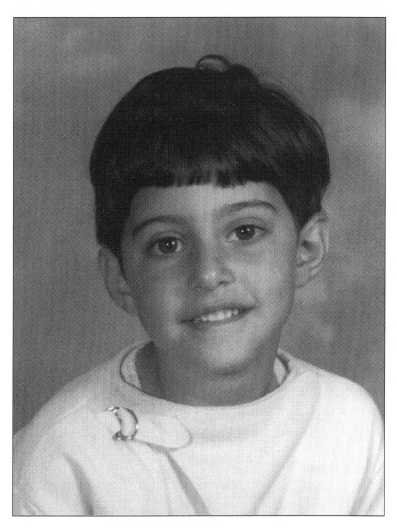

September 1988: Five years old

1995: Me, Mom, and Yas. Bedtime reading ritual

Summer 1998: Uncomfortable in front of the camera

July 1999: Me with my protector/best friend, Cookie

PART TWO
CRASHING

OCTOBER 13, 2012

IN LESS THAN A MILLISECOND, my car is spinning out of control. It happens so fast I barely have any time to see or process what is happening, but in the moment I do manage to look out my front window, I see a massive black SUV barrelling towards me. If it hits me, I will go over the cliff. I will die.

"Please, please, God, let me live."

It's a beautiful, sunny warm October day in Napa Valley. I'm driving to Sonoma on Highway 121 and I'm just 10 minutes away from seeing my good friend Claudia for lunch. She's in town from London and I can't wait to spend the entire Saturday with her sipping beautiful California wines and eating delicious California cuisine. I pass by Yountville, a picturesque little town that I would classify as a foodie's paradise. Definitely my kind of place! It is home to one of America's most famous Michelin-starred restaurants French Laundry, as well as one of my favourites, Bottega, which is helmed by award-winning chef Michael Chiarello. I could eat their *costolette brasate e affumicate* three times a day and never get tired of it!

I drive by Domaine Chandon which is known for its sparkling wine and beautiful lawn area, where you can eat and sip wine while looking out at the mountains. I can hear the Napa Valley Wine Train in the distance, which takes you on a scenic ride aboard an antique train that has been exquisitely restored to evoke the spirit of luxury rail travel in the early 1900s.

I normally travel everywhere in Napa and Sonoma by bike as I recently bought an absolutely gorgeous Specialized-brand road bike with a lightweight powder blue frame and pro gel saddle that is heavenly. I refer to my new wheels affectionately as my baby "Roxy." Roxy and I go everywhere together! Today, however, Claudia and I are planning to head to San Francisco after lunch to meet some other friends, so Roxy stayed at home.

The group of us will spend the evening together in the city, showing Claudia our favourite spots and cutting loose. I know it will probably get a little bit rowdy, and I can't wait! I never really had much of a social life back home, so these types of outings are a treat. I feel less like an outsider now, and I'm more comfortable in my own skin than ever. Life is good.

The drive on Highway 121 is beautiful. The road winds dramatically through lush green hills and valleys, and around every bend there is a new breathtaking view. It's a slower drive, as there are only two lanes, and because the road winds so much, you have to be cautious. You can never know what's around the next turn.

I see the SUV swerving into my lane and am suddenly jolted from my calm, leisurely state into an instant panic. I honk, and yell, "MOOOOVE!" The SUV is getting closer still. "MOOOOOOOVE!" I scream again.

This all happens in just a few seconds, but it feels like an eternity. I can feel my breath quicken, I grip the steering wheel so hard it feels like my hands are fused to it. If the SUV hits me, I will surely flip out of control and fall over the cliff to my right. My only option is to try and avoid it by swerving into the oncoming traffic lane to my left. I notice that the car behind the SUV is another SUV—even if I avoid one I will hit the other.

No matter what I do, I will be hit. No matter what I do, I may die.

I have to swerve. It's my only chance. As soon as I do, I lose all control of the car. I try to steer my way back but it's pointless, the car is spinning like a top.

It's like I'm floating inside my car in slow motion. I think of all the things I want to live for. All the things I have yet to do.

I've been missing home so much. I want to be successful, and I've fought so hard to make a place for myself here. I hate to think of going back to Toronto and people thinking that I've failed somehow. That I'm just coming back with my tail between my legs because I can't handle being on my own. I always imagined that when I did finally go back to Toronto, I would be CEO of a major corporation, with my first million in the bank. All I've got right now are few new lines on my resumé, nothing that impressive. Despite my hurt pride, I am missing home painfully. I want to be a strong, independent woman, to be the type of badass that takes no prisoners and can make it work ANYWHERE she goes, but I'm not. What does it say about me that I'm lonely and missing home so much?

Daddy must have noticed something was up because last week when we spoke on the phone he gently told me, "Dina, darling, you know you can always have Toronto as your home base and travel for work and pleasure."

I knew as soon as he said it that yes, I do want to come home. I've travelled the world and now I want to put down roots. I want to be with my family again—Mummy and Daddy and Yas. I miss our tea time and our family dinners. I miss our big family parties with all my aunties and cousins.

I want to tell my dad how excited I am to move back to Toronto in December. I want to tell him that as soon as I hung up the phone with him last week, I had started researching jobs there.

I want to tell my mom how much I'm looking forward to her homemade lobster curry, and more important, one of her hugs.

Yas is heading to China in early December for her MBA class trip. I'm so excited for her! She'll be visiting Thailand after the school portion of the trip for some R and R with her friends. I looked up some interesting things for her to do there, but I haven't emailed her the suggestions yet.

My car is still spinning, the cacophony of car horns outside is deafening, and I'm suddenly drenched in sweat. All I can think about is sending that email …

I feel the impact of the airbag and hear a thunderous CRASH. Everything goes black.

"Please, God, let me live. I'm not ready to die …"

34

MARCH 2002

"D ... THE ENVELOPE FROM the University of Toronto has finally come! Open it, open it!"

My mom can barely contain her excitement as I walk through the door. She almost pounces on me, waving the letter excitedly in my face. My stomach sinks and my heart starts to race—I've been waiting for this letter for months! What if I don't get in? A part of me doesn't even want to open the letter—if I'm rejected, at least ignorance will be bliss!

Deciding where to go to university has been difficult. I was accepted at all of the schools I applied to, including Queens (in Kingston, Ontario) and Western (in London, Ontario). A part of me wants to have the full "life on campus" experience. Leaving home, living in a dorm, being independent—it all sounds amazing. There is another HUGE part of me that is beyond terrified of leaving home. What if I completely flame out and fall to pieces? I shudder to think of what I might do, how I might act with all of that freedom. I've learned that I need structure in my life: a routine, a schedule, a plan that I can follow. To be suddenly thrust into a completely foreign environment with no friends? No parents to guide me and make sure I don't revert to bad habits? I fear the worst.

Most of all—and it's hard for me to admit this to myself—I'm terrified of this thing I've heard of called the "Freshman 15." Apparently, everyone who goes away to school and live in residence gains weight. When I went to visit Queens and Western, I toured the residences and facilities, including the cafeterias. When I saw the brownies, chicken fingers, burgers, fries and pasta—I immediately panicked. I wouldn't be able to control myself! "Freshman 15?" I'd gain something more like the "Freshman 50."

I am making a lot of progress by vocalizing my feelings and learning slowly how to eat a healthy way. The voices in my head have quieted. I feel better than I have in years. And yet ... the deciding factor of where I will go to school is determined by the thought of how much weight I will gain at each one. The University of Toronto (U of T) it is! At least there, I can still live at home and avoid the daily temptation of burgers and fries at the student cafeterias.

Mom and Dad believe that I deserve the best education I can get and they will pay for my tuition, but they have told me that if I choose to live away, I have to pay for it. I have no concept of how much rent, bills and basic necessities cost, and perhaps most important—I have no money! Dad is fixated on the fact that the University of Toronto is "one of the BEST schools," so really, there is no reason for me to go away.

Ultimately, the fear of the "Freshman 15" and a completely unscripted life away from home led me to want to choose U of T. Waiting for this letter since I made my decision has been excruciating! Now, the telltale moment has finally come. What will my future hold?

I tear into the package ... Mom's eyes are bugging out of her skull as she nervously studies my face for a reaction. The silence for those few seconds is filled with nervous anticipation.

ACCEPTED! Not only that—I've been offered a scholarship! I will officially be going to the University of Toronto this coming fall. I'll be a model student: straight A's and on all the sports teams. I'll get to know all of the students and make new friends. I'm even going to finish my bachelor's degree a semester early! Then, I'm going to be accepted into medical school on a full scholarship and be a doctor just like my Aunty Katy and Aunty Dhun. I'm going to have the best university experience ever!

Life is going to be perfect. It *has* to be.

35

SEPTEMBER 2002.
FROSH WEEK.

I'M JUST BEGINNING TO UNDERSTAND what a massive school U of T is. There are seven "colleges" that make up the entire school, which (according to my frosh leader) has a total of roughly 60,000 students. Holy shit! Harvard has only 25,000 students, and it always seemed like the biggest school in the world in my mind!

I will be a part of University College, which is right at the heart of the downtown campus. Walking around, the buildings make me think of Hogwarts from the Harry Potter books. They are mostly built in the Gothic or Romanesque style, so everything looks beautifully aged and almost mythical. I imagine this is what Oxford or Cambridge would look like (I also like to imagine myself attending med school there on a full scholarship, the pride of the Pestonji family!).

It's halfway through frosh week and I'm having a great time. I live on campus this week, which is such an eye-opener! I really feel like I'm living in the "big city," a welcome change from the suburban vibe of my North York neighbourhood. The campus is close to College Street and Kensington Market, both neighbourhoods with lots of cool cafés, restaurants, bars and shops. You can see the skyscrapers of the financial district and the CN tower from the middle of campus. It's all very cosmopolitan, and I'm loving it!

I'm sharing a dorm room with two other girls named Laila and Maddie. I practically do a double take when I first meet them—they're basically giants! I've always felt so self-conscious about my height, but at 5'5, I'm a hobbit compared to them. Laila is 6 feet tall and Maddie is 6'1, and both of them are beautiful and slim. They're pretty much perfect I would say. Both of them are very athletic and have been at school for a week already for the women's volleyball team orientation. They have so many stories already about the team and each other—it seems like they've known each other for years! I feel a little left out whenever they talk about volleyball (often), and a bit jealous of their closeness. I shake it off and consider trying out for the team so we can be a trio of unstoppable best friends ...

We decide to work out together in the morning before frosh activities start that day. As we jog together around campus for the first time, I can't help but notice that while I am sweating like a pig in a sauna, they seem to remain perfectly coiffed and kempt! It's actually hard for me not to stare at them constantly. I envy their clear complexions, their toned and shapely bodies, their amazing summer tans. They can probably eat and eat and eat whatever they want and still stay thin ... I want to hate them, but I can't!

I hear Yassy's voice in the back of my head scolding me, "Dina! STOP staring at these girls all the time. You'll make them uncomfortable!" How can I not stare though? It's like I'm living with the supermodels whose pictures I used to idolize and tape to my bedroom mirror. It feels like déjà vu. School hasn't even officially started yet and I already feel like I'm somehow "less than" the other students around me.

I'm enjoying all of the fun frosh activities—scavenger hunts, campus tours, social events—but at the end of the first day, I feel my stomach churn as our frosh leader tells us we'll be eating a buffet meal together at the dorm cafeteria.

I try to not drool over the buffet. It has EVERYTHING: fries, burgers, chicken fingers, pasta, salads, bread, desserts ... Admittedly, I'm nervous. I generally avoid buffets at all costs because I inevitably want to gobble everything up. Laila and

Maddie waste no time filling up their plates. It takes every ounce of my strength to keep walking past the lasagna, mashed potatoes and cheese pizza and instead load up my plate with salad greens, fish and steamed vegetables.

Laila notices my plate when we sit down to eat. "Oh my gosh, you're so good. I'm going to start eating healthier, too."

I explain to her and Maddie that I'm really serious about healthy living, that I want to join a sports team as well (maybe track and field) and how I consider myself to be "in training" all the time. They nod their heads appreciatively. It makes me feel good to be thought of as the responsible "healthy one" among us.

Over the course of frosh week Maddie, Laila and I work out together, have all of our meals together, stay up late and chat all night, go to the local pub for drinks at the end of the day, and generally have a blast. I'm grateful for my new-found friends. I imagine the three of us celebrating our many milestones throughout the year: cramming for our first midterm exam together, getting back our first grades (all A's of course!), picking out new courses together … It makes the newness of everything seem less overwhelming.

I'm a bit devastated when frosh week comes to an end. I have to move back *home* now? At the end of the week, Laila and Maddie sit together and watch me as I pack up my things.

"We'll totally see you, like, every day, Dina," Maddie promises.

"Now that you've lived here you can tell your parents how much you love it, and maybe they'll let you move in next semester!" Laila giddily suggests.

We hug goodbye and make plans to check in with one another and go for coffee on the first day of classes.

I see Laila and Maddie a couple of times during the first month of school, but after that we mostly lose touch. Apart from the occasional lunch date or random encounter at the athletic centre, I rarely see them at all.

36

SEPTEMBER 2002. FIRST DAY OF UNIVERSITY.

"WELCOME, STUDENTS. THIS IS BIOLOGY 101. Everyone look to the person to your left, and again to your right. Now ... let's see a show of hands. How many of you are planning to be a doctor? Now, everyone look to your right, look to your left. This is your competition. MOST of you want to be a doctor, but very few of you will actually succeed. Some of you will drop out after the first semester. Even more will either flunk out or leave this program after the first and second year. It's only a VERY small percentage of you that will even be eligible to apply for medical school. So remember: you've got to work hard—harder than you've ever worked in your life—if being a doctor is really what you want. Now ... let's get started with Biology 101 ..."

My heart sinks as I look around at the 1500 other students with me in Convocation Hall. I feel so discouraged. My vision of a blissful and breezy university experience and my dream of becoming a doctor feels shattered in mere moments.

I don't think I can do this. I don't think I'm going to be one of the ones who makes it ...

I hear my parents' voices reprimanding me, "Dina, nothing ever comes easily. Don't be so negative. You have to be strong. How can you give up before you've even started?"

I guess it's just the way I've been raised, but fear of failure— fear of any kind really—is just not an option for me. I choke down my feelings and make a decision then and there to BE

STRONG. Always. I don't even completely understand this choice I'm making, but I do know that in my mind, being weak is the worst thing a person can be.

I will succeed at university. I will have a great university experience, ace all my exams, and I will become a doctor.

I will NOT be weak ...

37

OCTOBER 2002

I'VE BEEN AT UNIVERSITY FOR over a month now and I can officially say: I hate U of T.

The campus is SO damn large! I spend all of my time running from one class to the other, and since the campus is so spread out, I barely make it to any of them on time. I'm always huffing and puffing, exhausted and sweaty, and feeling like I'm going to have a heart attack most days. By the time I arrive at each class and catch my breath, the professor has already given the important details about the lecture that day (which I've missed, because you can't hear when you're heaving loudly to catch your breath). I try to get the attention of one of the other 1500 students in Convocation Hall, hoping that one of them will be kind enough to tell me what I've missed, but I might as well be invisible. No one looks at me; no one even acknowledges my existence!

How is it that with over 60,000 students on campus, I feel so alone? Everyone is rushing from one class to the next or buried in books at the library. At first I found this odd: Why don't any of these people want to talk, for heaven's sake? I thought that university was supposed to be this incredible time in a person's life, where you not only study and learn but also forge lifelong friendships and discover new things about yourself and the world. HA! I have been living in a naïve little bubble, but now I understand: there is no *time* for any kind of "life" when you are barely managing to keep your head above water! With all of the reading materials, note taking, research papers, weekly tests and chemistry labs—the thought of "socializing" becomes a long forgotten dream. During frosh week, I excitedly signed up for soccer, the running club and the public speaking club. I mean, what was I thinking? Who the heck are those people who manage to participate in these extracurricular clubs, anyway? Clearly, they aren't pre-med students. They *can't* be! It's 6 p.m. and as I'm heading to the subway station to go home, a young woman taps me on the shoulder.

"Excuse me, miss. Can you tell me how to get to Robarts Library?"

I try to get the words out to answer her, but my voice is so hoarse, nothing comes out. I clear my throat a few times and (sounding like a frog who's smoked about a hundred cigarettes) give her the directions. As I continue on toward the subway, it dawns on me—I have actually not said a single word today. I have not spoken to a single person. In fact, I have not really smiled, laughed or had an engaging discussion with anyone this whole week. It occurs to me that this is actually quite normal. Between the 1.5 hour commute to school in each direction, to sitting in classes, lectures and labs, running across campus, coming home and studying, to making and eating my meals each evening, my life is pretty much solitary.

It's lonely, and it sucks.

When I get home that evening, I am desperate for some conversation—any conversation! But our family's schedule is so different these days, our paths rarely cross. I make my supper in silence and think of the family dinners I hated and avoided for so many of my teenage years and start to get emotional. What I wouldn't give to sit around the table with everyone and talk about nothing!

I feel the tears welling and stop myself.

NO feeling sorry for yourself, Dina. Don't be such a wuss. Don't be weak.

Okay. I suck it up. I can handle not having a social life. This is what it takes to be a success. All I need to do is study hard, get good grades (starting with my very first midterm exam), get into med school and be a super specialized in-demand doctor at the best hospital. At the moment I'm envisioning myself as a pediatric-oncologist at SickKids ... What an important person I'd be!

38

DECEMBER 2002.
MIDTERMS.

THE MASSIVE ATHLETICS CENTER AT U of T has been transformed into exam central. There are rows and rows of desks with numbers on them. I look at the list posted at the front of the gym for my student number and corresponding desk where I will write the exam. Everything feels so impersonal and cold. I don't even have a name. I'm just known by my student number, "UC-5720561."

Everyone is seated and a voice bellows over the speaker. The professor will be here for the first hour of this three-hour exam so if you have questions, this is your only opportunity.

My gosh, this professor has a few thousand students taking this exam and what, he's such a busy guy that he has some place better to be?

The exam begins and I notice all the stone-faced invigilators walking up and down the rows of desks. It's as if they are waiting to pounce on any student and accuse them of cheating! I'm scared that if I even glance up, I'll be expelled, which will definitely not help my chances of getting into medical school.

I hate these multiple choice tests. Unfortunately this is how all of my first-year classes test students so I get to look forward to another four exams just like it! Lucky me.

First question: "Solve this formula. Choose answer A, B or C." And … I have no clue. Okay, moving on. Time is of the essence, Dina. Just keep going, not all of these questions will be unfamiliar. You can do this.

Second question ... and again, no clue as to the answer. Third question ... nope. Fourth question ... fuck.

This is not good. I keep working my way down the page but it's not getting better. What is happening right now? All I've done for the last four weeks is take notes, study notes, read chapters, study chapters, then take more notes, then study more notes. My life has been nothing but schoolwork and studying and yet, I have NO idea what any of the answers on this exam are?

The memory of that first lecture at Convocation Hall echoes in my ear, "*Very few of you will actually succeed ... Some of you will drop out after the first semester ... Even more will flunk out ...*"

Flunking out is suddenly a very real possibility. I'm not used to this—at all. In high school, tests were a breeze for me. I got straight A's. Now, I can barely process or retain any of the information I'm getting in class. I actually do not understand most of what I am being taught.

I feel the sweat pooling under my arms and my pencil becomes slippery in my hand. What will my family do when they learn that I'm doing so poorly? I'd be such an embarrassment. I imagine Daddy telling Aunty Dhun that his apparently smart daughter is actually failing, and sadly, will amount to nothing. There's no way I'll ever be a doctor like her or my cousin Sabrena.

"Forty-five minutes left," the mediator yells out. Wait, what? I seem to have hit a time warp because it does not feel like I've been here for two hours. I'm barely halfway through the entire exam! I frantically pick up the pace and do my best to answer or, more accurately, guess the answers to the rest of the questions. There are students who are getting up from their desks and handing in their papers already. They're done early? I want to cry as I watch all of these clearly superior students get up and leave. I honestly have worked hard, but it doesn't seem to matter.

"Pencils down," the exam invigilator calls out. My heart sinks.

If I don't get into med school, what the hell am I going to do?

39

DECEMBER 2002.
CHRISTMAS HOLIDAYS

"MOM, I'M GOING TO BEN'S house now for the reunion. I have a lot of material to read for next semester, so I won't be back late."

One of my high school classmates, Ben, lives in a massive house and has super cool parents, and they've invited the entire high school graduating class to come over for a little reunion. I cannot express how excited, and yes, *thankful* I am that I will be getting to see everyone, and more important, talk with everyone! Finally, I can vent about my shitty start at U of T and talk with some people who can relate.

I step into Ben's house and a warm feeling of familiarity washes over me. I recognize everyone. Everyone recognizes me. How different this is from my life now, where I walk past what feels like thousands of people daily at U of T but don't really know anyone and can't talk to them.

For the next half hour, everyone is hugging and saying hello. I walk into the kitchen to get myself some snacks—carrots and cheese—to munch on. As I return to sit on the couch in the living room, Lisa, who is at Western University, is already mid-sentence and all I hear is, "He is SO wonderful. Dave lives on campus, two buildings away from me and we are *so* in love."

Alice, who is at Queen's, chimes in upon hearing Lisa's story. "OMG! That is so cute. I totally know what you mean. My boyfriend also lives close by. We do everything together and he is on the track team. He's coming over tomorrow so my family can meet him! Can you believe it?"

Julia and Crystal, both studying at Guelph, chime in with similar stories about new boyfriends and how amazing life on campus is blah, blah, blah ...

I mean, seriously, I think to myself, you all have boyfriends? You all have *time* to spend with them? HOW? I barely have time for myself, let alone a boyfriend.

Wait ... Is there something wrong with me?

I feel a ball of emotion well in my throat. I don't have any cool boyfriend stories to share. I'm relieved when I hear Clara, who is at McGill, talking about something else.

"Me and my five new best friends are all planning a trip for Reading Week. We're so excited!"

Wait a second ... she has five new best friends? So, she not only has a social life but also has the time to go on a trip? Like, "leisure" time"? I was planning on getting ahead on my school work during the break! Well, great. I totally can't contribute to *this* conversation either. I could not feel like a bigger, lamer, dork. Smile and nod, Dina, just smile and nod as if you know what they are talking about ...

I'm trying so hard to be enthusiastic and happy for everyone but, honestly, I'm not. I'm fucking jealous!

Then, Ashley and Cindy who are in the same classes at Waterloo say, "We loooooove our program and we're doing soooo well on the tests!"

Umm, seriously. Fuck this. Am I on a completely different planet? I have no boyfriend, barely any friends, no social life and I'm scared to death I'll flunk out.

I look around at my high school friends. We have very, very different lives. As I try to hide my seething jealousy, I notice most of the girls have gained a few pounds. Ashley has gained at least 10 pounds. I know it's bitchy of me but I find some comfort in the fact that I have not gained any weight.

Take that! You can have your parties, and boyfriends, and dorm room cafeteria dinners where you have all these new best friends to eat with and stay up late with, BUT ... you have also succumbed to the dreaded "Freshman 15!" At least I win in that category!

I secretly want all of what they have, but what can I do? I brush my jealousy aside and console myself with the knowledge that they have packed on the pounds while I have remained slim and trim.

40

JANUARY 2003

ENOUGH IS ENOUGH. I HAVE no idea how to meet guys at school, but everyone seems to have a boyfriend and I'm sick of it! I see girls around campus who wear high heels (High heels?) and miniskirts to class and wonder if that's what I need to do? My school "uniform" is typically Roots sweatpants and a hoodie, with my hair up in a ponytail and zero makeup on my face. Or, if I'm at the gym, it's baggy shorts, a T-shirt soaked through with sweat and a greasy forehead. I guess the mystery of why I have no boyfriend is solved!

At this point, I expected to be kicking ass in school, life and love, but I'm falling short in all three departments. Something's got to give! I've heard that people go on the Internet to find dates so I look into it.

I trudge down to the basement where our family desktop computer is, which already feels a bit clandestine. I would be mortified if my dad discovered what I'm up to! Yas would also *never* let me live it down. I type "online dating," and "dating Toronto," into the search engine and a dizzying number of websites and articles come up on the subject. As I click through the links and comb my way through profile after profile of "eligible singles," I can't help but laugh. It kind of seems as if online dating is only for older desperate woman. NO one my age does it. Yikes. No one can ever know about this! It's *so* embarrassing.

I see the website for Lavalife come up pretty consistently as the best site to go to for dates. I create a profile, and after going through a long-ass questionnaire that asks me everything about my behaviours, personality and interests, the site instructs me to write a short "blurb" about myself. Crap. How can I spin "dull, failing student with no social life" into a sentence that will inspire guys to get in touch with me?

"Active, smart girl who loves to laugh," is all I can come up with. It's somewhat true. I am active and while I am not really smart anymore, I was smart in high school. And although I can't really remember the last time I've laughed, I do love to do it!

The site asks for my credit card information. I'll have to make sure I check the mail every day so Daddy doesn't see the payment. How awkward would *that* be?

I've officially become a "desperate woman." I have a real online dating profile! I feel like a complete and utter loser, but I'm also excited and curious about who I will meet!

I sit and watch the screen for over an hour, waiting for notifications. Note to self: this is what desperation looks like.

Midterm test marks came back a little while ago and as I suspected: it's not good. I didn't flunk (thank heavens), but my mark is nowhere near what I need it to be. C minuses certainly won't get me into med school! I have no idea what I'm going to tell my parents. I hate so much to let them down in any way. They are so supportive and loving, and I haven't forgotten—they are paying for this whole thing! My only job is to show up and get decent grades. I have no idea how so many students manage to work part time and pay for school, which makes me feel like even more of a failure.

I feel terrible—literally. Every time I start to stress over grades, my (non-existent) social life, my sad little online dating profile, I just want to run screaming in the opposite direction from everything I'm feeling! The old voices in my head have definitely subsided but there's a new one that seems almost worse: my own. I hate, abhor and loathe the pathetic girl who whines every other second about her shortcomings, but I can't get her out of my head! I would really prefer to just get on with things and focus on the positive, but she is constantly pulling me back into a perpetual state of self-doubt.

I am honestly so fucking tired of myself.

It's been a long day and I realize that I haven't actually eaten anything. No wonder I'm so exhausted! I could probably just go home and there would be some kind of curry or pasta in the fridge, but I decide to treat myself to some takeout. At least this shitty day can end with a tasty meal from one of my (secretly) favourite restaurants, Red Lobster. We used to go as a family to the one near my house at Sheppard and Warden, and it was always the biggest deal for me and Yas. Forget fine dining—for me, nothing compares to the kids' menu at Red Lobster. It's the ultimate comfort food, and I could seriously use a little comfort right about now.

I drive to the nearest Red Lobster and decide (since I'm alone and have no desire to sit and eat by myself) to order takeout. I go straight for the kids' menu and decide I'll order chicken fingers with all four sauces (pina colada, sweet and sour, ketchup and tartar sauce), some Cheddar Bay biscuits, and an order of the "Brownie Overload," which is a giant slice of fudge-y walnut brownie drenched in warm fudge sauce.

I know I'm not a "kid," so ordering off of the kids' menu is a bit of an ordeal. What if the hostess calls me out for it? "Uhh … you're way too old for this menu, young woman. I'm afraid I can't let you do that." How humiliating would that be? My heart is actually racing as I play out this worst-case scenario in my mind. I quickly invent a story I can tell her in case she gives me grief: it's my little brother's favourite, he's just getting over a cold … As she approaches me, I feel the panic rise in my chest. I NEED that delicious food and I'm gonna get it!

"What can I get you miss?" she asks cordially. I quickly ramble off my order in the hope she won't notice anything is amiss. I decide to tack on a few extra biscuits and some fries as well for Yas—she'll love me for bringing a little home for her. Screw it—today I'm going to indulge. I'll get back on track tomorrow, but tonight? I deserve a pick-me-up.

"Okay, about 10 minutes and that will be ready," she tells me. Sweet relief, I'm safe!

Once my order is ready I gun it out of there as fast as I can so as to avoid any suspicious looks. I reach the car and can hardly wait until I'm safely inside to rip open the takeaway bag and devour a biscuit. They're warm, fluffy and buttery in the middle, with a perfectly toasted golden brown top that's obviously brushed with butter so it crisps up nicely. I could eat an entire meal of only Cheddar Bay biscuits and be perfectly happy! I quickly devour another one, and then another ... I haven't even left the parking lot and I've already eaten five biscuits.

I'm pretty full now, but I don't care. I crack open the fries and place them on my lap for easy pecking access. I snack on my delicious, salty, crispy fries along the way, eagerly shoving a few of them at a time into my mouth. Before I know it, they're all gone. It's like I've inhaled them.

Since I've eaten everything I was going to give to Yas, there's really no turning back. I've messed up my healthy eating so I may as well indulge to the max. I make a plan to hit the gym tomorrow an hour early, and I'll also make a healthy meal plan for the next few days to help me get back on track. In the meantime—I take advantage of a stoplight and bust open the brownie. It's pretty messy but that doesn't stop me, and, if I eat it now, I can stop at the Tim Hortons drive-through before I get home and order some glazed Timbits (mini doughnuts) and an oatmeal raisin cookie. I've got to get all of my cravings out of my system so I can start fresh tomorrow! In fact, tomorrow I'm going to start practising a healthier lifestyle overall. I'll definitely have to cut out ALL processed food, and research "macrobiotics," which I've heard is Gwyneth Paltrow's or some other celebrity's secret to staying so fit and trim.

Half of my order of chicken fingers and six chocolate glazed Timbits later, I pull into my driveway. I am so stuffed, I can hardly breathe. I feel disgusting. I look at all of the takeout containers and bags littering the passenger seat of the car and panic: What if Mom or Dad or Yas came out at this very moment and saw this? I picture them staring at me, shocked and revolted. The amount of calories I have consumed in the last hour is probably the equivalent of a three or four days' worth. I want to be sick but I've been down that road before and the thought of it is enough to stop me from doing it.

Even if I work out like crazy, even if I starve myself, I can't undo what I've just done. I feel so gross and pathetic right now, I just want to shower it all off and forget.

I head inside and bolt upstairs to my room. I can't look anyone in the eyes right now or let them see me like this. If they knew that I'd been cramming all of that junk food down my throat like a pig, I don't know if I could handle the shame.

What the *fuck* is the matter with me?

41

MAY 2003

I WANT TO CRY. I get my grades back and feel lost. I'm close to failing and I've never seen such horrible grades. I used to love school and now I hate it. My dream of medical school feels completely out of reach.

I arrive home and Mom sees my face. She can see the devastation in my eyes and hugs me without saying a word. I go to my room, change into comfy sweats, and then take a seat at the top of the staircase where I just start sobbing. Yas comes and sits beside me as Mom and Dad look up at us from the bottom of the staircase.

I don't have to even say it, they already know: I am so, so unhappy.

The pace of university feels so fast—so many new subjects, styles of teaching, different types of assignments and these horrible multiple choice exam determining my overall grade—I didn't have time to adapt to all this newness.

I feel a COMPLETE loss of control. The normal A, A+ grades that I was used to receiving in high school have now become C's and D's faster than I can blink. I am so overwhelmed and have no idea how to get myself back to the A+ level.

I tell my family through sobs that I feel like a failure. I tell them I am spiralling downwards academically so rapidly that I feel the need to starve myself. I can't tell them about the binging, though, that's just too disgusting and I'm too ashamed.

Mom and Dad come to the top of the staircase and sit beside me.

"*Jaanu,* this is year one of four. You are in a very challenging program. You are in a very different environment compared to high school. Don't be discouraged. You have worked very hard. This is a time to learn and it is okay. Next year, classes will be smaller; you can go to more tutorials and ask for help from the teaching assistants. They have been through it and they will help you. It's okay. It's just a rude awakening. This is normal and I promise you will be just fine. Now … let's wash all those tears off your face, and then we will have a nice dinner and celebrate the fact that you have made it through first year."

I can hear the devils in my head getting louder. "NO," I tell them. "You are NOT welcome in my mind! I'm better and I've got this! I am strong and I am healthy now. Everything is FINE."

"I'll do better next year," I tell my family as I wipe away tears.

42

MAY 2004.
END OF SECOND
YEAR UNIVERSITY

SINCE THE TIME I WAS about 15, I thought I would be a doctor, just like Aunty Dhun and Sabrena. It never occurred to me I would, or could, do anything else.

Imagine my surprise when, after almost two years in pre-med, I realize that I hate blood, I find human bodies revolting and "icky," and the notion of "healing people" is something I have no connection to whatsoever. I hate listening to Sabrena's gross stories about "surgery" and "treatment." In fact, I usually plug my ears and hum loudly to drown her out.

I don't want to be a doctor.

Holy crap. What on earth do I do now? I'm in a pre-med program. I don't like U of T. Can I even transfer into another program? If I can, what program do I want?

I frantically search my mind for the answers to all these questions. The voices in my head chime in, asking the most unbearable question of all,

"Who the hell *are* you?"

I have no fucking clue. I essentially do the mental equivalent of "LA-LA-LA, I CAN'T HEAR YOOUU ..." and erase the difficult questions from my mind.

"Who are you, Dina? If you're not a doctor, who are you?"

No matter how hard I try, I can't drown out the voices, their awful questions, and the painful answer ringing clearly above it all:

I'm nobody. I'm nothing. If I'm not accomplishing something, I'm less than nothing.

I feel the tears welling and I push them down. Stay positive, Dina! Strong people find solutions, they don't waste time worrying or moping about their feelings!

BOOM. It dawns on me. I'll become a businesswoman! Aunty Dhun recently won an award for her business endeavours, and we all went to the gala and watched her accept her trophy. She was amazing! I always thought that in order to emulate her, I had to be a doctor, but now I see! She is also a remarkable businesswoman!

I can be like her as a businesswoman. Question answered. Done. Hooray!

I'll enroll in a business program, stat. I start researching business programs to apply to. Western and Queen's have good programs, but if I transfer schools, they will not allow me to transfer my courses, which would essentially mean I go back to first year. Screw that! I am not willing to do another four more years of university.

After a long chat with my parents, we decide that the best option is to stay at the University of Toronto and finish my science degree, but I will fast track. I'll take courses over the summer and finish my undergrad degree in a year and a half. I can't wait to get into the working world and discover my true career path.

I set some new goals: I'll be CEO of my own company by the age of 23. I'll be the youngest female CEO ever to end up on the Fortune 500 list.

I'll be way more than nothing now. I'll be extraordinary, or I'll die trying!

43

JULY 2004

"MOM, I *CANNOT* GO INTO the working world looking like this!"

As if I don't have enough going against me, in a matter of less than a week, my face has become horrible! It started with just a few blackheads, then a few bigger pimples, and now—AGAIN— my entire face is covered with painfully inflamed acne.

I cannot go through this again. I'm about to head into my final year of university, which means that very soon, I'll be heading out into the workforce. How will I be taken seriously in the professional world if I'm covered in zits? It's a fact: no one wants to look at someone's pimply face.

When I first started Accutane, I was warned that some individuals require multiple treatments. I always hoped I would not be one of those people, but apparently I am. Mom sympathizes and we make an appointment with the dermatologist for the following week.

I do the math: I have just over a year to get my skin clear again. That's when I will most likely be going out on interviews for jobs. I MUST have a clear face, exude confidence and be a superstar at whatever career I decide on. I'm ready for the next phase of life! My face is apparently on a different wavelength, but I'm praying that a second round of Accutane will put it back on track.

While I don't particularly like U of T, there is a plus side: most of my classes are still very large, so I can hide at the back of the room where no one can see my horrible-looking skin. I always quickly slip out and run to my next class and avoid people's gaze as much as I can. I guess there is an upside to feeling invisible.

44

SEPTEMBER 2004

THE SECRET'S OUT: I MET a guy on Lavalife. His name is Steven. We've been dating for months.

I literally want to poke my own eyes out as my parents ask me to explain "What is this Lavalife thing?" and the whole concept of online dating. I lie and tell them that everyone meets online nowadays; it's totally cool ... The reality is, if it weren't for the fact that they noticed the charges on my credit card statement, I never would have told them anything. I'm so embarrassed! No one else knows about my Internet exploits except for them (and Steven), and it has to stay that way!

I'm not quite sure what to call my "relationship" with Steven. I can't pinpoint a time that he's actually called me his girlfriend or even insinuated that we are in a relationship. Sometimes I know when I'll see him and other times I'm in the dark. Sometimes he calls and sometimes I don't hear from him for days. I never used to take my phone to the gym, but I do now, just in case. I am always waiting for him.

And wondering: Why isn't he calling? What did I do wrong? Does he not think I'm smart enough? Or pretty enough?

He's six years older than I am and is already working on Bay Street for a big financial firm. I enjoy talking with him, learning about the business world, so when he disappears or acts indifferently toward me, I let it go. I'm lucky he's interested in me at all!

I try my hardest not to think about it, but I wonder why he doesn't want me more. Why isn't he proud to call me his girlfriend? Why does he keep me at arm's length? Why doesn't he want to meet my family or friends?

I get upset when I think about these things, and so I'll just ignore them and tell myself that he does love me, in his own way. The truth is, I'm scared there isn't anyone out there who will actually love me the way I want to be loved. Maybe this is as good as it gets?

As I explain to my parents the ins and outs of online dating, I pray that Mom doesn't see through my bravado and ask me the dreaded question she always asks when she suspects something is up,

"Dina, are you happy? Does Steven make you happy?"

Thank God, she doesn't ask. If she doesn't ask, I don't have to admit it to myself that I'm miserable, and that this guy treats me like shit.

In the end, Steven answers the question for both of us. He unceremoniously dumps me and I resolve in that moment to put off "relationships" and "love" until I'm established in my career.

Relationships are such a waste of time! Especially at my age, when I should be focused on getting ahead in the world. Having a boyfriend and being in a relationship might stifle my career. What if I get offered a job in another country? I wouldn't want "love" to get in the way of that decision. Furthermore, I have a very specific routine and I don't want any man interrupting that. I NEVER want to be one of those people who "gets comfortable" and "lets themselves go," as many people do in relationships. Being fat is not part of my plan.

Relationships are for pathetic needy women. I am strong and I will never let a guy get close enough to mess me up and make me get fat ... never!

When I see girls gazing at babies with their dreamy eyes, I want to throw up. All the "awws," and baby talk is crap! I have ZERO desire to have one of those rug rats. Pregnancy weight? I don't think so. I am just not meant to have kids or be in a relationship. At least for now. They would just mess up everything! I resolve to stay laser focused on what I want—becoming a CEO and being rich!

45

OCTOBER 2004

WITH A RENEWED SENSE OF direction and purpose, I begin my final year of school with a concrete plan in my mind. I tell myself: the plan is everything. I cannot deviate from the plan. To do so would be to jeopardize any chances I have of success. I just have to keep my head down, ignore all of the voices steering me off course, and be resolute. You have a goal, Dina: to be the most successful businesswoman in Canada within two years. You can do it!

I maintain a routine no matter what. It cannot be tampered or shaken up. It's MY routine and it keeps me sane.

I always wake up early. I have never woken up past 7 a.m. and even that was pushing it. I always have the same breakfast; over the years that has changed, but right now it's egg whites and a cup of fresh fruit. It makes me a lean, mean machine and I know I'm starting my day off right!

Then I work out. My day MUST start this way. I do not allow anyone to mess with the start of my day. It is ME time.

Whether I am at school or work, I ALWAYS pack my lunch and snacks. I never want to be so hungry that I resort to buying foods that will tempt me. When I make my own lunch, I know the portions I want, the protein content to ensure I'm not too hungry and it allows me know what I am eating. I always make my lunches the night before so I'm never scrambling to get it done in the morning.

I will have dinner around 7 p.m., which is extremely important for a few reasons. First, I'm usually hungry at this time. Second,

I have a peaceful relaxed dinner and I have enough time to digest the food, sometimes take an evening stroll and go to bed. Having a good dinner at an appropriate time allows me to go to sleep early, have a good sleep, and wake up rested for the next day.

NOTHING can change my routine! It's a cycle that is important for me to function effectively. If anyone tries to do anything to tamper with my routine, I not only get extremely anxious but I'll avoid that person.

When I chose my university courses for the year, I purposely chose courses that would allow me to peacefully eat my meals. There was no way I was going to attend a 6–9 p.m. lecture—that's dinner time!

Some of my chemistry labs are from 9 a.m. till noon. I just plan backwards and wake up at 4:30 a.m. so I can run, shower, and calmly eat breakfast (Rushing meals to me is a CRIME!). The idea of grabbing a coffee and a muffin on the way to work is absurd to me.

I will never sleep in. If I sleep till noon, I'd effectively miss breakfast. I can never miss a meal. I look forward to EVERY meal every day. There is such a joy in looking forward to each meal. When I'm done lunch, I count down till dinner. My life revolves around food and exercise.

Even if I go to clubs and stay out late, I will ALWAYS wake up early the next day and go to the gym. I can never just waste a day.

My routine has effectively silenced the devils in in my head. Thank God! The constant battle between them is so draining. I know that if I keep sticking to my routine, they'll stay quiet.

However, there are two new voices that have replaced them.

First, there is the responsible voice. It's the voice that shines bright 90% of the time and keeps me in line. It's the calm voice of reason reminding me to eat in moderation, avoid binging, be in bed by 10 p.m., and to push it to the max on the treadmill so I'll feel great after my morning workout. Some would refer to this as the rigid, Type-A, routine-driven, neurotic voice. I like structure so I'm glad this voice reigns supreme most of the time.

Second, there is the reckless voice. It shows up around 10% of the time and tells me to be more fun and let loose a little. It's the voice that says, "You've been awesome this week, Dina! Have that extra piece of bread! The extra shot of tequila! Enjoy that street meat after the club! Go out and have fun and stay out way past your usual bedtime!"

Usually, they talk amongst themselves. For example, "Okay, she can have the extra three drinks tonight at the bar and have the burger and fries after, and wake up an hour later as long as you know her tummy won't feel good, she might have a headache and she'll need to push herself to get a good workout in ..." They make the deal and we're good to go.

The problem is—I'm bad at moderation, or being sensible, or really any behaviour that's less than 100% all in. I'm a "black or white" person. There's very little grey area. I'm either in 100% strict healthy mode, or completely off the wagon and binge eating as if it's my last meal. I decide that the reckless voice has got to go. There's no in between, and I can't risk failing at something yet again.

To be a perfect 110 pounds, carefree, and able to do everything in moderation really seems like such a dream.

46

DECEMBER 2005

THIS DAY COULDN'T COME FAST enough, and now, here I am, and I'm terrified.

I finished my final semester at U of T. School is officially over. I should be celebrating! But ... I'm not even close to where I want to be! Everything I had envisioned my life to be by this point—forget about it. I have no idea what I want to do career-wise. I'm ridiculously lonely, and to top it all off, I'm still living at home.

I want to be rich and successful but have no clue as what industry or role I should look into. I don't even know what relevant skills I possess or what employers are looking for. I can't imagine I have any qualities that a boss would deem "useful."

University has felt like a very solitary experience. What about those so called "lifelong friendships" that you're supposed to forge in university? What a load of crap! I've got a grand total of zero close friends.

I know I chose to stay at home and go to U of T, but I worry that I've missed out on so much. Yes—I didn't gain the "Freshman 15," which I am grateful for, but I'm plagued by the fear that I'm too sheltered, that I should have been more independent and moved away or at least lived on my own.

I feel so unprepared for what's ahead—and I hate being unprepared! Despite my best effort to plan out every little aspect of my life, I feel lost. I feel like I have no control over my destiny.

I feel the urge to binge eat, and starve myself, and scream, all at once. Instead, I take a deep breath, and hit the career centre on campus. It takes all of my strength, but something inside of me gives me the strength to take this next step. I may feel hopeless about my job prospects, but I'll never know what is possible if I don't start looking.

I beef up my resumé as best I can, and fire it off to about 30 different employers. There's no rhyme or reason as to which positions I apply for—if it sounds interesting, I apply. If it pays well, I apply. If the company is well known, I apply.

And then I wait.

Remember, deeeeep breaths, Dina. You never know what could happen. Be strong. Have faith.

47

MAY 2006

"WOW! THAT WAS A GREAT interview, Dina. You've got the job! Get ready to head to New York."

Excuse me? I've got what now? I'm going where now? I can't believe it! I did it! I really did it! I got my very first job in the real world. I'm completely flabbergasted!

When I was called to interview with a worldwide financial company, I couldn't believe it. It was my very first interview and miraculously, I landed the job. Man, I feel TOO lucky! I would have never guessed that I would ace my very first interview in the real world. This is exactly the confidence boost I needed. I feel like a rock star, ready to tackle my first job in the corporate world!

The BEST part of my new job? I'm moving to New York in a few weeks! There will be 50 new graduates just like me and we will all be together! I have never lived away from home and this is exactly what I've been waiting for. The chance to be on my own, answering only to myself! Pure freedom!

I am ready to start the next chapter of my life. I decide that this is MY time! It is my time to make up for all the years that I didn't live life to the fullest.

I will be an "account manager," which means I will be managing the existing relationship with clients who buy our financial products, while also trying to get new clients to buy our products. Frankly—if they had told me I would be scaling fish all day, it wouldn't have mattered! I'm going to New York City! I am so excited to start this brand-new chapter of my life that nothing can hold me back.

I have become that (annoying) girl that is SO happy, giddy, and up for anything. The world is my oyster now. There is so much I want to experience. Picture the *Friends* episode with Alec Baldwin ("The One in Massapequa") where he plays Parker, Phoebe's overly enthusiastic boyfriend. That is me, times a thousand! I know my enthusiasm might be irritating to some, but I don't care what anyone thinks. Thank gosh I don't have a needy boyfriend or any kids to hold me back!

New York, here I come! Mumzie, I don't think you even need to ask the question ... It's so obvious—I'm ecstatically happy!

48

JUNE 2006

TODAY IS MOVING DAY! I am leaving Toronto to start my new life in the Big Apple! I really can't believe I'm getting paid to live in New York—even my rent is paid for. I'm pretty sure this is what winning the Lotto 649 must feel like.

I feel as giddy as I did as a five-year-old girl, wondering what toys Santa would bring me on Christmas morning. I wonder what new adventures, possibilities and people I will meet when I wake up in New York tomorrow. I just can't wait for my adventure to begin.

My small alarm-clock radio is on full blast as I sing along to Justin Timberlake's "SexyBack," and bust a move to Shakira's "Hips Don't Lie." My tone-deaf voice and my lame dance moves are laughable but I'm too happy to care how silly I look.

Mom, Dad and Yas pass my room every few minutes asking if I need help packing and although I know they are sad that I am leaving, they are very happy and proud of how far I've come in the last five years. I don't think they could have ever imagined such a bright future for me; I know this is all WAY beyond even my wildest expectations.

Toronto is my past and New York is my future. My new life is beginning today and as Mace says, it "Feel So Good!" Today, I'm grabbing life by the horns. I want to try every restaurant including Katz's Delicatessen, Lombardi's, and Bamonte's. I LOVE musicals, Broadway and theatre, so *Wicked*, *Jersey Boys*, and *Mamma Mia!* are on my must-see list! I want to run in Central Park, explore the cozy dining options in the East Village, take pictures of the grand architecture in the Flatiron District, finally learn about this Hell's Kitchen, shop in SoHo, and sip coffee on the tree-lined streets of the West Village. I want to do it ALL.

We get to the airport and I feel like I'm racing to the ticket counter, weighing my bags and eagerly running to get through customs. Mom and Dad hug me every few minutes and are trying to hold back tears. Meanwhile, I cannot stop smiling and picturing my new life. It's as if I've eaten an entire gingerbread house and all the sugar is making me bounce off the walls. I have so much energy!

We get to the security checkpoint and I have to say goodbye to my family as they can't come any farther in the airport with me. I hug and kiss them and feel so loved. They tell me they will wait there. As I move farther in the security line, I look back and wave and blow them kisses. I used to be so embarrassed of my parents, but now I cherish them and feel so proud to have them and Yas in my life.

I turn back to see them still waving and smiling. I now have to head to my gate so send them all one last goodbye wave and kiss. I get to my gate and take a seat before boarding. It's time for my new beginning.

49

AUGUST 2006

I'VE BEEN LIVING IN NEW York for over a month now. Every single day, Frank Sinatra's song "Theme from New York, New York" plays over and over in my head.

"If I can, BOOM, make it the-e-e-re, I'll make it, BOOM, anywhe-e-e-ere ..."

I have to pinch myself every day. I CANNOT believe I'm in New York! I MADE it! After what feels like an eternity of suckitude, I'm finally getting a chance to live the fabulous, extraordinary life I've envisioned for myself. I AM going to be a top CEO, earn tons of money, and NO ONE will stand in my way.

My old life in Toronto feels so long ago. I have so much energy here. I'm so eager to prove myself. I'm the first one to arrive at work every morning and the last one to leave at night. I somehow manage to always meet friends and colleagues every evening for drinks as well as work out every morning.

Being in a relationship is the LAST thing on my mind. Don't get me wrong—I definitely enjoy flirting and hanging out with guys and doing fun activities, but ONLY when it is convenient for me. I don't want any guy coming into my life on a consistent basis and messing up my routine. I have to work out each morning, be at the office early to prove that I am the best employee, go out and have fun with my colleagues and go home to make a healthy dinner. If, on a Saturday, I have some free time and want to walk around the city or discover a new restaurant, that's the only time I'll see a guy.

I share an apartment with my only other colleague from Toronto, Ken. He introduces me to takeout food and Ben and Jerry's. I have never ordered Chinese takeout before. Wow. It's just so easy! It comes in teeny tiny containers so I can order a variety of dishes and not feel (too) guilty. The pork dumplings, sweet-and-sour chicken balls and crispy spring rolls are to die for!

The convenience store just below our apartment has these small-sized Ben and Jerry's tubs. Man alive! Every bite is a taste of heaven. Chocolate Fudge Brownie and Chunky Monkey make me so happy. The only problem is I can't stop eating it. I'll put a few scoops in a bowl and tell myself the rest is for another day. As I devour the last few bites, I tell myself, just two more scoops and I'm done. Then, there is only a scoop or two left, so I may as well not just take up space in the freezer with one tiny scoop, right? And just like that, my perfect healthy routine is tainted—and I can only attribute it to my male roommate. Stupid boys ... they just mess things up!

At this moment, I don't feel like anything is missing. Of course I miss my family but my focus is just experiencing life and discovering new things! No boys, relationships or any of that silly nonsense!

Dominic, my boss here in New York told me yesterday, "D, you are SO New York. You're moving here. Let me discuss options with the lawyers."

AHHHHH ... Is it possible that things could be going THIS well? Dom wants me in New York so it's definitely a done deal. I'm going to be a New Yorker! Just a few forms from the lawyers and it will be official.

I pester Dom every single morning when I see him open his office door. "Dom, have we gotten official word from the lawyers? Dom, it's happening, right? Dom, can we follow up with the lawyers? Why are they not responding?"

It's the middle of August and things are sailing along, but something odd happens this particular morning—Dom looks at me and waves for me to come to his office. This is different from our usual morning routine. He isn't his cheery self. In a split second my heart sinks. I already know what he's going to say.

"D, I've tried everything. The immigration lawyers can't find a way to allow you to stay. But as soon as we reach the one-year mark, we will get you on the next flight to move here."

Dom and I have a great relationship and I know he has done the best he can. I fight to hold back my tears. I'm angry and frustrated by the bureaucracy that stands between me and my new home.

He explains that that I have to work in my "home office," back in Toronto. Only after a year there, can I make the move back to New York.

I love living in the bright lights of New York. How can I possibly leave this vibrant exciting city? I'm scared ... scratch that. I'm TERRIFIED that I'll lose my new-found zest for life if I move back to Toronto. New York to me is a place of opportunity. It's exciting and cool, and let's be honest—it sounds pretty badass to tell people "You're a New Yorker." Toronto is just a dull grey, stagnant, boring place. What's more, I hate the idea of returning with my tail between my legs. What will people think? They'll obviously think I couldn't make it here.

I think of the Frank Sinatra song again, and then I think, if I can't make it here ... I can't make it anywhere.

We have a conference call with the lawyers. I have just two weeks to prepare myself mentally and accept the fact that I am moving back to Toronto.

50

SEPTEMBER 2006

COMING BACK TO TORONTO HAS been pretty devastating, but I tell myself, "Dina, don't feel sorry for yourself. No one likes to be around sad people." Okay, then! I commit to being upbeat and happy all the time. Toronto is amazing! I love it here! I will make the best of my time back here and in less than nine months, I'll be living in New York again. That's the new plan, and nothing is going to stop me!

I don't have enough money to move out on my own and I only have nine months till I move to New York again, so I have no choice but to live at home. Don't get me wrong—I love my family but ... What a fall from grace. Overnight, I've gone from "rising star New Yorker" to "grown woman still living in her childhood bedroom." Pathetic.

This "upbeat and happy" all the time thing isn't so easy. I'll just have to try harder!

I start up work again in Toronto and my boss Vincent tells me some exciting news—I'm going to be paired up with a "mentor." Her name is Ivana, and she is one of the top sales executives. I'm so happy to get this opportunity as not everyone at my level is assigned a mentor. I feel quite special—management must see some potential in me!

Ivana and I meet for lunch in the boardroom to get to know each other. I listen to her story, all her accomplishments and let her know how excited I am to learn from her. With her guidance, I know I can kick butt here in no time! I feel hopeful about my future at this company.

Things don't go exactly as I had hoped.

I think Ivana hates me. Whenever I ask for help, she always has something "better" to do. I am quite capable of working with clients and closing sales, but she takes over in all our meetings and doesn't allow me to speak.

I scheduled a meeting with one of my new clients last week and asked Ivana to come and observe so she could give me some feedback on my performance. I barely had the opportunity to introduce myself before she took complete control of the meeting. It's like I'm not even in the room. I'm invisible again.

She makes me feel stupid and dismisses my input at every opportunity. I try to explain to Vincent in a professional manner that I'm not getting much out of this supposed "mentorship," but Ivana can do no wrong in Vincent's eyes. She brings the company a LOT of revenue. I'm too junior for anyone to really care.

It only gets worse. Months pass, and nothing changes. Ivana seems intent on stifling my career here, but I'm stuck with her. Getting through the workday becomes more and more of a challenge. I check the clock often. I secretly long for the days she's on vacation.

I'm pretty sure Ivana talks shit about me to Vincent and the higher-ups. Before her, I was always being commended for my performance, and given new opportunities to grow within the company. It's been months since Vincent last mentioned New York to me. I get the distinct feeling that possibility is off the table.

So if I'm not going to New York, what the hell am I doing here?

I think of Mom and her question: "Are you happy, Dina?"

Another lightbulb moment. I think I hate it here. No, actually, I'm sure. I hate it here!

I'm not happy. At all. I want to stick it out for a few more months just in case New York could still happen, but this place is killing me! I've got to make a change.

I wonder if financial product sales is really a field I want to be in. Maybe I'm meant to do something else as a career. Maybe a job in marketing will allow me to better utilize my skills. To be honest, I don't really know what specific skills I have yet. This is my first real job! My first year in the full-time workforce! I'm still just figuring out what I'm good at.

I have always been good at math. Maybe accounting would be a good career move? I love learning about finance so perhaps I should network and get to know what jobs are out there in the financial world. I also feel a new battle brewing – going after a career that focuses on money, prestige and status, or a career that contributes to bettering society in some way. Right now, the former holds more weight. I'll make my millions first, and then do some good in the world!

I start researching other career possibilities online, and while I'm at it happen to discover a program called "Bridge to Business." It's a one-month-in-residence program designed to bridge the gap between arts and science and business. Talk about serendipity!

The program is part of the Rotman School of Management and all the courses are taught by the MBA and EMBA faculty. I look further at the different subject areas and see macroeconomics, ethics, accounting, strategy and marketing. This sounds SO exciting and exactly what I'm looking for. There are also career sessions to ensure we find jobs after the program. And an added bonus ... everyone in the program has to live in the on-campus residence for the duration. I can move out of my parents' place!

I submit my application and hope and pray I'll get in.

51

MAY 2007

I AM ACCEPTED INTO THE Bridge to Business program! I even get one of the two scholarships offered.

At the same time, I'm currently training for my very first half-marathon. Back in January, I didn't feel challenged at work, so I found a different type of challenge and joined "Team in Training." I don't really feel I'm contributing to society in a meaningful way, so the opportunity to raise money for a great cause and also do something active was a no-brainer.

I'd love to say the reason for me joining Team in Training is 100% because I want to help others in need, but the truth is—that's not really the main reason I chose to do it. I think long-distance runners have fantastic lean bodies. The fact that I had to raise money for leukemia was a small price to pay to learn how to run a half-marathon and hopefully trim down.

In order to train with this team, I have to raise over $2000 for the Leukemia and Lymphoma Society. I asked my family, friends and even went door to door but I still have about half of the amount left to go so am slightly nervous. How will I raise that kind of money?

I have a genius idea!

My company will be rolling out a brand-new financial software solution and we need to convert every client to the new platform. The catch is that if they don't switch and choose to go to our competitor instead, we have lost a client and therefore lost revenue.

I overhear a conversation that there is a group of 40 or so very difficult clients that "someone" needs to take. No one wants these clients because they are extremely stubborn and older. These clients do not like change, especially changes in technology, and they will not want to move away from the simple financial platform they have been using for at least 10 years.

JACKPOT! This is my opportunity to leave the company on a high note. I plan my pitch carefully and set up a meeting with Vincent.

"Vincent, I'm so grateful for the opportunities you have given me, but I've been accepted into a business program at Rotman. I'll be leaving the company in June."

He is disappointed, but gracious and understanding. Then—I hit him with my proposal:

"I know I can convert those challenging clients to the new platform. I can do it! If I manage to convert at least 80% of those accounts in the one month I have before I leave the company, will you sponsor my Team in Training run?"

52

JUNE 2007

FORTY-ONE OF 42 ACCOUNTS CONVERTED—CHECK. Boss asking me (once again) if I will reconsider and stay with the company—check. Company admitting that pairing me with Ivana was not the right choice—check. Company sponsoring my run—check. Leaving company on great terms—check!

As I walk through the company door on my way out, I feel proud. I am happy that I found a way to make the best of a challenging circumstance. I am also happy that I was able to contribute to my company and make a difference. I know that I won't be moving to New York anymore but there are other opportunities that will reveal themselves at the right moment.

I love the fact that I will finally be living on the University of Toronto campus even though it's just for one month. Our residence is Woodsworth College, which is a brand-new building on the corner of Bloor and St. George Street. The building is very modern! There are about 100 students in my program and we all live in suites with four to five other students.

My parents drop me off at the residence, and I settle into my new home for the next month. My roommate's name is Sophie. We both start unpacking and we must have been on the exact same wavelength because we both blurt out, "I need to go grocery shopping!"

I am relieved to discover that Sophie is actually super cool! We have a lot in common. We both have Type-A personalities, want to reach the top (career-wise), are single and have tried online dating. I feel instantly I can share anything with Sophie without being judged and it's a wonderful feeling. As we talk more and get to know each other, she suddenly asks me,

"Dina, did you ever have an eating disorder?"

This is weird. How did she know? I'm taken aback but at the same time, I know I can tell her this secret. I tell her that yes, I have struggled with an eating disorder in the past.

"Me, too," she tells me.

We don't speak about it again. Knowing that we share this unspoken bond is enough.

I really had no idea I would love being a student again. My four roommates and I cook, study and celebrate together. Our classes are held at the Rotman Building, about a two-minute walk away from our new home. I feel I'm getting a small glimpse into what living on campus must have been like in university.

The residence we live at is a five-minute walk from Yorkville, one of my favourite areas. It has cobblestone streets lined with trees and colourful potted plants, quality restaurants and very chic boutiques in Toronto. Much like New York's Fifth Avenue, Chicago's Magnificent Mile and Los Angeles' Rodeo Drive, Toronto has Mink Mile with luxury retailers like Hermès, Gucci and Cartier; not that I can afford anything in those shops!

I find it pretty cool how quickly we all feel like family. I feel like I actually belong, which is something I did not encounter in high school and university. My new friends listen to my suggestions, care if I'm at the party, want to know which Saturday activity I would like to do … It's new but it's a feeling that warms my heart.

I really enjoy learning about business. I'm just fascinated by all our subjects and take it all in like a sponge! After finishing the Bridge to Business program, I decide that I want to do an MBA. I'll have to make up a few bachelor degree courses that I did poorly in and get my grades up, which means two or three semesters back at U of T. I'm kicking myself for not doing better in school before! Doesn't matter—if this is what I have to do, I'll do it. I hunker down and focus on getting my grades up.

I contemplate applying to Rotman's MBA which would be the obvious choice. I thought of all the other business schools in Ontario as well as some in the US but nothing felt quite right. I want to experience a life outside of my parents' home, Toronto and North America in general. I want to push myself and go beyond, way beyond my comfort zone and see what I can do on my own.

I come across a unique school where I can study business abroad with people from around the world. The program is divided into two parts, which are spent in two different cities, and you get to choose which cities you would like to study in. My eyes practically pop out of my skull when I see what choices are available: London, Berlin, Madrid, Paris, and Torino. This is it! This is exactly the type of experience I am longing for. After New York, and this past month living in residence, I know what I still need. I need to get out of my parents' house! Out of Toronto!

I apply for the program and receive a scholarship to boot. I choose the London campus as my base city, and within a few months, I'm on a plane.

In barely a few minutes of meeting my new flatmates in London, I know it my heart that I made the right decision. I meet my tiny, very properly dressed Austrian flatmate, Emma. I love her accent. I meet Andreas, a man three years younger than I am and in a different business program. He is from Cologne, Germany. I thought my humour would be lost on him but he totally gets me and I feel I've known him all my life.

Then there is Elif, the very quiet, studious girl from Turkey and Vasily, the tall, thin man from Russia. I feel at home almost instantly when I meet Jannik, the extremely enthusiastic and talkative German fellow and Sofia, my hilarious new Greek friend and many others.

I notice how we all embrace each other and are fascinated by each other's cultures, traditions, language and beliefs. We want to all learn about where the other person came from, our hopes, dreams and aspirations. There are no groups, cliques or divisions, but rather a sense of togetherness. We quickly become thick as thieves. Inseparable!

We, fifteen friends from many different countries, all decide we are going to celebrate American Thanksgiving together. We decide on all the different dishes we will make and shop for all the ingredients and, together, cook a fabulous holiday supper.

As we toast to our great meal, I think to myself, I finally feel like I belong. All the years throughout childhood, high school and parts of university, the times that I felt alone, lost, ugly, different ... They are all a distant memory. Here—we are all different! That's what unites us. It's amazing.

53

NOVEMBER 2009

I'M AT THE SPIRIT OF Christmas Fair in London. It's a massive fair with everything from handmade jewelry to toys to beautiful festive caviar baskets.

As I walk to the next table, something catches my eye. A lovely-looking girl, maybe a few years older than I am, is sitting on a large couch. This girl and her sister are playing with a young girl who must be about three years old.

Then I see an older lady, who must be the sisters' mother, playing peek-a-boo with an adorable little girl who looks to be about a year old.

My heart skips a beat and I smile just looking at this family. Is this what I want? I didn't expect to have this feeling, as I've always thought of men as things that will just impede my career and kids as little messy rug rats that I definitely do not want at all.

As I look at them, I picture having my own "girl's day" with my daughters. We would take a picnic basket to Edwards Garden in North York. Mumzie would be pushing Ava, my adorable one-year-old while Yassy and I each hold one of Olivia's hands, my three-year-old. I'd also be holding on to a leash as Bailey, our Great Dane, is always with us.

Ava and Olivia would grow up with my parents and Yas, who I know would be the best aunt, as well as her kids.

It's the first time I've actually thought about a relationship and having children. But it is just a thought. Career is most important right now, so I quickly brush these weird new thoughts out of my mind.

I head back to Toronto for the Christmas holidays, but just for a few days! I want to party in London for New Year's!

Mom and I are getting dinner on the table for my last dinner before I leave. In passing I tell her about my experience at the Christmas Fair.

"Maybe I do want to get married and have kids … Maybe. Not now! In the future. I think maybe I would like that. MAYBE … totally not thinking about it now. Just a silly fleeting thought," I confess to her.

"Well, this is new, Dinsi," she tells me. "Whatever makes you happy, *Jaanu*. Whenever you are ready. Popsi and I are happy with you and Yasi. We'll always support both of you and whatever you decide, kids or no kids."

I just wanted to mention it. Not quite sure it's what I want but decided to tell Mom anyway.

54

MARCH 2010

MY SECOND SEMESTER OF SCHOOL is in Paris. There is an exchange program with a business school in India there, so I'm excited to meet the 15 Indians who have chosen to come to Paris.

Almost every day that I live in Europe, I have to pinch myself. I would have never guessed that having picnic lunches under the Eiffel Tower, and sipping great wine with my diverse group of friends would be a common occurrence. I am utterly fascinated when the 2010 FIFA World Cup games start.

A large group of us gather at the Champ de Mars which is a free, outdoor lawn that is broadcasting the FIFA games daily. It really warms my heart to see such diversity and different people all together respectfully cheering on our own country.

I relish in European life with its emphasis on slowing down to enjoy life, spending hours enjoying a great meal and the value that is placed on a work-life balance. I feel alive here!

There's only one problem. I'm getting fat.

Seriously ... WTF? There are pretty much no gyms in Paris and the one I found is ridiculously expensive! Apparently gyms here in Paris cater to elite millionaires and not poor students! Stupid gyms!

Fine. That means I will run every day and do circuit-type training in my teeny tiny studio apartment that is 200 square feet. No clue how I'm going to manage that in my itty-bitty place where I barely have room to move.

My first week of running in Paris is HELL! Paris has beautiful gardens and scenery, but I can't enjoy any of it on my run because

I'm looking at the ground to avoid all the dog crap! When I finally do manage to look up, I'm getting cigarette smoke blown in my face. Are people here oblivious to poop and SCOOP!? And my gosh … EVERYONE smokes!

My routine is getting thrown way off course. I start to feel on edge, panicky, and uncomfortable. How on earth am I going to maintain a healthy lifestyle here?

Many of my Parisian classmates buy breakfast at school five minutes before class begins. I do NOT understand. They have a teeny little espresso and three bites of a croissant! I stare at them in complete awe. How on earth do they not at least eat the WHOLE croissant? It baffles me every day. I'd eat the whole thing and probably have to order five more.

I've gained about 15 pounds living in Paris. I'm so ashamed of myself and feel disgusting. I've decided I'm moving back to Toronto to get back to my routine and slim down. Paris is not a "livable" city. French women may not get fat but apparently North American women, specifically me, DO get fat.

I have always thought of myself as a very healthy, active and fit woman. It's who I am! Living in Paris has stolen that part of my identity, and I already have enough trouble figuring out exactly "who I am."

I have to get out of here. Back to my routine and being slim once again.

55

MAY 2011

IT'S BEEN CLOSE TO ONE year since I moved back to Toronto after business school. Just like many of my friends and colleagues, I was drawn to the prestige factor of having a consulting job. I feel I should have made more of an effort to look for a role that I *actually* wanted, as I don't really feel a passion for my consulting job.

I feel I've gotten a swift kick in the butt to ignore how a certain job will make me look in other people's eyes but that I need to follow my heart, really understand the role and if it will excite me. I feel we spend so much of our lives working and that I need to do something I enjoy. Dreading hearing the alarm clock on a Monday is no way to live.

When I came home after Paris, I lived with my family and made the one-hour subway ride downtown every day. I love my family but I want my freedom. I don't have enough money to move out but in our culture, you ONLY leave your parents' house when you get married. I've NEVER associated living in Toronto with having my own place. I would only live on my own if I lived in a different city. It would just be a "waste of money" if I lived on my own in Toronto. It is such a ludicrous idea and not prudent.

Many of my North American peers, friends and colleagues say that it's "known" that once you reach 18, you're out. You live on your own and your parents cut you off. It's baffling to me because my parents want me to stay and want to take care of Yas and me. When we get married, that's when we know we'll leave my parents' house, but until then, we live with our parents. And they've always told us, no pressure or rush to get married and leave. They LOVE us living at home.

At the current moment, I don't like living at home and do not like my job. I miss my life in Europe with the freedom of living on my own, all my friends and the more relaxed way of life. London is one of my favourite cities and I want to move there again.

I have managed to get a work visa that grants Canadians under 30 years of age a two-year work permit for the UK. I am choosing to think of the here and NOW. I don't know what I will want in the future, whether I will move back home when this visa expires, but for now, I want to move away. I know that I am sacrificing family life, but I want to keep exploring. I thought that doing my business school abroad would have satisfied my regret of not living away for university, but I guess it hasn't.

I'm not ready to be in Toronto. It's not my time. I don't feel I've made up for the life I lost when I was anorexic. I still need to experience more, see what I can do and be on my own without having the safety net of my family.

Most companies won't sponsor me and I'm finding that search firms are reluctant to take me on as I'm not a permanent resident. Even though I've got a work permit, that's not enough for them which is incredibly frustrating! However, the harder it is, the more I want to find a job and move to London. I must be a total sucker for punishment!

I had a phone interview with a worldwide food and beverage conglomerate in London and got an in-person interview. I'm happy but that also means a rather expensive flight to London. I want to move to London so I hustle and set up in-person interviews with other companies. I will stay with my good friend Aimee for two weeks in London. I've got to make sure one of these interviews work!

56

JUNE 2011

THE INTERVIEW WITH THE FOOD and beverage company went well but I am overqualified for the role and the pay is extremely low. I have no clue how I would even be able to live in London earning so little money! I'm completely dejected. I also don't have time to waste because I now have about eight days to find a job I love, interview, actually get the job and find a place to live. Such pressure! Why I do these things to myself is beyond me.

I interview with another three companies but don't feel there is a fit with these companies, either. I'm at a loss of what to do. I want to live in London!

There's another potential company—a startup—that seems interesting. I feel ambivalent about it, but since I'm already here, I may as well try to get the manager to meet me.

The company is Naked Wines, which, as I learned from my initial meeting is an online wine retailer. The company's customers (called "Angels") support independent winemakers by investing £20 a month into their Naked Wines account, to spend whenever they want—in return for discounts, freebies, exclusive wines and more. It's crowdfunding. All the customers and winemakers interact online, posting feedback and reviews. It's a cool concept that allows customers to try wines that are not available in stores that they would have never otherwise tried.

In addition, your wine is delivered the very next day and they have an excellent call centre.

This seems closer to what I want out of a job. I like that the company funds winemakers who are small that would not exist without their help. I really like the concept!

"You're hired. Can you pack up your stuff in Toronto and be here in London to start in less than two weeks?"

I am sitting in front of Rowan Gormley, who has just blown my mind with his question. He is the Founder of Naked Wines and from all that I read about him, a brilliant man who used to be Richard Branson's right-hand man at Virgin. Rowan is dressed in shorts and a T-shirt much like everyone else in the office. I definitely feel out of place in my pinstripe black suit and black pumps. *Note to self: dress CASUAL for first day of work!*

I try to sound cool, calm and collected. "Yes, of course!"

Less than a week ago I was so discouraged at my prospects of working in London and the actual roles at these other companies and, now, I can't believe it's all falling into place. It feels so surreal. As I walk out of the office and out of sight so no one can see me from the window, I set my handbag down and leap in the air and squeal in excitement! This is really happening!

57

DECEMBER 2011

IN LONDON, I WORK FROM my flat, as the company is based in Norwich, which is about an hour north of the city. Rowan and I meet whenever he comes to London. I love the setup I have in London—the gym is a five-minute walk from my flat, I work from home so I don't have to commute, and I am enjoying a great balance between work and personal life. I miss my family but other than that, London suits me perfectly.

I'm just about to leave for the airport to fly home to Toronto for the Christmas holidays. I can't wait to see my family and celebrate but I have to quickly meet Rowan before I go.

"Dina, we're going to launch the company across the US. We'll be based out of Napa Valley. How would you like to start it up with me as Head of Sales?"

WHAT? Me? Move from London? I was just starting to feel like this place was my home! Wait a sec ... Did I actually hear him correctly?

I sit on the couch, literally at a loss for words. It's clear from the dumbfounded look on my face that I'm a tad shocked. Rowan graciously gives me an out: "Just think about it. Have fun with your family back home and we'll talk after the holidays."

As much as I love London and was planning on living here permanently, and as much as it looked like I had to think about it, the second he asked me, I knew I was moving. How could I pass up the opportunity to launch a company with this brilliant man?

As I am leaving, he says, "Did you know that Napa Valley has the most Michelin-starred restaurants in a single mile? Just saying ..."

Sneaky move. He knows I love great restaurants. While I have a million details to sort out in my head, I know that I have a brand-new exciting chapter ahead of me.

58

MARCH 2012

WHEN I FIRST MOVED TO Napa, I didn't know anyone except the CEO and the new staff we hired, so I joined different "meet-up" groups to try new things and meet like-minded people.

My first "meet-up" was a one-day white water rafting trip. I felt a little nervous getting into this all by myself, but I met some amazing women right off the bat. Many had also just recently moved to San Francisco (and surrounding areas), were single, driven, had a sense of adventure and wanted to meet new people.

I make some great new friends on the trip, including Christine. We are both into food, activity and travel. We love exploring and we spend most weekends together hiking, biking, trying new restaurants, and discussing topics ranging from career, men, politics, world affairs and what we want in life. I cherish these types of meaningful relationships where I can speak my mind and know that the other person can see my point of view. It's stimulating and I feel like I grow in many areas including intellectually, physically, and emotionally.

Herein lies a major conflict. During the week, I work and live in Napa. My social life is minimal to nonexistent. I don't enjoy going to the bar every evening with colleagues and it seems like that is all they do. I don't care to hear "when I was drunk" stories night after night. I also find it very hard to relate to my colleagues. Many have never travelled beyond California, are not very educated, and lead very simple lives.

I realize I'm not meant to live in a small town but I'm unsure what to do. I enjoy my career and I love working for a visionary

like Rowan, but I want to have a social life and have fun! I'm 28!
I feel the life is being sucked out of me.

I never thought I'd feel this way, but I don't want my career
to be my entire life. Money and climbing the ladder is not everything anymore.

I'm tired of being on my own. I'm tired of proving to myself
that I can be successful career wise. I'm tired of taking care of
myself, not leaning on anyone for support and not really allowing
anyone to enter my life or get close to me. I'm tired of coming
home to no one.

It would be nice to come home to someone who I respect, can
be silly and laugh with, celebrate the little daily moments with,
someone who makes me feel safe, allows me to be vulnerable
and wants to take care of me. I would love to meet my "partner
in crime." I'm done proving to myself that I am an independent
woman. I'm even growing a little tired of travelling! Staying put
in a place that feels like "home" sounds pretty good.

Last week I brought up the idea to Rowan of moving to San
Francisco and coming to Napa once a week. He flat-out said "No."

Later that day, I call Daddy. It's been a while since I've asked
for advice from my parents. I wanted to show them, and myself,
that I could survive on my own. I don't need them to swoop in
and save me every time I have a problem in my life! It's hard for
me to admit—I really need help.

"*Jaanu,*" he tells me, "you can always come home, get a great
job here and travel as much as you want. But at least you will
have a home base in Toronto."

I'm sure Daddy has said this to me several times before, but
I actually hear him this time. I WANT to be home. The life I envision *includes* my family. Skype and phone dates and seeing my
family one to two times a year is just not enough. What I wanted
at 22 and now at 28 are very different.

I want to live in Toronto with my family. I will never have
a truly balanced life if my family is not part of my daily life.

It's decided. I will find a good, steady job where I can start saving to buy a house, hopefully meet the right person and start a family. I will create new friendships and build on existing ones. I will continue my healthy, athletic lifestyle as I've always done.

Here we go! My new life in Toronto is going to be amazing! Perfect! Nothing can stop me!

First things first. I have to work up the courage to ACTUALLY leave my job and life in California.

59

SEPTEMBER 2012

ROWAN, I AM SO THANKFUL *for the opportunity. Rowan, umm ... so ... I love my family ... Rowan ... SHIT, SHIT! Rowan ... I know you have given me the chance of a lifetime ... So Rowan, I know how much family means to you ... so ...?*

I've been rehearsing this speech for weeks. How am I going to tell the most brilliant man I know that I want to move home? How can I give up my position of Head of Sales across the United States? This man has taught me more in a single year about business, running a company and how to adapt than all of my years at university and previous jobs combined.

I feel so conflicted. I LOVE my job. I LOVE my life in California. Now that I think about it, I've loved every single place I've lived for different reasons. But, there's one thing that is missing from every city— my family.

I miss being curled up in my PJs on the couch and watching a chick flick with Yas. I miss seeing the twinkle in my dad's eyes when he sees me come home from work, or when he remembers a joke and tries to tell it to us at the dinner table but is already laughing so hard that he can't even make it through the joke. We all end up in hysterics just from seeing him laugh so hard at his own joke!

I miss my mummy's hugs—those hugs that take away all my daily stress. I miss my mom's *dhunsak* and meatballs and her chicken *vindaloo.* I miss how comforted I feel just by seeing her smile. I miss those moments when Yas and I are in the sunroom having tea and watching Mom and Dad tend to their garden, seeing them so happy, laughing and enjoying retired life together.

The lawyers are currently at work to get Rowan and myself visas to permanently work in the US. I can't put off this conversation any longer.

* * *

"Rowan, I can't adequately express how much I learn from you each and every day. You have entrusted me with so many responsibilities and had faith in my decisions. I'm not sure I would have known what I was capable of if I didn't have you as my boss and mentor. I love this company and know we are in the process of getting our visas and permanent work status for the US, but I need to please ask you to stop the process for me."

He must be noticing how shaky my voice is and that I'm having a great deal of trouble getting the words out because when I finally finish rambling, he gives me a hug. I can tell he knows that my decision was not one I took lightly.

He may have known this time was coming. Perhaps it's due to the fact that I talk about my family ALL the time. Or, the fact that I've asked Rowan at least once per week since we arrived in California if there was any possibility we could launch the company in Canada (say, Toronto) and that I'd be up for running it.

In any case, I feel a huge amount of relief of finally making my decision and vocalizing it to him. We decide that I will stay till the end of the year and tell the rest of the team the plan and we can all work together to welcome and help my replacement get up to speed so we get a strong start to the 2013 year.

It feels a bit like I'm leaping off another cliff, into the unknown. I'm giving up such a great opportunity here, for what exactly? I have to keep reminding myself, I WILL get a great job in Toronto.

I WILL continue my successful career. I WILL start a great new chapter of my life. I'm scared but I just have to truly believe it.

After breaking the news to Rowan, I start moving at warp speed. I spend my evenings and weekends scouring the job market in Toronto. I reach out to people I know, contact people on LinkedIn, and bookmark every job I see that looks interesting.

I'm also looking at the downtown condo market in Toronto. I've lived on my own now and I need to be free! My parents realize how important this is to me and we all decide that the most important thing is that I create a life in Toronto that I enjoy. Living in downtown Toronto on my own is a huge part of that equation.

I'm going to get a place downtown, get my new dream job and spend many happy days and nights with my wonderful family.

It will all work out, it will all work out, it will all work out …

60

OCTOBER 13, 2012

THIS WEEKEND, I'M TAKING A break from my job and condo searches in Toronto because Claudia is here! She is a good friend from London and she is in northern California this week for work. She's got the weekend off, so we are going to reconnect.

I can't wait to show her around Napa, Sonoma and San Francisco! I am too excited to start our fun weekend together. I have a list of all the restaurants and bakeries I want to take her to, the wineries I know she will love, and many unique, "non-touristy" spots in San Francisco to show her.

I have a quick Saturday morning run and get ready to meet her. It's picture-perfect sunny weather. I put on my favourite baby blue capris and a flowy summer top and hop in my car to go and meet her. We are having lunch at noon at a beautiful winery in Sonoma.

* * *

"MOVE!" I cry out. The woman driving the car has now passed the yellow line into my lane. There is no guardrail on either side of the one-lane highway.

"MOVE!" I yell again! Why isn't she looking up as she is driving? I honk my horn frantically trying to get her attention, but the pathetic *honk* on my old Nissan Versa is not loud enough to get her attention. She is going to hit me.

I need to do something quickly. If I don't move, she will crash into me. If I swerve off the highway, I will plummet to my death.

Talk about being stuck between a rock and a hard place. I either get hit and die or swerve off the highway and die. Oh God, please give me another ... ANY other ... option. Please!

In a split second I decide to steer my wheel to the right as she comes barrelling towards me. Her car barely avoids the crash but now I face falling off the highway.

I try to steer the wheel to the extreme left but my car is now spinning out of control.

I hear a loud *BANG!* and everything goes black.

• • •

"Miss! Miss! Are you okay? Keep breathing. Deep breaths. We're going to get you out. Just stay with us! Stay with us!"

As I try to understand what is happening and cry out for help, all I can see is white. My face and body feels crushed under the weight of—what exactly is that? I realize my airbag has gone off. It actually knocked the wind right out of me. I am pinned between the bag and my seat. I am trapped.

My mind starts to race, and the panic begins to set in. *"Okay, as long as I have my legs. Do I? I can't feel anything. My legs ... WHERE ARE MY LEGS?"*

I am trying not to panic but I can't help it, I'm in total shock. I can't move my head but as I shift my eyes, I notice there are at least 20 people surrounding my car trying to open the doors. They are all crushed shut and I can hear many voices yelling different ways they could try to get me out.

I can't feel my body, and now I see blood everywhere.

I start hysterically crying. I can't control my breathing. I am hyperventilating and I feel like I only have a few seconds before I go unconscious.

I hear sirens. I feel like I am suffocating. I am trapped and can't move. Every second I am stuck alone in my car feels like an eternity. My shirt feels wet—is it sweat? Or blood?

The sirens are getting louder and louder. Hallelujah! That MUST mean help is on the way! All the bystanders have surrounded my car and are talking to me through the windows to try to keep me calm but I really, really just want the police or paramedics to get me out of this goddamn car.

They arrive. Ambulance, police and the fire department. Even though I'm crying uncontrollably and hyperventilating, I feel relieved. I know these professionals have the means to get me out of my car and keep me safe. I don't know if I have whiplash or if I've broken anything but I trust these men and women to help me.

"Ma'am, we are going to get you out," a police officer tells me. "Just stay with us. We're going to cut the door so don't move or be alarmed when you hear the noise. Stay still and we will get you out."

I hear the *whirrr* of some kind of machine and at that point, I lose consciousness. Next thing I know, I'm on a spinal board in the middle of the road. Paramedics surround me. They seem to be perplexed at where all the blood is coming from. I feel like I'm fading in and out of consciousness because I can barely hear them. I am too scared and think my mind has had enough and so I fade. I have no idea what is happening but I have no energy to even ask. I'm too shocked to even put together a coherent sentence.

• • •

The next time I open my eyes, I'm in an ambulance. I fade out again and wake up in a hospital bed with doctors and nurses all around me. As soon as I open my eyes, I start shaking uncontrollably. I'm not sure if I'm in shock or if I'm cold but the nurses are wrapping me in huge blankets and trying to get me to stop shaking.

I have about five wool blankets covering me so I must be warm, but I can't stop shaking. I want to apologize but I can't. I have nurses on either side of my bed holding my hand and trying to get me to lie still but my entire body is shaking. I'm still hyperventilating and my lips are chattering away.

When I finally get up the strength, the only words out of my mouth are, "Legs? My legs?"

My mind is filled with terrifying thoughts. All I want to know is if I will be able to RUN. I NEED to run and work out. I have to. Please, please, please, I don't want to be confined to a wheelchair. I can't. I'll die. If I can't exercise, I'll get FAT. I will get FAT. Please let me know that I'll be able to run ...

The doctor tells me, "Yes. Your legs are fine," but like a broken record, I keep repeating, "My legs? Will I run again?" I am not sure why I keep saying the same sentence but I can't stop. I think I must have faded for a few minutes because when I open my eyes again, I'm still shaking but feel more aware of my surroundings. The doctors explain that I have a hairline fracture in two spots in my back and in my nose but I am going to be just fine.

They tell me I will be staying in the hospital tonight. As a nurse takes me to my new room, I realize I am alone. I need my parents. I am so scared and don't see any familiar faces. I wish my parents were right beside me but they are a six-hour flight away.

I feel like I've regressed to being a baby. I want my mommy. I'm a 28-year-old independent woman but I still need my parents. Who knew? The odd part is that I'm okay with it. Maybe it's the shock of the car accident, or maybe I was starting to accept it when I made the decision to move back to Toronto, but I'm not ashamed that I need my parents.

The doctor tells me I will be fitted for a brace that I must keep on for the next month so that my fractures can properly heal. The physiotherapist will see me tomorrow to assess my walking abilities and set a plan for me going forward. They will also set up an appointment with an ENT to assess the damage in my nose and what I'll need to do for it to heal.

"But wait, I have to go to these appointments alone?" I ask in a panic. "I can't do this alone? Can't we wait until my parents get here? I need my mom. She's a nurse. I WANT her here!"

I slowly calm down and stop crying. One of the nurses hands me a few clear bags. "These are your clothes, dear."

My blue capris that I love, my flowy white shirt, my bra and my underwear. They all are stained with blood and appear to be cut up. I am taken aback. What on earth happened?

She notices my confusion and explains.

"When they got you out of the car, they couldn't find where all the blood was coming from and they needed to find the source of the bleeding. So they needed to cut the articles of clothing as they searched."

I put two and two together (finally). I am covered in blankets and timidly take a peek underneath all these blankets. I'm naked! FULLY naked! That means I was naked on the Napa State Highway. I can't believe it! There were SO many people around me—police, firefighters, paramedics and all of those bystanders …

I look upward (to the proverbial "man upstairs") and think to myself, "Naked on a highway, eh? Thanks a bunch!"

I have to laugh.

A very kind-looking man, clearly a police officer, comes to my room to check on me. He tells me that my car is completely totalled and asks if I have my purse on me. I completely forgot about my purse but he tells me he will go back to the accident scene and search for it for me.

He tells me the lady that was coming into my lane was distracted because she was trying to change the radio station. She remained on the scene and did not try to flee and completely admitted to being at fault. The car I collided with was a black SUV and had two people in it—a middle-aged couple. He told me they were fine. I basically took the brunt of the accident.

He tells me that if the collision had been even one inch to the right, I definitely would have died. Even though I don't have my phone on me, there's one number I know by heart. He is going to call my parents but I reiterate to him about 10 times:

"My parents are very protective and will be very scared so please, please, please tell them FIRST that I am okay. I don't want them to be worried. They are a six-hour plane ride away and I know they will feel helpless being so far away. They NEED to know I'm safe, in the hospital and I will be fine. Please promise me that when you call them?"

He calls my parents and gives them the hospital phone number so they can call me. Just from their voices I can tell they are scared out of their minds. No parent should ever receive a call like that. But I keep repeating, "Daddy, I am okay, don't worry. I'm being taken care off at the hospital. Don't worry."

Daddy tells me Aunty Nilufer (travel expert and consultant who my entire family and community entrust with all travel needs) sprang into action instantly and has booked them on the next direct flight to San Francisco. I can't imagine how scared they must be but am relieved that Aunty Nilufer is helping and taking that worry off their plate. I hate being so far from them. Even though they are on the next flight, I'm scared because the flight isn't until later that night. Then it's a six-hour flight and they still have about a one-hour drive from the San Francisco airport to Napa. Meaning, it will be almost 24 hours until I see them.

Within an hour, the officer comes back with my purse (Thank God!) and tells me I have quite a few calls, texts and voicemails. I only know my parents' home number off by heart but rely on my phone for every other number.

I realize Claudia must be wondering where I am! We were supposed to meet for lunch hours ago.

When I call her I can hear the worry in her voice, too. I tell her what's happened but I plead with her to enjoy her day with the other girl she's with and to go to San Francisco and continue with the plans. She tells me in a very stern voice she will most certainly not and she will come to the hospital instantly. I know Claudia: when she's made up her mind, there's no point in arguing.

Next up, I need to call Rowan. How can I tell him my company car is totalled? To my surprise, he's calm and collected and happy that I am safe. He says he will contact the insurance people and lawyers and that I just have to focus on getting better.

My mind is thinking of a million things. We had just found a replacement for my job and I'm still training her and want to be at work on Monday so we can continue. Do I have any calls scheduled with companies in Toronto or application deadlines? What happens next in terms of the car accident? Who is paying for my time here in the hospital? How many hours till my parents arrive? How long will I stay in the hospital? Exactly how many days do I have to wait to get back to the gym and running again?

Claudia arrives with her friend and I can see the tears in her eyes. The many questions running through my mind disappear when I see her. I tell her I am fine and I will stay here. I want her to go enjoy San Francisco but she refuses to leave. She pulls up the chair beside my hospital bed and plants herself there and holds my hand. She's not leaving.

The physiotherapist comes in and wants to assess my mobility and see if I can walk. As she helps me to sit up and get out of the bed, I am fairly certain that I am flashing everyone in the hallway. My rear-end is getting a lovely breeze and I become acutely aware I have no underwear on! As the physiotherapist watches me, Claudia helps keep my fanny hidden by holding the back of my hospital gown.

The physiotherapist fits me with a brace and I am told to not talk or laugh because the entire front upper half of my body was battered pretty badly. Breathing hurts and I feel like my ribs will break if I move too much. It is excruciatingly painful.

Every little while a nurse comes in and gives me different meds and scans my hospital bracelet. I laugh (in my head) every time because every time I hear the *beep* of the scanner, I feel like I'm on a checkout belt at the grocery store.

The next day, Claudia is back at the hospital and has a present for me—underwear! I've never been so happy to get the package of granny panties from Fruit of the Loom.

She stays with me for the morning and then leaves to catch her flight back to London. I feel so grateful for her concern. It is terrifying to be alone in the hospital without my family but having Claudia there really comforted me.

It's almost lunchtime and I hear two familiar voices! I start yelling, "MUMMY! DADDY!" I can hear them talking to the nurses and doctor but I'm too excited! I want them NOW!

I remember those days when I was barely two years old in daycare and that feeling of complete joy when mom came to pick me up. I'd drop whatever toy I was playing with and run as fast as my little wobbly legs would take me and jump into her arms.

My eyes twinkle with joy as they wrap me in a huge bear hug. Mummy smells like her lavender baby powder that she always wears and Daddy smells like his GQ aftershave. I don't want to let them go. Now that they are here, I can take any news that the doctors tell me. Now that my parents are here, I feel safe.

My parents come into my room with the nurses and we go over what has happened and how to take care of me going forward. I have to wear the brace at all times. I am also not allowed to lift my legs because it can affect the healing of my back, so the nurse explains that getting in and out of a shower or bathtub is a no-go. Mom can see my look of disgust when I hear this and she assures me we will find a way to make it all work. She was a nurse so I feel a small amount of comfort in her words.

I'm also not allowed to do any exercise except walking and the doctors advise me to limit that to 30 minutes a day. Morning workouts and a shower are key to starting my day, so I'm very worried about this.

I'm also not supposed to climb stairs, which is going to pose a slight problem as I live on the second floor of my residence complex and there are no elevators.

The next day, a nurse wheels me out of the hospital. Daddy helps me stand up and we wait for the special cab that reception has called for. As soon as I see the cab, I know I have to get in the vehicle. My heart beats faster; I feel my palms are sweaty as I tighten the grip on Mom's hand.

I can't get in. What if a car hits me? I can't be inside a car. I look to Mom pleading that we just walk to my apartment. She holds me tight and reassures me that it will be okay. We've got a three-minute cab ride and they will be there with me.

Dad helps me get into the cab and Mom keeps telling me, "Deep breaths, we are almost home. You can do it, *Jaanu*."

Three minutes of terror are finally over. Phew! When we get back to my place in Napa, I realize how difficult the simplest activities really are. Dad carries me up the stairs. I cannot bend in any way due to the brace so Mom has to help me with both removing my clothes and then putting on my PJs. It is hard to bend over the sink to brush my teeth. It hurts to even breathe, let alone laugh, as my entire stomach is bruised very badly due to the impact of the airbag. I plead with Daddy to stop telling me jokes because it hurts so much, but he is such a funny guy!

It takes me and Mom about half an hour to determine how to get me to lie down in bed. I can slowly sit on the edge of the bed, then she helps me put my head on the pillow and roll me over to my side and put my legs on the bed. Then I can roll from being on my side to lying on my back. She will sleep beside me because I can't actually get up on my own. Since I can't use my stomach to get up, I need her help to move to my side or get out of bed.

It's quite the ordeal but I'm so glad my parents are here with me. Since I don't have a car anymore, we're lucky that there is a Target, CVS, Trader Joe's and Whole Foods within walking distance. For everything else, we need to take a taxi. I ignore the doctor's silly "only 30 minutes of walking a day" suggestion. I feel so much better by moving around. There's no way I can just sit still and twiddle my thumbs.

For the next two weeks, our days are filled with police station meetings, hospital checkups, calls with insurance agents and claims adjustors. It's very draining and it scares me each time I have to recall the accident. The only thing that helps me is knowing that I can lean on my parents for support— whether it's venting my frustration, Daddy cheering me up with his funny jokes or Mom's hugs that seem to melt away the anxiety after each phone call.

We make sure to balance out these not so pleasant experiences with having amazing wine tastings at unique vineyards, sampling exquisite restaurants in Yountville, and plenty of walking around lovely downtown Napa.

Throughout everything, I take comfort in knowing that in just a few days and I'll finally be home, in Toronto. The night before we leave, I sit snuggled in my Mom's arms. As if on cue, she asks me, "Are you okay, Dina?"

These last few years, I've heard her voice in my head, asking me this question over and over again, but there's no substitute for the real deal. Having her with me, in the flesh, is the best feeling in the world.

"I'm okay now, Mummy. Thank you."

I know that eventually we will have to get up or change position, but for the first time in years, I don't want to move a muscle. I want to stay right here, in my mom's arms, forever. This is home. Family is my home.

It's almost shocking to me. It seems like every other year, I'm in a new place and a new job making a new plan for myself. The thought of staying put in one place was completely unappealing. Scary, in fact. In a way, I have known that staying in one place would mean letting people get close, and I'm not sure I'm ready for anyone to see me for who I really am.

But here in my mom's arms, everything is okay. I am able to forget about my uncertain future for a few minutes and take comfort in her.

"Everything will be okay, Dina," she tells me. "We'll be home soon."

May 2007: Crossing the finish line of my 1st half-marathon in Ottawa Canada, with Team in Training

**Spring 2010: Living in Paris for second
semester of business school**

2012: Hiking Mount Tamalpais near San Francisco

PART THREE
THE STROKE

JANUARY 5, 2013

"GET MY SISTER A DOCTOR ... NOW!"

Yas is yelling at the top of her lungs to anyone who will listen.
We're in the emergency room at Toronto Western Hospital. The
right side of my face is numb, I can't feel my right arm and my
body is now shaking uncontrollably.

We were *just* here less than 24 hours ago, but the admitting
department still insists on having me fill out a form and be
evaluated by a triage nurse.

Yas bellows out again and I can hear the panic in her voice.
"GET A DOCTOR. GET A DOCTOR ..."

I feel my legs give way. The shaking has now turned into full
on convulsions. The nurses see me drop to the floor and come
running. They strap me into a gurney and wheel me into the ER.
All of a sudden I see at least 20 people surrounding me. I frantically search the crowd of white-coated strangers for a familiar
face until I find my mom and dad, Yas and Aunty Dhun. They
look terrified.

The convulsions stop. I must be okay, right? I'm okay now?
I'm completely exhausted and can barely muster the strength
to move at all, but the doctor wants to do some reflex tests so
I manage to pull my body up to a sitting position.

*"Dina, use your left pinky finger to touch your nose. Okay, now
try the right hand. Sit on the edge of the bed and straighten your left*

leg so it's 180 degrees. Now do the same with your right leg. Use your right hand and show me where your face is numb. Point to my pen. Touch my tie. Point to my watch."

After the doctor finishes, the medical students start. Two by two they ask me to repeat the tests. It's very tiring and after the tenth medical student, Mom is getting fed up.

"Will someone *please* tell me what is happening with my daughter? What is going on?"

Without warning, the convulsions start up again. I'm scared at how my body is shaking but at the same time, I'm utterly fascinated. I stare at how fast my legs are vibrating back and forth and the lack of control I have as my arms flail about.

The convulsions stop about a minute later. I'm in total shock. I look to my mom, speechless. Yas comes and holds me on my bed. Mom is stroking my hair and Daddy is holding my hand. I know the convulsions must have been very scary for them to watch. I have no idea what is happening but I feel comforted because my three favourite people are right beside me. Aunty Dhun, Dr. Hodaie and the nurses are all talking beside my bed.

Their voices start to fade until I can't hear them at all. The room starts to go dark ... I can't see them now, either. I'm fading. I want to fight it, but it's too strong. I must be dying and on my way to heaven ...

61

OCTOBER 31, 2012

TODAY WE HAVE OUR FLIGHT back to Toronto. I have sold all my furniture in Napa and given everything else I had to friends. I look around at my empty apartment and enjoy the clarity this barren view provides: a clean slate, a fresh start ... but the feeling is bittersweet. I truly love Napa and San Francisco—the mountains I can run up every morning, the trails I can hike every day, the delicious wine and beautiful vineyards at my doorstep ... It is hard to say goodbye to this place.

As we load up the taxi, I know in my heart this is my final move. After so many cities, countries and continents, I'm finally coming home. It's the place I want to be and settle down for good. I want to put down roots. I'm done with running from place to place, chasing the "high" of new, new, new ... I chuckle to myself a little when I think of what an old fuddy-duddy I sound like! Still, the nomadic chapter of my life is complete. I'm eager to get my life really started in Toronto. I'm a little scared—I know it means admitting a lot of things aren't quite so rosy and perfect in my life—but I think I'm ready to get the ball rolling.

But first ... I need to survive the one-and-a-half hour cab ride to the airport. I've gotten used to the 5-10 minute cab rides in Napa but the thought of one and a half hours in a car is quite terrifying. And what if there's traffic? Or worse? I'm going to need every ounce of positive reassuring energy to get through this. Last week when we came home from a dinner in Yountville, I had to get out of the car because I was starting to have a panic attack, and that ride was barely 10 minutes long!

My parents prepare the driver by letting him know that I've recently been in a car accident and give him instructions: no unnecessary lane changes, drive at a steady pace and no tailgating. I feel a bit badly for the driver—he's really under the microscope! My parents must be making him so nervous!

It's hard on my back to sit for so long in the car. I can't turn my body or change positions because the brace keeps my back in place. My back is starting to feel achy and at the same time I'm completely on edge as I watch the rest of the cars on the highway. I feel like every single car that passes will hit me. Either they are too close or not paying attention. I breathe a sigh of relief every time a car passes that doesn't crash into us. I just want to get out of this car and plant my two feet on the ground!

"We are almost there, *Jaanu*. You can do it," Daddy tells me. I've been trying to be strong and grit my teeth through this excruciating ride, but I should know better! Nothing gets by him—he knows me too well. Mom holds my hand tight and reminds me to breathe.

I finally see the signs for the airport and tears well up in my eyes.

We're so close. So, so, close. Please, please, please get me to the terminal so I can get out of the car. Please, please, please ...

We park the car and the huge weight on my shoulders is lifted. Daddy helps me maneuver my body to step out of the cab. The relief of being on solid ground has me shedding tears of joy. Mom exits the cab and just holds me tight. She knows how hard it was for me to be in a vehicle for that long.

She just lets me cry and know that we got through it while Dad pays. I'm okay, I survived the car ride! I did it!

Next up: the airplane.

My victory is short-lived as a new wave of panic starts to set in. Will my back be able to handle the almost six hour flight we've got ahead?

The stewardess kindly finds me a row on the plane with no other passengers sitting beside me. She points out different areas I can stand in if my back gets sore. I treat my back like I would a baby. It's fragile and I need to tend to its every need! If I don't, if it doesn't heal—I might not be able to run and exercise. If I can't exercise, I can't eat. I've never enjoyed just sitting for hours, being lazy, watching movies or playing video games. I LOVE moving my body; whether it's my Saturday kick-boxing class, taking a long walk with a friend, training for an upcoming bike ride or half-marathon, or going rock climbing. I am happiest when I'm active and doing blood-pumping, adrenalin-filled activities that keep me moving. I *have* to keep moving.

Aunty Dhun has set up an appointment with a spine surgeon and specialist back in Toronto. She knows that I'm anxious about being able to run again. Until I see someone who can tell me that I'm healed and gives me that green light to lace up my running shoes, I won't be able to think about anything else.

My mind is racing for many other reasons. I have a job interview tomorrow. I go through possible interview questions in my mind:

Dina, tell me about yourself. Why did you leave your previous job? Let's discuss your strengths as well as your weaknesses. Why do you want to work for our company? Why do you think you are qualified for this job? What do you know about our company and our products? What is your understanding of the role? Why did you leave your previous job?

If I don't get this job, I can't move out of my parents' place to an apartment downtown. My life in Toronto will be stalled. I have told myself I have one year to make it work in Toronto. If I can't find a great job, the perfect apartment downtown, and be happy here in a year, I'll have to start somewhere else all over again. I don't *want* to do that, but the thought of sticking around for everyone to witness my failure is too much.

My mind spins uncontrollably like a top, the questions are nonstop: What exact neighborhood will I live in? What do I need in my apartment? How many square feet is my minimum? What if it doesn't have a gym? How much can I afford? I don't even have a job ... What do I want to do for work? What is the pay? Benefits? Overall compensation package? Is the bonus capped or structured?

I also want to know the exact date I can start running and training again. The next two days waiting to see the spine surgeon will be tough—I want to know *now* what I can and can't do, and when! Then I can start looking at different running and cycling events in Toronto and start my training. I remind myself to look at different running clubs in Toronto.

I feel an ache in my back and get up to walk up and down the aisle for a bit. It feels nice to stand, and for a brief time, get away from the racetrack of my mind.

We land in Toronto at about 8 p.m. Despite the cold weather, it feels refreshing as I take a gulp of air and stand and walk. Back to business. I've got a TON to accomplish tonight. No time to waste!

I've got to get home, unpack, figure out my outfit for tomorrow, continue preparing for my interview, as well as take a shower, which is going to be a huge mission in and of itself.

Tonight will be the first time I take off my brace and shower. Hallelujah! And yet, I'm petrified I will inadvertently twist and hurt my back. There are so many potentially dangerous movements I could make that normally I would never think about. This shower will require 110% concentration. I have to keep my back perfectly straight as I wash my hair. I cannot even bend to wash my feet, and shaving my legs is out of the question. Thankfully, Mom understands how much I need this. I have my interview tomorrow and this shower is the beginning of my "getting ready" ritual. She sits on the toilet waiting for me, making sure every other second I'm okay. "Do you need anything,

Dina? Should I hand you the shampoo? Don't reach for anything, okay? I will get it—you don't want to hurt yourself!"

She hands me my towel and helps me put the brace back on. She has a chair ready for me, and proceeds to wash my feet and shave my legs. I have to admit—I feel a little embarrassed, but also, it's quite nice to be babied in this way again. I love my mummy!

I feel a million times better and am so happy to have the walk-in shower. But man, that was one lengthy process! My normal 10 minute showers have now become a one hour event.

The front of my body is still black and blue from the bruises from the airbag and I still need help to get into bed and actually lie flat. I move like a mechanical robot and I sit on the bed, keep my body at a 90 degree angle, while mom helps me lower myself into a perfectly flat 180 degree angle. She tucks me in and tells me to have a good night's sleep; she will wake up early to help me get dressed tomorrow for my interview.

62

NOVEMBER 2, 2012

I'M UP BRIGHT AND EARLY. Everything takes about 10 times longer wearing this brace so I need the extra time. I brush my teeth (10 minutes), get dressed (20 minutes), do my hair (20 minutes), then proceed to make my way downstairs to the kitchen for breakfast (10 minutes travel time, half an hour eating). My mind is all "Go, go, GO!" But my body says "Slow, slow, sloooow ..." It's torture!

I have to wear my brace to the interview, which makes me quite self-conscious. I am not supposed to wear pumps, but I feel like I have to make the extra effort to appear strong and "normal." I assure my parents I'll be fine despite their protests.

Daddy doesn't want me taking the subway in rush hour as he fears someone will push me or I might fall and injure my back. He's very protective and just wants to keep me safe. He drops me right at the office entrance and promises to be there to pick me up when I'm done. I'll barely be walking, which helps ease my parents' worry about the high heels.

As we start the drive, there is a lot of traffic so the fact that we can't travel very fast actually eases my mind. I tell myself that a lot less harm can be done on the highway if everyone is going 40 km per hour instead of the usual 100 km per hour.

Dad knows I want to use this time in the car to mentally prepare and feel confident. He lets me be quiet and use the time to focus.

My interview is with a large financial information data provider, and the role is very similar to my very first job. It feels very odd to have come full circle. I've worked in financial sales, education sales, consulting, as Sales Director, and I've completed a certificate program as well as business school. All this just so I could come back to a similar role at a similar firm? I laugh to myself. It reminds me of the episode of *Friends* where Chandler decides he doesn't like his job but doesn't know what he wants to do:

Chandler: "Eight and a half hours of aptitude tests, intelligence tests, personality tests ... and what do I learn? 'You are ideally suited for a career in data processing for a large multinational corporation.'"

Phoebe: "That's so great! 'Cause you already know how to do that!"

It's taken me six years of discovery, exploration and trying many new things to get me here—right back where I started.

As I walk into the office, the receptionist tells me the manager will be with me in a few minutes and invites me into the boardroom to wait. Perfect! I have time to remove my jacket slowly so I don't twist and hurt myself, sit down carefully, and be all ready before he enters. Awkwardness averted! Unfortunately, he walks in the room barely a minute later. Dammit! I casually say I'm freezing and will keep my jacket on for a few minutes.

Halfway through my back is starting to ache. Crap, why can't we be done? I can't twist my body as the brace is keeping me firmly in place and I can't just stand up in the middle of the interview. What would I say? "I was in an accident and my back hurts. Poor me." No way! I don't want to appear fragile and wimpy. The office is all men and I want to be seen as a strong woman that can get along in the "boys' club."

The interview ends and he says he will let me know if got the job by end of next week.

Thank heavens! I can finally stand up. Daddy is waiting downstairs for me and has brought me flats, which he helps me put on before driving home.

We've barely moved out of our parking spot and I'm already thinking about all of the other interviews I have lined up in the coming weeks. I hate this feeling of being "unsettled." Can we just skip this whole part and move to the "Wow, Dina! You're incredible! I can't believe how quickly you got that executive position and amazing condo, and you just won the waterfront marathon? That's incredible" part?

63

NOVEMBER 3, 2012

I CAN'T GET TO THE hospital quickly enough. I need to know how my back is doing and more specifically, when I can run again. The spine surgeon examines my X-rays and explains that I'm healing. I should be good as new in another two weeks! I LOVE this doctor because he is super athletic (I can see his muscles through his shirt) and can tell he understands how much it is killing me to not work out. We talk about running, races we've done, and some exercises I can do at the gym that will actually strengthen my back. He is very patient and answers all of my questions so I'm feeling a lot more relieved after seeing him.

I can finally concentrate on all of the other things on my mind—that one-year countdown clock is ticking! I need a great job, a great apartment, then I'll get into the best shape of my life, and then I'll be ready to meet a perfect guy that my family will love and everybody will be envious of. Someone like this doctor would be great ...

A couple of days later, I get a call. I've got the job! There's a teeny problem ... I've also got interviews with three other companies and I want to wait to see which one is the best fit. It's an important decision. Whatever company I choose will be my "home" for the next long while—I'm done with all of the moving around and the startups. I want a steady paycheque, a predictable schedule, and a place to grow. I reply to the offer letter saying that I'm currently interviewing with other companies and require some more time to contemplate all offers before making my decision.

Immediately, the company rescinds the offer. WTF? Okay ... Now I have NO job.

I could kick myself. I'm filled with anxiety because the other three companies I'm interviewing with are all working on their own timeline which does NOT fit with mine. I need a job *right now.* These people are in no hurry to hire anyone at all, it seems.

My next interview is with a company called Salesforce. The office is right downtown, which is a huge plus. I could walk to work! I prepare like crazy for the "mock sales presentation" portion of the interview. I need to nail this if I'm going to move forward.

I walk out of the interview with Salesforce and I know I didn't get it. I sucked. Badly. They didn't reject me on the spot but I know what's coming. Sure enough, two days later I get an email confirming it: I won't be joining Salesforce.

I'm trying not to panic but I have this nervous feeling growing in my chest that won't go away. What if I can't make it work in Toronto? I probably should have never left. I'm up against job applicants who are the same age as me, who probably came here or stayed here right after finishing university so I'm at a disadvantage. I look at my resumé and imagine what employers must think about me: New job every year ... Always moving ... Not able to stay in one place ... No wonder I'm having no luck.

I wish I could go for a run and shake off this panic but I'm stuck in this stupid brace and high impact exercise is still off limits. Instead, I start a new to-do list and think about how I can rewrite my resumé to make myself sound more appealing to employers. I hear the countdown clock ticking louder in my head ...

64

DECEMBER 2012

"DINA, DID YOU GET ALL the decorations from the basement? I found a few extras that I know you love. *Jaanu*, go take a look in the sunroom ..."

"Ahh ... Mummy. I LOOOOOVE!"

There's the red sleigh filled with cotton balls to look like snow that Yassy made as a child. On one corner there is the ceramic train set that links four cars together where you can open up each car and see a present inside. My favourite is the 10-inch figurine of Mrs. Claus with her spectacles and bag of presents. Mummy also found the angel that we always place on top of the tree.

I just love this time of year! I wish Yas was here to help us decorate but she's in China for her MBA class trip. She'll be back home on December 24th and I know she will love how warm, cozy and festive the house looks.

We hang our Santa stockings by the chimney just like we have always done. Mom sewed a "Y" and a "D" on them when we were babies. We hang a huge multicoloured "Happy New Year" sign above the mantle. Some might think all the decor looks gaudy, but we love it. All the bright colours make me smile.

Christmas music is playing while Daddy hangs a green garland with small white lights and red bow ties around the sunroom door. There are also two stockings by the front door, in case Santa decides to take a more civilized approach this time. One can never be too careful, and we must give Santa all opportunities to give presents.

There is a beautiful green garland Mom always puts around the mirror above the entrance table and two gold reindeer for the table. Mom puts her finishing touches on the two large outdoor planters that go on either side of the front door, filled with tiny winterberry stems, dried baby's breath, shimmery silver pinecones, and red plaid bows. I think Santa would approve.

I am so happy to be back home. I can't wait for Yas to be back so we can make some holiday cookies! I'm thinking cranberry-orange shortbread is a must!

65

DECEMBER 4, 2012

I GET SOME MUCH NEEDED good news: I let the company that initially offered me the job know that I really wanted to work for them and was hoping they could reconsider offering me a position. It turns out, they haven't found anyone else yet, and so they invited me to re-interview. I'd love it if they just sent me a contract already, but whatever. At least I still have a shot! The interview went well and I'm just crossing my fingers that Santa will deliver an early Christmas present to me: a JOB!

I'm worried about Daddy. He said that on his way home from the gym, his eyes felt odd and it looked like there was a halo around the traffic lights. He visits his ophthalmologist the very next day and the doctor tells him to just ignore it. I can tell Daddy is still concerned but is doing his best to downplay everything, probably for my sake.

I finally get an official job offer and this time, without hesitation, I accept! Thank God! I was lucky, but man, oh man ... The amount of anxiety of the past few weeks has been painful. I'm not convinced I will LOVE this job, but it ticks all of the boxes in terms of money and benefits. It will allow me to move into an apartment downtown and build roots. It's a good, stable job.

The countdown clock is a little quieter now. I'm making progress. I'm back on schedule.

The company gives me what seems like a mountain of paperwork to go through. There are documents to read, sign, copy and have witnessed ... Then there are websites to review and onboarding material to have completed before I start. I'll tackle this homework with gusto—I have to make up for not accepting their first offer right away. If I nail everything they send my way right out of the gate, I'll be back on track for an executive role in no time!

My first day on the job will be Monday, January 7, 2013. That means I have just over a month to find a new apartment downtown. I feel like I'm now officially in the race. The starting gun has just fired and ... GO! I start scouring the Internet for apartment rentals.

Daddy mentions that his eyes are still bothering him. He has seen this "halo" around traffic lights another two times but the ophthalmologist doesn't seem to care. I hate to see him worried and I know the timing bothers him—there is so much driving to do this time of year, and the weather and roads are trickier in the wintertime. I wish he'd find a new ophthalmologist.

66

DECEMBER 19, 2012

THE COMPANY I WILL WORK for are just a few days from closing for the Christmas holidays, so I work like crazy to read all of the documents and sign all the paperwork. If I get everything done before they close for the holidays, I'll look like a rock star.

As I'm doing that, I'm still searching for a new apartment. My friend, Perry, who is also a top real estate agent, takes me around the city to see different options.

After seeing about 20 places, I fall in love with an apartment at Bay and College. It's perfect!

I feel like a chicken running around with my head cut off. I sign the rental contracts, have to go downtown to not only meet the landlord but personally give him my post-dated cheques, get the keys, call Hydro and other utilities and have them transferred into in my name, organize my cable and Internet hook up, and shop for everything I'll need to move in.

For every single place I have moved into in the other cities I've lived in, I shop and have everything sorted IMMEDIATELY! Everything from dish gloves, cups, groceries, toilet paper, shampoo, and furniture must be purchased right away for me to start feeling like I have a home. I admire people who can take their time and do it slowly, week by week, but I am not built that way. I give myself two days max to have everything in my apartment sorted and ready to go.

Mom and I start shopping for things I will need for the kitchen and bathroom and when we return home, we all head to the apartment so Daddy can measure the dimensions for the bed, couch and dining table, which we plan to buy on Boxing Day.

After dinner, Mom and I do research on the Internet to see which furniture stores have the furniture that will best suit my taste and style.

When we get tired, I switch to doing research on the company, and check out various websites regarding financial data and sales objectives.

I try to fall asleep but I can't. There is too much I need to accomplish and I feel I have NO time. My mind keeps racing and racing. The countdown clock keeps ticking loudly. I'm actually dying for my alarm clock to ring at 5 a.m. every day so I can continue marking off things on my to-do list.

67

DECEMBER 22, 2012

MY ALARM GOES OFF AT 5 a.m. and I'm alert. Christmas is still a few days away and I've got WAY too much to get done. Mom and I will go shopping again today to get everything from dishes and cutlery to towels and non-perishable food items so my kitchen is all stocked.

By the time we get home, we're both exhausted. Five hours of shopping was a success. My parents' living room is filled with boxes that we will take and put at my new apartment on our next trip over.

Thank God Mom had already made dinner because we are both starving. She's always so prepared and totally knew shopping would take this long.

After dinner I try to stay awake so I can read more of the websites that my new company sent to me but I can't. I start drifting off and dreaming of Christmas ...

Christmas is my absolute favourite time of the year. Every Christmas Day is a cherished tradition. Everyone wakes up and has breakfast. I'm always first to wake up so I patiently and eagerly await everyone else to be up. Once everyone is done breakfast, Yassy and I open our stockings. We always know what is most likely in them but there is still so much anticipation. There are a few three-pack chocolates, usually Lindt, Pot of Gold, Ferrero Rocher and always Guylian for Yas. Mom will search every store to find Guylian because it's Yas' favourite.

If there is any chocolate with salted caramel, I'll usually trade those with Yas because she LOVES that flavour. It makes me laugh seeing her eyes pop with excitement.

There's always a puppy calendar (even though Mom knows we use Google calendars now). I still love them and put my calendar up on my wall to look at the adorable puppies. There are always socks. I get the thick, fuzzy, warm ones as I'm always cold and Yas gets the thin ones. One year mom got me these huge puppy dog slippers to keep my feet warm. I love seeing the variations of socks she's chosen each year.

Without fail is an envelope containing a few Lotto 649 tickets. The morning after, we all race to the paper to check the Lotto numbers and see if we've won. I think the most anyone has won is a mere $10. Mom also packs a few scratch-and-win tickets for instant gratification.

There are always bath gloves and a few beautiful smelling soaps from The Body Shop. Mom knows my hands are always dry so, there are also a few amazing fragrant moisturizing lotions for me.

Every year there is a different small surprise—whatever Mom finds that she knows we will love! Last year she came across a family-run bakery specializing in shortbread cookies. They were beautifully packaged and so delicious!

Once stocking time is done, Yassy and I head to the gym for a great workout. Sometimes on Christmas Day, there is a high-cardio group fitness class which we go to and if there isn't, we'll do our own cardio and weights together.

Then we shower and have lunch together in the sunroom. Since everything is closed on Christmas Day, Mom gets our favourite "cheese knot" bread from Michael's Baguette in Fairview Mall the day before. Dad makes bacon and breakfast sausages, fresh orange juice, as well as a kettle of perfectly steeped chai along with eggs and a bowl of fresh fruit.

After lunch is present time! For years and years when we were younger, Mom would go shopping and find us different clothes and toys and pack them all in separate boxes as there was an immense joy in tearing off the wrapping paper and boxes. On most occasions, we would then go back to each store (smart Mummy kept all the receipts) and we would exchange what she got us.

As we got older, she was so relieved to be free of shopping, so she and Daddy now give us the BEST gift. No boxes, wrapping paper or ribbons. Just that small envelope and card with a cheque—EXACTLY the gift Yas and I love!

After lunch, Mom and Dad nap while Yas and I curl up to watch a holiday movie. We invariably end up napping as well—I think we have seen the first half of *The Sound of Music* about 20 times!

Later we will head over to Aunty Dhun and Uncle Farokh's house. Cousin Sabby always messages me and Yas to come over earlier. We all get ready and we all have to wear something red. Since Sabrena and I have lived away from Toronto for so many years, it's one of the few times we are all together as a family.

The entire house is decorated with wreaths and bows, but the most impressive thing is the spread in the kitchen. Uncle Farokh always takes me and Yassy around the huge kitchen island to show us what's cooking. Many years it's been turkey and ham, but one year it was delicious Cornish hen with wild rice apricot stuffing. Uncle Farokh is a master chef and we always trust what he makes. There is always so much flavour and he always puts unique twists on each dish. Two years ago he made cornbread stuffing with pecans and sweet sausage. It was SO good!

As soon as everyone arrives, we start off the evening with exquisite champagne and a caviar plate that includes a few different varieties of caviar surrounded by small bowls of chopped egg, lemon wedges, red onion, chives, crème fraîche and either blinis or crisps. It is served in an elegant plate with a mother-of-pearl caviar spoon. Our Christmas dinners start off in such style!

Then, all the appetizers take over their kitchen island. There are bacon-wrapped sausages, mini quiches, vegetables and dip, baked brie with caramelized onions, sausage rolls, spinach dip and warm pita, and the extravagant cheeseboard.

Sabrena loves to bake, so after Uncle Farokh explains the main courses, Sabby will show us ALL the dessert. Sometimes she makes carrot cake with cream-cheese icing (Hands down—BEST carrot cake ever!), different types of cheesecakes, shortbread, and my favourite is her rugelach. She makes so many delicious variations including cinnamon and orange-cranberry.

Our Indian family is very loud and you have to speak up to get a word in. Everyone wants to talk, share stories and laugh.

It's my favourite day of the year by far—full of food, family and laughter. I've been looking forward to Christmas so much since I got back, I can almost taste it! Just a couple of more days ...

But first, I have to finish this to-do list.

68

DECEMBER 24, 2012

I'VE DECIDED TO CONTINUE SHOPPING for my new place today. I have a list of furniture places and did all the preliminary research online to find the pieces I need. If we can get everything at Boxing Day prices, I'll be all set up that much sooner!

Daddy drives, but after about three minutes he pulls into Fairview Mall to rest. His vision is blurred and he doesn't feel that it's safe for him to drive. So, Mom and Dad change seats and she drives.

We pull into the parking lot of the very first furniture store parking lot and I'm all ready to jump out of the car and find my new dream couch when suddenly, I can't move. I get horrendous shooting pains that start from the top of my neck and go all the way down my body to my feet. I wince in pain and let out a little shriek; it's that bad.

Then, comes this massive headache. It's like someone has reached into my head, grabbed my entire brain, clenched down and won't loosen their grip. I shut my eyes tightly to try and will away the pain somehow. I've never had a headache like this. Mom notices me grimacing in the back seat and puts her foot down. We're going home and I will go to bed. I know the look she gets—there is no arguing with her.

We get home and although I am weary from the headache, I also don't want to be alone. It's Christmas Eve for Pete's sake! I insist on sitting in the living room with Mummy and Daddy. It's early evening now and I am surprised by how dim it is in the living room. Mummy explains that Daddy's eyes are irritated by the light. We all sit quietly in the darkness.

Mom calls Aunty Dhun for advice about Dad's eyes. Dr. Nguyen, Aunty Dhun's friend and a well-regarded ophthalmologist, is away in the US for Christmas vacation. Next best option is to go to St. Michael's Hospital, which is downtown. It's a bit of a trek and they anticipate the Christmas Eve traffic downtown will be nuts, so they decide to wait until morning.

Yas calls to say she's landed back in Toronto after her MBA trip. Every single flight that Yas or I go on, Dad and Mom always drop us off and pick us up from the airport, no matter what. Mom takes one look at Dad and me curled up in pain on the couch and tells her, "Yasi, why don't you take a cab? There will be lots of traffic so it will be faster."

She doesn't want to tell Yas what's happening over the phone. Yas thinks it's very strange that no one is coming to the airport but after a 14-hour flight from Asia, she's too tired to care.

A little over an hour later, Yas arrives at home. "Did I just walk into the house of death? What on earth is going on?" she asks.

The lights in the living room are out, I'm in the fetal position on the couch and can barely lift my head, and Dad is in the recliner chair gripping the arms fearfully as the vision in his left eye is getting worse and worse by the minute.

Daddy is our main concern. I just have the stupid flu but we are all trying to do what we can for Dad.

I slowly try to lift myself to the seated position so I can talk to Yas. I know she must be dying to tell us about her MBA trip to China, as well as the Thailand trip she took with some friends. I finally hoist myself up and ask her for a big hug. I've missed her. While we talk, email or text pretty much every day, it's been nine months since we've seen each other. The last time was when she came to Napa to visit me.

She is just about to start describing her trip when the shooting pains start raging through my body. I can't help but cry out in pain. The headache comes on right away. After two long minutes that feel like an eternity, Mom gives me Tylenol and helps me slowly walk upstairs to my bed. She tucks me in and I pray to God that I can sleep and the pain doesn't start up again.

I have no idea what's happening. Mom calls Aunty Katy. We can't figure it out. The only plausible explanation is that I must have a severe case of the flu. What else could it be?

Okay, all I have to do is make sure I eat, even if I don't have an appetite. Drinks lots of fluids. Load up on Vitamin C. Rest. Stop being such a wimp. You are a machine. This is just a glorified cold. You run half-marathons and can move across the world. This is child's play. You've got tonight to get better. Tomorrow is Christmas! There's no time for sitting and sleeping in bed! There is way, way too much to do! Sabby is back in town, so you better be ready for fam-jam time. We'll nip this stupid cold in the bud!

69

DECEMBER 25, 2012

MOM COMES INTO MY ROOM at 7 a.m. to see if I need any Tylenol for the pain and to tell me she is now taking Daddy to St. Mike's emergency. He can't see at all out of his left eye now.

I'm even more worried for him but I barely have enough energy to lift my head up. Mom has never driven downtown. She is not comfortable on the highway and doesn't have the best sense of direction. I should be driving! She can see the fear in my eyes and says, "Don't worry, *Jaanu.* We're leaving now and we'll go slowly. There's no traffic and Daddy will guide me."

Yassy comes into my room at 10 a.m. and tells me she is heading to the gym. I let out a whimper because I want so badly to go with her but can't move. She rubs my back and says, "D, it's so much better to rest because you'll feel better this evening. Sab just texted and we'll all celebrate soon. It's okay, babe."

She asks if she can make me any food but I have no appetite. She brings me orange juice, apple juice and water and tells me she'll be back in an hour and she'll make me some lunch. As much as I want to protest and come to the gym, I know she's right.

Yassy comes back from the gym and comes to check on me. She says she's talked to Mom and not to worry, they found their way to St. Mike's. Since it is Christmas Day, there are no ophthalmologists in the hospital, only residents. The ophthalmologist in training measured Dad's intraocular pressure and it was 64 (normal is less than 20). She immediately put in drops, and they have to stay in the ER so the doctors can monitor the pressure in his eye every two hours.

Around 5 p.m. I hear the door open and that must mean Mom and Dad are back. I sit up and manage to get out of bed. I've had enough of this lying around nonsense. It's Christmas Day and I want to see Sabby and my family.

Mom tells me that Dad's eye pressure is still high but has now come down to 38. The resident sent them home and told them to come right back to the ER tomorrow morning. She has given Mom a detailed list of four different eye drops and the precise time to give each medication.

She tells me Daddy is very scared and she's going to go downstairs to make him some dinner and that we need to keep the lights dim as they bother his eye. She shows me the page-long schedule of eye drops and timings—it looks insanely complicated. At least Daddy can now see shadows out of his left eye, so that is progress.

She questions my strength and isn't convinced I'll be okay at Aunty Dhun's house. She says she and Daddy will not come to dinner but she will drive us. I am adamant that I am completely fine and will go to Christmas dinner. I can't show Mom or Yas any signs that I am in pain or they'll tell me to stay home and rest. This stupid flu is not keeping me away from my favourite part of the season—Christmas dinner!

Despite the pain, I somehow manage to muster enough energy to dress myself in something festive. Everyone is talking, laughing and the feast begins at Aunty Dhun's house. All of us gather in Aunty Dhun's huge kitchen. The chatter is deafening! In my family, you have to be loud to get a word in and while I am normally talkative, exuding energy and excitement, I can barely whisper.

I see the elaborate cheeseboard with some of the finest cheeses, including parmesan reggiano, stilton, camembert, creamy goat's cheese along with some delicious jams (fig is my favourite), grapes, caviar, an assortment of crackers and baguettes and tasty cured meats. It's killing me that I have no appetite.

Uncle Farokh always has the finest wines and I'm dying to have a glass of bubbly to go along with the cheese plate. I tell him I'll just have a glass of water and then I'll be ready for some wine.

As I go to fill my glass of water, I collapse. Everyone shrieks and gathers around me, helping me up off the floor. It's clear I'm in pain and as much as I want to stay, my cousin insists on driving me home to rest. My uncle tells me he will make me a big care package with all of the cheeses, appetizers, turkey, stuffing and all the delicious accompaniments and desserts that I love. I'm so mad! I am finally home and get to be with my family on my favourite day and this stupid flu is ruining everything.

As I walk into the house, Mom can see the frustration in my eyes as well as the pain I'm feeling.

"Come, come, *Jaanu*. Come sit with Daddy in the living room. I'll just put his next dose of eye drops in and we'll sit and have some tea on the couch. Can I make you *charvalu edu* and toast (eggs and toast)? Eat something so you have some strength."

I nod my head yes. I'm going to fight off this darn flu so I can at least enjoy New Year's Eve!

DECEMBER 26, 2012

I HAVE SO MUCH TO get done but I can't bring myself to wake up at my normal early-bird hour. I feel so discouraged. I'm wasting valuable time lying in bed. The countdown clock in my head is going haywire. You missed Christmas! You're late for Boxing Day! You'll miss New Year's! The stress of it all combined with my aching head is excruciating.

Mom and Dad head back to St. Mike's. Daddy needs to have his eye pressure measured and see if the drops are working. He still can only see shadows and although he isn't saying too much, I know him, he's scared.

Again, Mom and Dad are in the ER for the whole day and only come home in the evening.

Yas makes Mom and Dad dinner when they get home. I put a load of laundry into the wash earlier on, but I can barely keep my eyes open long enough to put everything into the dryer. I ask my mom if she can do it for me, but for some reason, I can't get the words out.

"Mum ... can you ... put the thing ... the thing in the ... in the thing?"

I forget the words washer, dryer, laundry. The words are just escaping me and I use the word "thing" for anything I can't actually name.

Mom and Yas can see me falling asleep so just brush it off. I can't find the words because I'm tired— that must be it. Mom tucks me into bed making sure I have water, juice, and Tylenol beside the bed in case I need it at night.

DECEMBER 27, 2012

DAD HAS ANOTHER APPOINTMENT AT St. Mike's today but before he and Mummy leave, they insist that I come downstairs to eat breakfast. I'm never going to beat this flu if I don't eat, so I agree.

Yas escorts me downstairs, watching me carefully the entire time. We sit down to breakfast and she goes to help Mummy.

"Mum, something is off with D. She's never sick ... I can't tell, but it's weird. I think we should call Aunty Dhun."

I try to ask how Dad is feeling but I sound drunk. I'm slurring my words and I can barely get a full sentence out. I can't be THAT tired. I've spent most of the past few days sleeping and wasting precious hours that I could be using to prepare for my new job or shopping for my condo. This flu is SUCH a waste of my time. I'm not completely panicking yet, because I know many of the Boxing "Day" sales become Boxing "Week" sales, so I should still be able to get most of my furniture at discount prices.

I can see that Mom is torn. My dad has to go back to the hospital as his eye needs taking care of, but I am obviously not well. I feel badly—this certainly isn't the holiday I had wished for! My poor mom, running around taking care of everybody, stressed out and worried.

"Jaanu, this flu is causing you to speak in quite an odd way so I'm going to call Aunty Dhun, just to be sure. We'll make sure you're back to your normal self soon, angel. I know this is bothering you."

She calls up Aunty Dhun, who wastes no time. "Shahnaz, you look after my brother; we'll look after Dina. Farokh will come to get her now."

Mom explains, "*Jaanu*, Aunty Dhun wants to see you and get a few tests done. Daddy and I are going to see the ophthalmologist at St. Mikes, and Yassy has a lunch meeting downtown for work, so Uncle Farokh will come pick you up and take you to see a doctor. Let me help you get ready because he is on his way over."

Uncle Farohk and I walk into Aunty Dhun's clinic and are quickly seen by a doctor. He's actually a neurologist, which I find odd. I'm sure he's just going to look at my throat, see that I have swollen glands or something and send me home with antibiotics. I'm really not sure what all the fuss is about.

I follow the neurologist into a room. He's pretty young—I'm guessing 35 years old, max. He's kind of cute, too. Man, I wish I'd put on cute clothes instead of my baggy sweats. Perhaps running a brush through my hair would have been a good idea as well. I silently laugh to myself. I always meet cute guys at the most inopportune times!

The doctor asks me to name a few objects, including his stethoscope, his watch and his pen. I'm not sure why I completely forget how to say the names of these objects out loud. He taps my knee, which I believe means he's checking my reflex actions. I keep wondering why he's not checking out my throat or glands but I guess he's the doctor and I'll just do what he says. All I really need are some pills so I can get rid of this flu.

After about two minutes, he says he just has to do a few things and asks me to wait with Uncle Farokh.

I go sit with Uncle Farokh and wait.

The doctor returns, and ever so calmly tells me, "Dina, I don't want to alarm you but you will be going straight to the emergency room at Scarborough Grace Hospital. They know you are coming, and Dr. Noria (Aunty Dhun) will meet you there, as well."

Excuse me, WHAT? How lovely that you don't want to alarm me but suffice to say ... I AM ALARMED!

My unflappable uncle just holds my hand and leads me to the car and says, "Don't worry, sweetie. Everything will be fine."

Aunty Dhun is already in the ER. I can't tell if she's worried or not. In most situations involving a hospital or health, she takes a very businesslike approach and gets stuff done. No time for tears and worry. Apparently I'm now scheduled to have a CT scan. My aunt doesn't want me to wait so after a few minutes of speaking with the ER staff, I get my CT scan done and she's already telling the doctor to read it to us so she know what the next course of action will be. She really has a remarkable way of getting things done, especially in the hospital environment. I always know that I'm in good hands with her.

"Sweetie, the doctor is just obtaining your scan and we will soon know what is happening. Just a few minutes," she assures me. In those few minutes, Mom and Dad rush in and hug me.

Mom tells me that she and Dad had come home after dad's visit to St. Mike's and Aunty Dhun had said to come to Scarborough General ER as I was getting a CT scan. Mom can read my mind as my eyes dart around the room. She tells me she called Yas who left downtown in an instant and would be here shortly.

The doctor's return with Aunty Dhun to explain my test results. "Dina, do you see this white circular shape on the screen? You can see the difference between the left side and right side of your brain? This is an abnormal mass—that large white circle— on the left side. It's about two centimetres in diameter. We have to find out why you have this mass. You will stay here for the night so we can monitor you and then first thing tomorrow, an ambulance will come and transfer you to Toronto Western Hospital."

Whoa, whoa, whoaaaa ... Back it up ... Back it up just a bit. I have a "MASS?" What is a "mass?" Why is it there? What does it mean? Do I have brain cancer? That's a death sentence, right? How long do I have? I want to go home!

Questions are running through my mind but no words come out. I am actually speechless. Mom takes one hand and Aunty Dhun takes the other and we all follow the doctor to the hospital bed I will stay in for the night.

"We've got you, *Jaanu.* It will be okay," Mom tells me.

I have not had any headaches or shooting pains for a while now and am starting to feel better, so I'm sure all of this is nothing. It's just really getting in the way—I have WAY too much to get done!

DECEMBER 28, 2012

MOM, DAD AND YAS ARRIVE early in the morning and bring me some real food for breakfast—thank God! The hospital food is basically fast-food mush. Yassy knows how important healthy eating is to me, so she has made an egg-and-cheddar-cheese sandwich on whole-wheat toast, with cut-up strawberries, kiwi and grapes on the side.

They all fawn over me and ask if I'm feeling better, tell me there's no hurry and I should take the time to rest, not push myself blah, blah, blah ... The whole time I'm basically preparing a revised schedule for the next month in my head:

Okay, today is Friday, December 28th. I start work in exactly nine days on Monday, January 7, 2013. So ... I'll spend one day at Toronto Western Hospital, max! Then if we go furniture shopping tomorrow, or latest Sunday, get everything delivered to the new apartment by Thursday, January 3rd, I'll have a few days to get used to the new place, get a feel for the gym in my new building, make sure all my meals are prepared for the week and my Internet and computer are all set up, and then I can go through all the different websites and information so I can wow my new boss on Day 1!

Since the doctors are insisting an ambulance take me to Western, we'll all have to split up. Yas will come with me and Mom in the ambulance, and Dad, Aunty Dhun, Uncle Farokh, Sabby and cousin Zub will meet us at Western. I wish they would just let me get up and walk. I HATE all this "sitting idle" time. It's so unproductive. I want to get up and MOVE!

We arrive at Western and Yas is messaging everyone what room I'm in at the hospital. Apparently today I will meet with doctors and residents and go through many tests. I shudder at the thought of all the waiting I will be doing today as the doctors go back and forth trying to figure out what's wrong with me. All I'm thinking is "I'm fine! Let's get this shit *done* so I can be on my merry way."

As they wheel me down the hall to start my day of "tests," I honestly think I'll breeze through everything in a couple of hours. How bad could it be?

Test 1: Mental Status

First up, the doctors will assess my "mental status." A neurologist, Dr. Steiner, tells me he will ask me simple questions designed to test my cognitive ability.

Sure, Doc, let's get moving. He starts: "Dina, remember these three objects as I will ask you to name them at the end of this exam."

Sure—bed, Q-tip, tongue depressor. Done! He then opens a book with some mathematical problems. I laugh to myself. My dad made me a math genius so I actually scoff as I quickly tell him the correct answers. He then gives me a cardboard clock and tells me to place the hour and minute hand in the correct position based on the time he indicates. Done and done!

He asks me to repeat a few sentences and remember the three objects he mentioned at the start. All complete and correct. Before I can even ask, "Cool, are we done? Can I go home now" the next test starts.

Test 2: Cranial Nerve Testing

One of Dr. Steiner's residents explains we will now do some tests to assess "cranial nerves." These are a set of nerves that relay messages between the brain and the head and neck and control motor and sensory functions such as vision, smell, movement of tongue and vocal chords.

I do appreciate these explanations but I also really want to yell out, "Dude! Get all this shit done and stop wasting time with all the explanations! The faster you just DO these tests, the faster I can get outta here and onto my LONG ass list of things to do!"

Dr. Steiner wiggles his finger starting at my nose, moving his fingers towards my ears to test if my peripheral vision is intact. He shines light into my eyes to asses my pupillary light reflexes. He uses the tongue depressor to check my gag reflex. Clearly those reflexes are just fine, as I almost throw up all over him.

The resident asks me to close my eyes and puts different scents below my nose to see if I can name the smells. He presses my cheeks, feels different points on my head and neck and continues to scribble out notes. I can tell that he is trying to see *what* area of my brain has been affected but they can't, so we move on to yet another test.

Test 3: Motor System

The resident, Dr. Ian, continues on to explain the purpose of each test. Next, they will look at my muscle strength and tone. I hike up my incredibly baggy hospital gown so they can look at my muscles. They ask me to sit on the edge of the bed and see if I can move my leg from 90 degree to 180 degrees, first on my own and then with resistance by pressing in the opposite direction. It's no biggie for me. I work out all the time, guys! I could kick you across the room with these quads!

Next, I have to get out of bed and walk along a straight line, first on my tiptoes and then on the heels of my feet.

Dr. Ian explains that evaluating the "Babinski response" is an important part of testing the motor system.

No problem! I'm knocking it out of the park! Bring on the next test!

Test 4: Sensory System

Dr. Ian tells me that my next set of tests will be used to determine areas of abnormal sensation, quality, and type of sensation impairment, and the degree and extent of tissue impairment. By this point, I tune out most of his long detailed explanations and just do what they say. Anything to speed things up. I'm losing steam, and the last remnants of my patience, by the minute.

Dr. Ian asks me to open my hands and close my eyes and tells me he will prick a certain area on my hand and I have to describe where exactly I think he is pricking. He then places hot and cold balls in my hands and I have to describe the temperature level I feel in that moment.

He also asks me to close my eyes again and uses a pen cap to draw different letters and numbers into my palm. I have to guess the letter or number.

"Okay, doc ... Are we done? Clearly nothing is wrong. Can I go home?" Apparently they *still* have more tests to go.

Test 5: Deep Tendon Reflexes

Next up are "deep tendon reflex tests" because alterations in reflexes are often the first sign of neurological dysfunction. He finally "dumbs down" the medical textbook talk and says "Dina, I'm going to use this soft rubber hammer to gently tap deep tendons, like around your knee, and see if there is a response, meaning you move your leg. This test requires nothing on your part." Bonus!

Test 6: Coordination and the Cerebellum

Not that I care to listen to his explanations of each and every single test but I know his superior, Dr. Steiner, is observing his actions, so I do my best to not look annoyed at how much of a waste of time I think all this is.

Dr. Ian informs me that the cerebellum is the part of the brain that controls voluntary movement and motor coordination, including posture. He asks me to move one finger from my nose to his finger and keep going back and forth. After he sees I can do that, he asks me to tap my fingers together. He later tests coordination on the lower half of my body by asking me to take my left heel and rub upwards and downwards on my right leg.

Test 7: Gait

"Dina, the last test I'd like to do is for gait, which is just walking."

The "last test?" Sweet music to my ears! He asks me to walk straight ahead, backwards, then on my toes and after on my heels, turning abruptly as well as running.

I turn to Dr. Steiner. "Doc, I've aced them all. I can be discharged, right?" He says there are a few more tests but it's so vague that I feel like I'm in the dark. I want to know exactly how many more tests, how long each of these tests are, and precisely what time I will be let out of the hospital! I *hate* not knowing exactly what is going on.

Another doctor, apparently a neurosurgeon, comes into my room and informs me I need to get some new tests done so the doctors can have a better idea of what's happening in my brain. She kindly tells me that they need to have a better, more conclusive set of tests.

I think she must be Type A and somehow understand how edgy I am because she tells me, in a matter-of-fact tone:

"Dina, we want to get you out as soon as possible. I promise we are not wasting time. Will you trust me?" Her straight up, calm demeanour and encouraging way of speaking make me like her instantly. I also notice my parents' reaction when she is talking to me. I feel as though my parents feel like a huge weight has been lifted off their shoulders. They seem to value whatever she says and look suddenly calmer.

Alrighty, Dr. Hodaie—I trust you. Let's get these tests done.

Test 8: Blood Tests

A short, sweet nurse named Mary with beautiful long red hair wheels in a "blood cart." All I see are rows and rows of vials, with different coloured caps and different types of needles. She explains that I'll only be pricked once using a butterfly needle and she will be able to get many different vials of blood as I will be tested for everything. Just one small prick and the pain will be done. I like her efficiency.

One small prick, my ass! Apparently I've got teeny tiny veins and after a few painful pricks of the needle, I'm ready to pass out. Figure it *out* already, lady! Prick number 5 is the charmer! Blood galore! I lose track as she swiftly changes the vials as soon as there is enough blood. Each vial is testing for something different but she tells me—they are testing you for EVERYTHING. I lose track around vile 11.

There is the complete chemistry panel and blood count which includes glucose, cholesterol, LDL, HDL and triglycerides. There is also fibrinogen, hemoglobin A1C, DHEA, Homocysteine, C Reactive protein, TSH, testosterone, estradiol, CBC with differential and platelets, kidney panel, liver panel, mineral and bone, as well as fluids and electrolytes.

Test 9: EEG

I learn that an EEG is a test that will measure and record the electrical activity in my brain. By the time they are done putting ALL the electrodes on my head, I look like a Martian. It takes forever to place all these electrodes in exactly the right place on my head. They use electrodes with some sticky goop, which feels odd on my skull.

I'm told to just lie back and pretty much be quiet as the technologist reads the recording and gets different data on the monitors to give them a full picture of my brain's electrical activity.

After two hours (TWO whole hours of *sitting still* ... KILL ME), I'm taken back up to my room. And yet again, they keep me in the bed and wheel me to my room. My legs feel like Jell-O. Fat wobbly Jell-O. I want to move and run but I'm pretty sure the doctors have not fit that into my strict schedule of tests, tests and more tests.

Test 10: ECG

Now I'm getting an ECG done. It seems similar to the EEG but the electrodes are placed on 10 different parts of my body (not only my head).

I wish they would warm up these electrodes. The ones on my ribs and close to my heart feel like ice cubes.

It will only take about 20 minutes and again, I'm told to just relax and lie still. I swear I'm going to punch the next person that tells me to "relax." I've been *"relaxing"* all damn day!

Test 11: Angiogram

Just when I thought we were finally done, I'm told I will now get an angiogram, which is an X-ray that uses a special dye and camera to take pictures of the flow in an artery or vein.

This is NOT a fun procedure. A thin tube called a catheter is placed into a blood vessel in the groin. The catheter is guided to the area to be studied and then an iodine dye (contrast material) is injected into the vessel to make the area show up clearly on X-ray pictures.

They tell me the test will take a few hours so I have to go pee one last time before it begins. It feels like each test is more painful, takes more time and is even more mentally exhausting than the last.

Test 12: CT

I had a CT scan done yesterday so I've got this one down! Not sure why they want to do it again as I don't think there would be any changes from the CT done yesterday, but I let them do what they want. It also takes no time at all.

A CT scan basically combines a series of X-ray images taken from different angles and uses computer technology to create cross-sectional images of the bones, blood vessels and soft tissue inside the body.

I just lie down on a movable table that goes into a very large scanner (picture a VERY large hollowed out wine barrel) and a few minutes later, I'm done.

Test 13: MRI

I'm in the MRI waiting room and Sabby and Yas are with me. I am informed that before the MRI, they will need to cut and remove my belly-button ring. I'm so sad ... I love that ring! The technologist uses a massive pair of plyers to cut my teeny tiny ring off.

Now Sab tells me we'll just wait till they are ready to take my MRI. From what I'm told, an MRI is painless and like a CT. I'm put into another scanner that produces much more detailed images of my brain and brainstem by creating images using magnetic field and radio waves. It creates 3-D pictures, so apparently this is more effective than a CT scan at detecting abnormalities.

I am actually scared for this one because I have to wear an uncomfortable helmet-like contraption and lie on a table in an extremely narrow tube. You are not allowed to move at all once you are inside the tube. I feel claustrophobic and fidgety before the table even enters the tube.

The technician monitors me from a different room but gives me a call button in case I need her to eject me or I need to ask her a question. I'm having three different MRI scans today, and if you can't stay still for the entire duration of each test, you have to repeat it. She gives me earplugs because parts of the test involve repetitive tapping, thumping and can get very loud.

Forty-five minutes later, I'm done and breathe a HUGE sigh of relief. I found that test to be quite difficult.

Test 14: Spinal Tap

I go back to my room where residents and my neurologist perform a spinal tap. I thought the MRI was bad but this is like torture. The spine is one's lifeline and I'm terrified that if I move while they do the test, I'll paralyze myself and not be able to move or walk.

I actually listen as the doctor explains why they are doing this test as I try to think of ANY way I can get out of having this test done. I really, really don't want to do it.

The doctor explains that they need to collect cerebrospinal fluid to examine in the lab. This information can help them diagnose serious bacterial, fungal and viral infections including meningitis, encephalitis and syphilis, as well as bleeding in the brain, certain cancers involving the brain and spinal cord as well as certain inflammatory conditions of the nervous systems.

I know that this test is a last resort. The doctors are wracking their brains to figure out what is wrong so I know I have to go through with it.

After a long and painful 45 minutes, we are finally done and I am exhausted.

I ask Mom if the nurses have told her when I can be discharged.

"Dina, they will keep you here and do more testing," she tells me.

"But ... why? Can't I go home? I feel fine!"

"No, *Beta,* they need to keep an eye on you and see if the mass is shrinking."

Why can't any of these doctors give me a straight-up answer? What is happening to me and why can't I go home?

73

DECEMBER 29 & 30, 2012

IT'S THE THIRD DAY I'VE been at Western and I'm going crazy. More precisely, I'm losing my mind!

First, hospital food is crap! I want to tell the nurse that I follow a paleo-style way of eating and these sugar-filled muffins, tasteless chicken breasts and fat-filled snacks really don't cut it. I know I'll sound like a snob so I bite my tongue. I have to eat as I'm on Prednisone (synthetic corticosteroid drug) to shrink the mass, and it must be taken with food.

I've been asked the same questions by about 30 different residency students and neurology fellows. After the tenth student asks me the same question yet again, I blurt out, "Don't you have my chart somewhere? Why are you ALL asking me the SAME damn questions? My gosh! With technology, can't you access the answers electronically? And on that note, WHY have I had every test done about five times? Clearly I'm fine! I have a new job starting in six days. I have WAY too many things to do and cannot be stuck in this hospital while you all play a guessing game!"

All my tests are negative. I feel totally fine and it's glaringly obvious that nothing is wrong. I just don't understand why I am *still* here.

They insist on taking me to every test via a hospital bed. It is so inefficient. I could walk down the hall in less than two minutes! My ass is numb from all the endless sitting. I'm either lying flat for an MRI or sitting for a CT or spinal tap. I want to walk, run, lift weights, anything that lets me *move* my body!

I feel like a couch potato, only there isn't even a good TV. It's a teeny little TV from (it appears) the dark ages with about three channels. Watching a 1950s cowboy movie is *not* my idea of entertainment. I'm bored out of my mind, restless, and extremely edgy. The nurses bring me books and magazines but I can't read the books because I'm too much on edge and the dumb girly magazines make me feel like I'm losing valuable brain cells that I should be using to read more about my new company, finance and how to be effective at my new job.

This is my new version of hell. Note to self: *Must* be a good person and get to heaven!

I picture myself in one swift motion suddenly standing up on the hospital bed, spinning around to reveal my superwoman cape and dashing out of the hospital. I'll fly through the air till I land at home (which takes about one minute with my super powers.) I'm going to need these powers because every day that they keep me in the hospital is another day I've lost in my carefully planned schedule.

74

DECEMBER 31, 2012

ONCE AGAIN, I FEEL LIKE a lab rat. Test after test after test, and still no answers! Today, I'm particularly annoyed because it's New Year's Eve. Ever since Sabby and I left Toronto years ago, we have made a tradition of celebrating New Year's together. Me, Yas and Sabby all wear comfy clothes, have delicious food and have our "us" time. We often watch Anderson Cooper and Kathy Griffin's New Year's Eve special. I cherish our time together and am so frustrated that I will be missing this.

Apparently the doctors want to keep me in the hospital despite the fact that every single test has come out negative *and* I'm already on prednisone to shrink the mass. I feel completely fine and just want to go home. My speech is fine and I am not having any headaches. I repeatedly tell the doctors that I was in a car accident barely two months ago but *no one* listens to me. They completely dismiss that idea that a car accident could have something to do with the mass in my brain.

Come on, people. They HAVE to be related. Can you at least look into the possibility? Am I talking to a brick wall? Hello-o-o?

Everyone is here surrounding my bed but when visiting hours are over, they have to leave and I know everyone will head to Aunty Dhun's house to ring in the New Year together. I fight back tears and everyone gives me one last hug before the nurse comes in, again, to tell them that visiting hours are over.

I feel so discouraged. I am finally back in Toronto and I really don't feel like I've gotten to celebrate the holidays at all.

Everyone leaves and it's 8 p.m. on New Year's Eve. I'm all alone. There's nothing to do but look at the dreary grey walls.

God, this is *not* how things were supposed to go. I had a vision ... This grey hospital wall was definitely *not* in my picture perfect vision! I was supposed to be enjoying furniture shopping, getting a comfy couch for my living room with bright-coloured accent cushions, a high-top queen size bed with a gorgeous white-and-red duvet set, a unique spiral lamp for my living room, an elegant glass modern dining room table so I can cook and have friends over for delicious meals. What am I supposed to do now? I'll be starting my new job in just a few days and that will require all of my attention and effort—there will be no time for "house-making."

I think about the first knock at my door. I would, of course, be dressed up in a very cute outfit, hair straightened and frizz-free, makeup done, and then I'd hear a knock ... I'd open my door to find a *very* handsome guy asking me for a cup of sugar. He was doing some holiday baking with his nieces and nephews. He would invite me to taste some of the cranberry-chocolate chip cookies he had made with his niece. We'd all spend the evening baking, laughing and talking and I'd be thanking you, God, for my amazing new apartment right beside my gorgeous, smart new neighbour. He'd give me a big hug and look directly at me with warm, kind eyes and ask me if he could take me out the next day for dinner so we could get to know each other better.

We'd have a wonderful date and I'd get to experience another one of my favourite days—New Year's Eve! It's an "us" day—Yas, Sabby and me! The three us of are in our comfy Roots sweatpants. Sometimes Mom, Dad, Uncle Farokh and Aunty Dhun are there, too, but some years they have their own parties to go to. But one thing is for sure: champagne and wine are flowing, Sab's famous cheese and caviar plates are there, there is a fabulous entrée cooking in the oven and an endless supply of cookies, pies and desserts.

New Year's Day is held at our house. We always start the year off with family, friends and great food. It's a must!

God, I was in a car accident less than two months ago, recovered, moved again and was *just* getting settled. Can you PLEASE cut me some slack? Seriously, this is *not* how my new life in Toronto was supposed to start.

This is one shitty way to bring in 2013.

75

JANUARY 2, 2013

IT'S SAB'S LAST DAY OF vacation before she has to head back to New Orleans. She has surgeries booked and unfortunately doesn't have much vacation time.

She comes to the hospital to hang out one last time before heading to the airport.

Yas has a team meeting later this evening for an upcoming MBA project and has a few group assignments due. I can see she wants to stay but I tell her, "Babe, I'm completely fine. This is all nonsense. You see that they've done every test. Nothing is going to change if you stay. I want you to go back to school and kick ass on your projects. I'm just a phone call away. Go ... I'm totally fine."

Mom and Dad are at the hospital with me every day. They have been going back and forth between here and St. Mike's and I can see how much of a toll it is taking on them. A few days ago Daddy saw the ophthalmologist at St. Mike's who told him to schedule an appointment with his receptionist for surgery. Mom and Dad have repeatedly tried to schedule an appointment but the secretary is (for some strange reason) uncooperative, which is only increasing their anxiety. I want to strangle this secretary! Doesn't she understand that my dad can't *see?* This is serious!

Daddy and I are frustrated together. Every time he gets back to Western after his time at St. Mike's, I'm more concerned about him and he's more concerned about me. We try to work together and get each other's minds off our frustrations. His sweet eyes and the way he'll always try to make me laugh does make me feel better.

Mom is taking care of both of us. I admire her strength. I can see she has no time to think or even cry. Between Daddy's fear that he is going blind (and the lack of answers we're getting) and my test results (which have not indicated *any* logical reason as to why I have a mass in my brain), Mom doesn't have time for herself. She really is the rock that is holding us together. She also has to keep Yas informed, not to mention take calls and update family and our numerous family friends. She does it all in stride, never complaining or even saying she's tired.

76

JANUARY 4, 2013

WOO-HOOO! AFTER ONE WEEK OF living in the hospital, I get to go home! I thought the one night I spent in a California hospital after the car accident was bad. Seven long days just plain sucks! I missed celebrating New Year's Eve, New Year's Day and didn't even experience Christmas.

I guess this means that I'll have to make up for all of it and start the celebrations now! It can only go up from here! As we wait for the doctors and nurses to finish all the paperwork so I can be released, the topic (of course) is what we will have for dinner to celebrate my first night home. My mouth is watering at the thought of having a home-cooked meal.

We go back and forth. Shall we have Indian or Western? Perhaps chicken *vindaloo* or meatloaf? Or shall we do tacos? Daddy says he'll even do salmon on the BBQ if that's what I'm craving. Or Daddy says we can go to any restaurant I want. We all come to a consensus—tacos it is! We will have a Mexican fiesta! All I want is to be home, in my comfy clothes, relaxing with the three people I love most in the world.

I think the hospital staff are relieved to see me go. Besides my parents, Yas, Aunty Dhun, Uncle Farokh, Sab and Zub, my room was constantly filled with other family and family friends. Everyone is very loud and demanding so the nurses had to update new visitors constantly.

As I walk out of the hospital, I'm on cloud nine. These silly shenanigans are finally over. It's freezing outside but all I notice is the beautiful sunshine beaming down on me. I haven't been outside in one week and am just inhaling the lovely fresh air.

We get home at the perfect time … tea time! Mom makes a sweet-smelling pot of chai. Yas should be home any moment. We decide that we'll go furniture shopping for my new apartment tomorrow. Then Sunday, I will get ready to start my new job, make my lunch and mentally prepare to start work again. I will live at home this week, which means a one hour commute to work in downtown Toronto, but we'll make sure everything is all ready to start living at my new place by next weekend.

For some reason I don't feel rushed to move. I'm happy I will stay with my parents for another week. Yas goes back to Ivey for her second semester of business school on Sunday, so I'm just happy to spend time with her before a busy January starts.

It's very unlike me to not be rushing around and trying to do a million things. I feel extremely calm and am just enjoying the laughter and time with my family.

As I get into bed, Mom comes to give me a giant hug, holding me tighter and longer today and somehow the crappy events of the past week feel like a distant memory. She pulls my blankets and folds them down, below my chin, as she knows exactly how I like my sheets. She tucks the bottom of the blanket underneath my feet and folds in the sides so my feet are all bundled up. "*Jaanu,* I'm so, so happy you are home and safe. We love you too much."

"Me too, Mummy … me, too," I tell her. While I am a very independent person who has travelled the world and done everything on my own, I don't think I'll ever get to old for Mummy's hugs.

77

JANUARY 5, 2013

I OPEN MY EYES AND glance at the time on my alarm clock. It's only 6:30 a.m. I've still got another hour before my alarm goes off but I'm awake and ready to get up. It's a glorious day and I am so excited to get it started! We're going to look for furniture today!

I must have slept funny because my right arm is numb. It figures—first night in my own bed, I must have slept like the dead and my arm got pinned underneath me for the whole night. I start punching it to get the pins and needles out but it stays numb. Hmmm ... this is strange.

I get out of bed and reach to turn the light on in my room but now my right fingers are also numb and I can't turn on the light. So weird. Oh well, time to go brush my teeth and get this day started.

Now I'm worried. I can't open the tube of toothpaste or hold my toothbrush. Okay, something's wrong. Now I'm scared.

I go downstairs and find Mom. "Mummy ... what's happening? I can't feel my right side. What do I do?"

She can see that I don't have any control of my right arm; it has gone limp.

Very calmly, she sits me down at the table and instructs me, "I am going to call the hospital and we are going to go to the ER. You cannot have the prednisone on an empty stomach so Daddy will make you eggs. Take the pills and we will go."

I don't know how to use my left hand to feed myself as I am right-handed, so Yas is now feeding me. I can see everyone is worried but trying not to panic. Within a few minutes we are all in the car heading back to Toronto Western. I can't believe my luck! I get home, and not even 24 hours later I'm going back to the hospital?

Yassy reaches and holds my right hand. I turn to her and smile. She looks at me and in a millisecond, her smile turns into a look of fear.

"D ... can you smile for me? Biggest smile ever?" She's calm but she must be noticing something weird that I cannot see.

I look up so I can see myself in the rearview mirror and try to smile so I can see what she is seeing.

HOLY SHIT! What's going on with the right side of my face? I can't smile on that side. I touch my cheeks, my eyelids ... nothing! It's all numb on the right side.

I must stay calm. Mom is driving and I don't want to make anyone panic and get into a car accident. She is still not comfortable driving downtown. I just keep telling myself that we're almost there. There's nothing to worry about—the doctors will figure out what's happening. Must stay calm. The hospital is just a few minutes away.

Mom pulls up to the ER, and we all get out of the car. Even though I still have my hospital card and we were at Western barely 24 hours ago, the triage nurse will not let us in. She insists that I have to register. Since I cannot feel my right arm, Mom, who is terrified and now has tears streaming down her face, is trying to fill in the form.

As she is filling in the form, we realize that our car is right in front of the ER and it has to be moved. The staff are telling my parents they have to move the car right away. Daddy has a patch on one eye and his vision is still impaired so he can't move the car.

Suddenly, I feel myself start to shake. Am I cold? No. The shaking is so strong that I drop to the floor.

Yas is yelling and crying. Mom is trying so hard to compose herself and finish the intake form so they'll take me into the ER. The ambulance personnel tell her again she has to move the car.

She is dazed and I have no idea how she is going to park in the massive hospital parking lot and find me. She is not the greatest with directions and even Daddy and I, who excel with directions, get lost in hospitals with their massive lots.

No matter how hard I will myself to stop shaking, I can't. I feel the cold floor on my back. Why aren't they coming to get me up already? I hear Yas bellowing at the nurses in the background and can feel all the eyes in the room on me.

Finally, the nurses come to get me. They put me onto a gurney and start wheeling me down the hall. I have people around me on all sides, checking my pulse, asking me questions, trying to hold my convulsing body in place so I don't fall right off the gurney.

The gurney stops. A swarm of what seems like 20 people descends over me. I don't recognize anyone. I suddenly feel very alone. All of these people are looking at me, but strangely, it's like they aren't seeing me at all. I'm also angry. I was fine yesterday. They told me I was *fine.* They let me *leave.* How come it's so much worse now? Why am I back here? I see Aunty Dhun among the crowd of medical staff and am relieved. She will definitely give someone hell for this!

I see Yas and my parents as well. I have never seen such looks on their faces. It isn't very reassuring. I know from their expressions that this is very bad. Furniture shopping is definitely out today. I won't be going home anytime soon. I try not to think of the very worst possibility: that I won't be going home at all.

The convulsions stop. I must be okay. I'm okay, right? I feel like I've just run twelve marathons, I'm so exhausted. I can barely lift my body but the doctors are urging me to sit up.

"Dina, use your left pinky finger to touch your nose. Okay, now try the right hand. Sit on the edge of the bed and straighten your left leg so it's 180 degrees. Now do the same with your right leg. Use your right hand and show me where your face is numb. Point to my pen. Touch my tie. Point to my watch ..."

After the doctor finishes, the medical students start. Two by two they ask me to repeat the tests. It's very tiring and after the tenth medical student, Mom, who managed to park the car and find her way back to the ER, is getting fed up.

"Will someone please tell me what is happening with my daughter? What is going *on?*"

Without warning, the convulsions start again. Thank God I'm in a bed and not standing up this time. It's surprising how much that hurt! I am scared at how my body is shaking but at the same time, I'm utterly fascinated. I stare at how fast my legs are vibrating back and forth and how my arms flail about. This is what a puppet must feel like.

The convulsions stop about a minute later. I'm in total shock. I look to my mom, speechless. Yas comes and holds me on my bed. Mom is stroking my hair and Daddy is holding my hand. I know the convulsions must have been very scary for them to watch. I have no idea what is happening but I feel comforted because my three favourite people are right beside me. I also notice Aunty Dhun, Dr. Hodaie and many nurses talking to each other at the foot of my bed.

Their voices start to fade until I can't hear them at all. The room starts to go dark ... I can't see them now either. I'm fading. I want to fight it, but it's too strong. I must be dying and on my way to heaven ...

78

JANUARY 9, 2013

I WAKE UP AND TRY to open my eyes. I can't open my right eye at all and can only see out of a small portion of my left eye. I'm groggy and confused. I try to shift my left eye to take in my surroundings but I can't see any light. It's dark and there is no window. It's a small room and I can see a computer monitor flashing red.

As I shift my eye, it seems that I have tubes coming out of every part of my body.

What the hell is going on? Where am I? Why am I here?

I would freak out, but I must be on drugs because the fatigue is stronger than the panic. I can't keep my eyelids open any longer and I fade out again ... Black.

JANUARY 10, 2013

MY LEFT EYE OPENS EVER so slightly. I catch a glimpse of a moving shadow and a second later, a small Filipino woman approaches and gently squeezes my hand. I don't know who she is but she has a soothing voice.

"Dina, you are in the hospital. Please stay calm. You are safe," she tells me.

I'd like to ask her questions but I don't even have the energy to keep my one eye open, let alone open my mouth.

Where is my family? Why am I here?

I start fading out again ... Black.

JANUARY 11, 2013

I OPEN MY LEFT EYE and from the very little I can see, I'm in a different room. There are tubes everywhere. As I look closer, I see that these tubes are attached to me. There are tubes attached to every inch of my body! I want them off. Now. I try to remove them. People that I don't recognize keep telling me to stop but I won't. I don't know them and they are invading *my* space. Who are they to tell me anything? They keep touching me and pushing me away every time I reach for one of the tubes. I'm terrified and use any strength to swat them away as hard as I can. For some reason I can't feel my right arm, so I gather any strength to use my left arm to get them away from me.

I start crying. Why are they attacking me? Please don't hurt me! Why are these people hurting me? I feel like I've been mugged and viciously beaten by a pack of thugs and they won't stop until they kill me.

I can no longer see faces and go into shock and panic. My left hand is handcuffed to a bed. They must have done something to my right hand too because I still can't feel it. I'm utterly helpless. These horrible thugs are going to kill me.

My body can't take it ... and I fade ... Black.

• • •

I wake up again in what looks like the same small room and immediately try to defend myself. I try so hard to move my body and feel like I've dislocated my left arm from trying to fight as my left hand is still handcuffed. I can't tell if this is a horrible nightmare or real. Please wake up, Dina. *Please ...*

I hear a familiar voice and I know, for a moment anyway, that I don't have to be afraid. It's MUMMY!

I can't see her yet because there are so many tears but she is here. I feel her. Maybe I'm not being attacked ...

The other people move and Mom places herself on the left side of the bed so I can see her through the small sliver of my left eye. She's crying and holds me, placing one hand on my shoulder and one on my stomach. She is trying to calm me down.

"*Jaanu,* we are here. You are safe. It's okay. Slowly breathe, slowly, slowly."

Why is Mummy crying? Am I on my deathbed? What is happening? Where are Daddy and Yas? Why do I feel so helpless?

This is all too much for me to handle and I fade again ... Black.

• • •

I wake up again and hear Mom still crying. Through the corner of my left eye, I see people trying to shove something down my throat. I can't swat at them because my left arm is handcuffed and I'm starting to think I don't even have a right arm anymore. I can't defend myself! What are they trying to put in my mouth? No. NO! I move my face violently from left to right. I will *not* let them put this tube down my throat.

Mom is sobbing so loudly I can't hear anything else. I've never heard her cry like this. I want to call out to her but I can't. I wish someone would tell me what is happening.

I hear another voice above her sobs. It's SABBY!

"*Aunty Shahnaz, go ... Go sit with my mom. I will help the nurses. D will be fine. Aunty Shahnaz, it doesn't matter if she punches me. I'm used to this tube. She will be fine.*"

I have no clue what is happening, but I do know my family is here. I don't know why they are here or what these nurses are doing, but Sabrena is *here.* I am safe. My family will protect me. She is helping them and she is a doctor, so I guess these people are not trying to harm or attack me.

I am in so much pain and crying uncontrollably, but I know I can't swat or hit anymore. I trust Sab and let them put the tube down my throat.

The pain! The pain is so bad that I pass out ... Black.

JANUARY 12, 2013

I OPEN MY EYE AND notice I'm in a new room. I see a window and sunshine streaming through. I'm lying in a bed and can't see trees or houses or pretty much anything other than blue sky and the sunshine.

I don't see anyone in this room and I'm all alone. Before the panic really starts to take hold, a beautiful nurse with her braids tied in a ponytail comes in. Her smile is big and bright. I don't think she is here to hurt me.

"Good morning, Dina! I'm your nurse today. My name is Jane. How are you feeling this morning? Do you know where you are? You are at Toronto Western Hospital. You are in Toronto. Do you know the date today?"

All right. This is all new information. I'm pretty sure she sees the blank stare on my face because she goes over to a whiteboard on the wall and points to it, explaining, "Today is Saturday, January 12th and we are in 2013."

I don't really know what the date signifies. I don't remember anything before so I can't put this date into context. *"When"* doesn't really matter, what I want to know is *why* am I here?

I try to say the word, "WHY," hoping she will understand me and explain what is going on.

I muster up all the energy I have, open my mouth, but no words comes out. I cannot speak. Where is my voice? I can't even make a sound. Nothing.

I'm confused, scared and alone with this stranger and I cannot speak. The fear is so overwhelming that I fade out again ... Black.

JANUARY 13, 2013

I OPEN MY EYE AS I hear about 10 to 15 people surrounding my bed. It's still dark out so I'm not sure whether it is very late at night or very early in the morning.

I recognize someone! It's Dr. Hodaie! She is here, so I must be safe. I'm trying to keep my eye open but I'm so tired. I want to ask her so many questions, but I feel sleep taking hold of me again.

"This is Dina Pestonji. Twenty-nine-year-old female …"

I gather these must be Dr. Hodaie's residents or fellows, as it looks like a scene from *Grey's Anatomy.* For some reason, I can't comprehend anything they are saying. I feel like the dog from *The Simpsons.* They speak, but all I hear is, "Wah-wah, wah-waaaah … Wa-wah-waah waaaaah …" Everything around me is very fuzzy and blurry. I'm either tired, or something is off with my memory or brain. I'm too tired to care and fall asleep while the residents continue talking.

• • •

This time, I open my eye and it's either sunrise or sunset. I have no concept of time. Dr. Hodaie sees that my eye is open and approaches me,

"Dina, do you remember your name? What is the date today? Dina, can you feel me holding your right hand? Dina, can you now feel that I'm squeezing your right foot? Your mummy said you are ticklish. Can you feel it? Your family was here today. They were all around but you

were asleep. They love you and they will be back tomorrow. Sleep, Dina. Sleep. I'll see you tomorrow morning, Dina."

I don't know why I can't reply to her. Have I lost my voice? Maybe I was at some event where I was yelling and lost my voice? Maybe I was yelling at someone who was trying to hurt me? Or I was angry? *What* is happening?

83

JANUARY 15, 2013

I CAN'T KEEP TRACK OF how much I sleep. I'm barely awake for a few minutes at a time before I fade out. I think I saw Mummy, Daddy and Yas yesterday but I'm really not sure. I'm never quite certain if I'm awake or asleep and dreaming.

Dr. Hodaie and her medical students walk into my room. I am starting to realize that this happens many times a day. They ask me the same questions every time:

"Dina, can you wiggle your fingers? Take my phone. Can you use your fingers and type a message? Dina, can you feel me grasping your right forearm? Can you try to lift your right leg? Your mom says you are ticklish on your feet. Can you feel my fingers tickling your toes?"

Things are becoming clearer now. I can't feel anything on the right side of my body. It's as if I have phantom limbs. Every time I try to ask for an explanation, nothing comes out of my mouth. No words, no sound at all. I know that this has been going on for a few days now, so I'm starting to think that actually, this isn't just a bad case of laryngitis. I have lost the ability to speak entirely.

Mummy arrives and hugs me. Hooray! At least I remember her. At least I know who my family is—I haven't forgotten that! She takes my blanket off to give me a proper hug and gasps, *"Jaanu! Your right arm? WHERE is it?"* The nurse rushes into the room after hearing Mummy's concern.

"Oh, my sweet child, your right arm is hidden beneath your body," the nurse explains to Mummy. I can't see or feel my arm so I trust she knows what she's talking about.

Mummy comes over to the right side of me and sits on the bed. She takes my right arm and starts to massage it.

"*Jaanu*, let's always make sure we keep your right hand on your stomach so we can see it and it doesn't get hidden again."

. . .

I wake up and Mummy and Daddy are gone. I hate these times the most—when I wake up all alone, confused and wanting answers, or *any* kind of explanation that will help me to understand exactly what is happening to me. I want to be strong. I want to be the no-fear go-getter Dina that I usually am, but I feel completely helpless.

A nurse enters my room. I don't recognize her—where is Jane? I hate having to deal with new people every day.

"Good morning, Dina. It's a bright day outside isn't it?" the nurse says, pointing to the window. I smile, nod and give her the thumbs-up sign.

"Dina, today we're going to try for a bowel movement. I'm going to give you a suppository." I have no clue what she is talking about so I give her my best confused look and shrug my shoulders hoping she can give me more of an explanation.

I've never heard of the word suppository but she says it will help me poop. Since I started gaining consciousness more, I've stopped trying to fight everyone off. I pretty much just lie in bed and let the nurses do as they please. I can't move or talk so, really, I have no choice but to comply.

I feel something cold and wet get shoved up my bum. I don't know what's worse—strangers looking at my exposed bum, or having something foreign put up there and having no ability to say "no" or "stop." She tells me the suppository can take some time to work and she will be back to check on me shortly. I give her the thumbs-up sign.

A few minutes later, my stomach starts making weird noises. I now understand what she meant! I need to poop! I don't have a diaper on so I need a bed pan—STAT!

I use my left hand and hit the red "call bell" to get a nurse. A nurse comes on the intercom, "Yes, what do you need?" For Pete's sake ... I can't talk! Get in here! NOW!?

"Hello? Hello?" the voice on the intercom repeats.

I'm desperate! I'm going to shit myself *right now!* I *need* a bed pan! I keep pressing the call bell frantically. Please! Someone come and help me!

There's no point. It's all coming out of me whether I like it or not. I start to cry. Here I am, lying in a pile of my own crap. I'm beyond mortified and tears are streaming down my face.

The nurse walks in and sees me and I'm scared she's going to be mad and tell me what a mess I've made. Or worse, laugh.

"My dear child, why all the tears?" she asks.

I lower my eyes and indicate the mess I've made.

"Sweetheart, don't you worry. I'll clean you up and you'll be fresh as a daisy. No more tears. You did good! Mummy and Daddy will be coming soon so let's get you all ready for them!"

I start to smile at the thought of seeing them. I feel better, but man oh man. I've sunk to a brand new low. I now shit my pants like I'm a baby.

I'm a grown-ass woman but I function like a fucking helpless toddler!

84

JANUARY 20, 2013

DR. HODAIE AND HER MEDICAL students walk in as usual. I get asked the same questions. It's like I'm stuck on a repetitive loop, doomed to repeat the same day over and over again for eternity.

"Dina, can you wiggle your fingers? Take my phone. Can you use your fingers and type a message? Dina, can you feel me grasping your right forearm? Can you try to lift your right leg? Mom says you are ticklish on your feet. Can you feel my fingers tickling your toes?"

After two weeks of this same set of questions, I feel dejected and sad. The answers are always the same. No, I can't wiggle my fingers. I can't move. If I can't move, I certainly can't type. I can't speak. I can't even make a sound. I wish to God I could feel someone tickling my feet! I always fight my mom off when she tickles me, but right now, I wish for nothing more than to enjoy the laughter of a major tickle session.

I just lower my eyes and shake my head from left to right. No, I can't feel anything. I failed before at things, but this failure stings more than any other. A *baby* could do these things. Why not me?

Stop. This isn't *me.* Come on, D! You have to *fight.* Think ... think! Imagine your right side moving. Picture it in your brain. Really, really imagine it. Just try. Take a deep breath and give it every ounce of energy to move your leg. One of these days it will happen. The doctors said so! Your body has to re-establish the connections in your brain. Picture the movement in your brain and your body *will* make it happen. It will! Don't get discouraged. You have way too much to do. This is *not* the end. You will move again.

You can *do* this.

• • •

I'm lying in my bed in my hospital gown. I've grown to love my hospital wardrobe. Big, comfy cotton gowns, no laundry ... I've always preferred sweats and T-shirts over pencil skirts and pumps, so this is really not so bad.

My nurse has just finished brushing my teeth, washing my face and giving me a sponge bath. She rubs a lovely rose-smelling cream on my skin so it doesn't dry out. She changes me into a fresh new hospital gown and I feel ready to start the day. Just a few more minutes until my parents arrive!

MUMMY! DADDY! Every day I anticipate their arrival. I count down the hours and minutes. It's the moment I wait for and cherish most every day.

Mom races to take her jacket off, quickly sets down the package of food she has brought, and runs to my bed to embrace me in a tight bear hug. By the time Mummy and I have had our hug-it-out time, Daddy has hung up his winter jacket, set his *Globe and Mail* paper down that he will read while I'm in my therapy sessions, and is right there so we can have our own hug time.

I *live* for those two hugs every day. They make me feel safe. They remind me that I'm not alone. There is so much love, warmth and positive energy in my parents' eyes. They give me the energy I need to get through each day here.

I understand that I am in the hospital but I still don't really know *why*. Something must have happened, but I don't feel any pain and no one really treats me like anything is wrong. I am surrounded by caring nurses, my neurosurgeon, neurologist and best of all, my family. They tell jokes, make me laugh, and encourage me. I can't talk (maybe that's why I'm here), but it's quite surprising how much we can get across using non-verbal communication.

There are many doctors and nurses who come into my room each day and ask me if I can feel my right arm, my right hand, my right leg and my right foot. I have no feeling, but maybe that's normal? I must be an infant. We learn to talk and crawl and walk when we are ready … right? So maybe I'm just not ready. Mom and Dad both take turns massaging my right arm, right hand, right leg and toes and explain to me that they are trying to get the blood flowing and stimulate the nerves to promote movement.

I can't move so I stay in my hospital bed in my room at all times. It's not so bad here. The sun shines through my window, Daddy has brought me many pictures of family and friends, and there are *so* many beautiful flowers.

Still, I'm starting to feel frustrated. I want to talk and get up and walk! I need to get out of this bed! This room! Last week a few family members came and wanted to all go downstairs to the cafeteria to get a coffee. It took about half an hour for my nurses to get me in the wheelchair and, by that point, I was already exhausted. By the time we reached the cafeteria, I was ready to pass out.

This is how it is every day. One moment I'm awake and in a matter of seconds, I'm passed out.

• • •

YAS IS JUST A FEW months from finishing her MBA at Ivey. She re-jigs her schedule so she can attend all of her classes during the week, and then races back to Toronto to spend weekends with me in the hospital. She will bring her assignments and papers and study materials to the hospital and work on everything while I'm asleep or in a therapy session. I have no idea how she does it. Not to mention the insane amount of driving she has to do going back and forth each week.

During the week when she is at school, she calls Mom every evening to get my daily update. Mom will tell her if I'm sad, happy, frustrated. I can't hold the phone, let alone speak, so Mom will hold the phone to my ear and Yassy just talks.

I love hearing about her day and what's happening at school. She always knows what to say to make me feel better and keep my spirits up. Yesterday, I was particularly frustrated. Things just aren't happening fast enough. I should be better by now! I get angry at myself and then depressed when I think of how far I have to go. I'm not even sure if I'll ever get there. I was crying, and Mom told Yas what was going on.

Yas said to me in the most matter-of-fact tone, "D, don't you *dare* let it get you down. You *will* move and you *will* speak. So what if you didn't do it today? You tried and you should be proud of that. D ... BE PROUD! Today is done. We have tomorrow. Sleep well, and you will be fresh and try again tomorrow. Promise me that you are smiling! You know I will not get off the phone till Mummy tells me you are smiling. Be proud of yourself, babe! I know that you are going to be better than ever and back to bossing me around like the big sister I know and love!"

Mom always tells me that my eyes twinkle when I hear Yassy's voice, and how much happier I look afterward. It's as if she injects this huge dose of positive energy over the phone. I can't speak, but I wish I could tell her how much she means to me and how she has this ability to make me feel so strong even when my body is so weak.

I'm not quite sure she understands how a few minutes of talking to her make me feel like I'm on top of the world when mere moments before, I was fifty feet below the earth in my grave.

I hope Mom tells her how much she means to me, and how much I appreciate all she is doing.

85

FEBRUARY 2013

I HAVE BEEN LIVING AT Toronto Western Hospital for just over a month. It's early evening and Dr. Hodaie comes in to say hi and check on me. She places her phone on my bed to see if I can grasp the phone with my right hand, but nothing.

"Dina, can you use your right hand to send a text message? Can you use your fingers?"

I take a deep breath and use all my energy to get my hand to move. It doesn't budge, but something else moves instead. *I wiggle my toes!* I can't believe it! My toes are moving! They have been asking me to do this for weeks now, and it's finally happened!

I still can't yell out to tell everyone, so instead I flail my left hand in the hope of getting my parents' and doctor's attention.

In a millisecond, there are about 10 people gathered around the foot of my bed. My gaze is fixated on my toes but I can hear Mom's squeals of joy and Daddy's "Go, Dina, go!" in the background. I'm in complete awe! Four weeks of feeling nothing on the right side and finally, *finally,* a glimmer of hope.

This is all I need. It is a sign that whatever happened to me will be fixed. If I can wiggle my toe, I will be *me* again.

In this moment, I know what I will do. It comes to me with such clarity, that there is no doubt in my mind it will happen. I have a plan. There are three things that I will accomplish before the year is out.

I will run a half marathon. I will see my sister receive her diploma. I will celebrate with my parents on their 35th wedding anniversary.

I feel alive and inspired in a way I haven't felt since I woke up. I want to get out of this hospital and I am ready to fight! I will fight because there is something waiting for me outside those doors. There is *no way* I will not succeed and achieve my three goals.

Wiggling my toe reminds me of the most important thing I had forgotten: I'm *me!* I'm not this bedridden girl who can't fend for herself. I get shit *done.* I don't *fail.* I set a goal, and I *get there.*

I want to tell my parents about my new plan, but I remember—I still can't speak. I will write it down! Wait … I am right-handed, but I still can't move that hand. I have to find a way to tell them about my plan!

I look in every direction and spot a napkin. Perfect! I use my left hand to point to a piece of paper. Daddy always has a pen in his shirt pocket so I grab it with my left hand. They are all looking at me. It's evident I have a plan so they are all waiting to see what I'm trying to communicate.

I try to write a letter but I notice something strange. I don't remember what letters look like. I have the words in my brain, but by the time the words go from my brain, down my left arm and into my fingertips, I completely forget what I'm trying to tell them.

Okay, I must find small words and really concentrate. I want to tell them that I will run the Scotiabank half-marathon, which is held every October in Toronto.

I point to my feet.

"Yes, *Jaanu,* you moved your toes! Amazing job. We are so proud of you," Mom says.

Yeesh. Let's try this again.

I take my left arm and swing it back and forth to look like I would while running. I must look awkward because the room goes silent and all I see is perplexed looks.

Back to the pen and napkin. Even though I have done many half-marathons and know the month each one is held in, my family doesn't know this.

I can't remember how to write or spell and it's frustrating the hell out of me. I continue to gesture and point but I'm getting nowhere. My dinner tray arrives so this amusing game of charades is done for the evening. I would keep trying, but I only have so much energy. Who knew that wiggling my toes would be such a workout!

Midway through dinner, Mom can see me fading so she tucks me in, holds me in a hug and says a little prayer as she does every evening. Mom tells me one of my aunties told her about "Kukadaru," who was a Parsi Zoroastrian priest in India who was best known for the power of healing.

She recites:
Ya nure' dastagir;
Ya dastagire' nur,
Karam kar karima;
Rehem karo ya parvadigar,
Madad karo ya nabi,
Zarthost teri padshahi!

Translation:
Oh, Sarosh Yazad!
Do thou grant assistance unto our souls in performing
virtuous and meritorious deeds?
Oh! Creator and Nourisher!
Have mercy on us for the atonement of our sins
and do thou help us whereby we acknowledge and
accept the sovereignty and Lordship of thy Holy
Prophet Zarathushtra!

Daddy says the same prayer as he hugs me. He says it slowly and tells me soon enough, when I can speak again, we will say it together each evening. I'm not sure what the prayer means exactly, so I silently say my own prayer as I nod off.

"Please, God, give me the strength to get through this. I want to run, and see my sister graduate, and give my parents' the anniversary present they deserve. I want to *live* ...

. . .

The next day when my parents arrive, I'm determined to get my message across. I've got it! I'm going to write "OCT," on the napkin, point to my feet and gesture with my arms that I'm running. The guessing game continues.

They look at me like I'm an alien! I know they are trying so hard to understand me. I can't believe how difficult it is to communicate when you can't vocalize your thoughts! It's been over four weeks that I have not said a single word. This is *me* we're talking about! I'm always talking. Loudly! If I ever get to speak again, I don't think I'll be able to stop!

Yassy is the one who finally cracks the code. As I continue my clumsy miming act, she suddenly jumps and asks, "Wait, are you trying to run, D?" She sees my eyes perk up and I try to gesture for her to continue on and elaborate. I keep pointing to my feet, then the letters "OCT" on the napkin. Yas finally says, "Isn't the Scotiabank half-marathon in October?"

I did it! I made them understand! Whether they think I'm delusional or not, everyone is excited and happy. This is real progress, and we all know it.

Now I need to tell them that I want to go to Yassy's MBA graduation in April. More important, I want to *walk* in, not be wheeled in with a wheelchair.

. . .

I must have fallen asleep because I wake up and Yas is sitting on my bed. Exactly who I wanted to see! I set to work right away. I'm going to use my left hand to roll up a piece of paper that I can only hope will signify the diploma Yas will get at her graduation.

I'm not sure why but I write "CON"—I'm hoping it will convey "convocation" from her MBA.

Mom and Dad are here now, too, so I've got three sets of eyes ready to start guessing. I point to Yas, roll up the piece of paper and give it to her. I point to the wheelchair and shake my head furiously. I think the head-shaking is making them more confused. I just point at Yas and the makeshift diploma. I know that Yas' graduation is in April, so I take Daddy's pen and grab the napkin and write "APR" and keep pointing to Yas.

It feels like it's been hours but, finally, they guess correctly. Yas gets emotional and we hug. I hope she knows that I want to be there for *all* of the important moments in her life. Nothing in the world could keep me from being there with her when she graduates and gets that diploma. I want to tell her how much I love her. I'm not sure I really tell her enough, but for now, it will have to wait.

• • •

My final goal is to take my parents out to a nice restaurant so we can all celebrate their 35th wedding anniversary together. I want to walk into that restaurant with my own two legs and not my wheelchair and make sure they get a break from all of this drama.

I point to Mom and Dad and continuously point to both of them over and over.

"Okay, *Jaanu*, you want to tell us something?" Daddy asks.

I shake my head no. "Something to do with Daddy and me?" Mom asks and I nod my head rapidly. We are on the right track.

I grab a napkin and try to draw a heart. I keep forgetting what a heart looks like and in the process, forget what I'm actually trying to do. Remembering anything, including my train of thought, is a challenge. Simple tasks like drawing feel harder than the university exams I used to sweat over!

I ignore everyone and really focus. I close my eyes and envision a heart symbol. I just want to remember this image so I can draw it with my left hand. After the fifth attempt, I manage to draw half a heart. Now that I see it, I can look at it and know what I'm trying to do! I just have to replicate the drawing of half the heart for the other side.

I finish the drawing, then I point to Mom, Dad and the heart, over and over again.

"Is it that we love you, *Beta*?" "I love Daddy?" "We love each other?" "You love us?" "Are we close, *Beta*?"

I know the last thing on their mind is their own anniversary so this is a tough one. Throughout this whole ordeal, I doubt they've spared even a moment to think about themselves. Every day, there are here with me, without fail. Even through all of Daddy's scary eye problems, he was still here, wearing an eye patch and never uttering a single complaint. And my mom! Taking care of him, doing all the driving back and forth—she must be exhausted. I want nothing more than to take them out for a fun-filled night where they don't have to worry about *anything*. I'll be out of my wheelchair, and they'll see that there is nothing to fret over and we can just celebrate!

I grab Daddy's pen. Underneath the heart drawing, I need to write "July 2," because that is their anniversary.

July has four letters but it takes me a few attempts before I figure out how to even write the letter "J." I manage to write the "U" but I'm getting impatient so I hope they can guess "JU" means "July." I write the number "2" next to the "JU."

I now point to Mom, Dad, the heart and "JU 2."

"Our anniversary?" Mom asks.

Yes! Yes! I nod my head back and forth happily. I take my left hand to gesture eating food and then take my left hand and gesture disco dancing.

Thank God they know me well because Yas pipes up, "We're going to celebrate Mom and Dad's anniversary?" I wrap my arms around her and we laugh.

I feel like I could fly! I'm still confined to this bed and this stodgy hospital room, but I know in my heart that wiggling my toes was the first step towards a full recovery. For weeks, I've been lying here just letting things happen—and that's exactly the problem! All I've needed to get back on track was a goal, and a plan. That's how I do things. That's how I will get better.

In April, I WILL attend Yassy's MBA graduation at Ivey and I will *walk* into the auditorium and cheer for her!

In July, I will find an amazing restaurant and we will celebrate my parents' 35th wedding anniversary!

In October, I will run my seventh half-marathon. And, I've decided to challenge myself even more: I'm going to beat my best time of 2.5 hours.

I'm going to get everything back and be better than I was before! *I have to.*

86

FEBRUARY 20, 2013

EVER SINCE I WIGGLED MY toes, my family and my doctors encourage me to keep on wiggling! I'm hopeful I'll get feeling back in my entire foot very soon. It takes quite a while just to get out of bed and into my wheelchair but when I do, I use all my energy to propel myself forward using my right heel. I often get winded after about one minute but I'm making progress. At least that's what everyone is telling me. All of this "wiggling" is fine and dandy but if it were up to me, I'd be light years ahead, already running and back to normal.

Today Mummy is in my room. She wants to get me up to see if we can try standing and putting pressure on my right foot.

Mummy puts the wheelchair right beside my bed and helps me move my body so I can stand on my left leg, then rotate my body and sit in my wheelchair. She then wheels me into the bathroom.

She helps me up and is holding me around my waist to ensure my right leg doesn't collapse.

Holy shit! I'm standing! I haven't stood on both feet for *so* long! It feels so wonderful. I keep looking down at my legs, surprised and overjoyed and proud! When I finally look up, I notice a mirror. There are no mirrors my hospital room so this is the first time I have seen my face in over a month.

My hair is split down the centre with a braid on either side of my head. The braid on my right looks normal, but on my left side there's a lot less hair. That's when I notice the huge indentation on my skull. I look like an alien! It's grotesque. I also see short wisps of hair like my head has been shaved. I'm extremely confused and try to rotate my head to examine the obvious differences between my left and right side.

I look to Mom, then back at the mirror, then back to her. She can see my expression shift from confusion to fear.

"Sit down in your chair, *Jaanu*. I will explain everything to you."

She helps me into bed and brings the top half of my bed into a seated position. She holds my hand and explains as calmly as she can,

"Dina. You had to have emergency brain surgery. Do you remember when we came to the hospital in December? All of the tests?"

I now remember and nod my head yes.

"There was a mass in your brain, but they didn't find any reason why it was there. They thought you would be okay and sent you home. Do you remember, *Jaanu*? Yassy came home and we had dinner together. We had tacos ..."

Yes! I remember!

"The next morning we had to go back to the hospital. Do you remember this?" she asks.

Yes! I do remember all of that. I motion for her to continue telling me more. At last, someone is explaining what happened to me.

"*Jaanu,* you fell unconscious. Dr. Hodaie told us that the pressure in your brain was building up so quickly that if you didn't have surgery to relieve this pressure, you might die. Daddy and I had to decide ... You had to have emergency brain surgery."

My jaw drops. Brain surgery? Like, they cut my head open? I almost died?

She goes on further. They had almost no time to weigh the options; my condition was that critical. Once they had consented to the emergency surgery, Mom got right on to the "Aunty Emergency Hotline." They called Aunty Dhun first. Aunty Dhun immediately called Sabrena, who promptly cancelled all her surgeries in New Orleans. Sabrena then called Aunty Nilufer who again leaped into action and had Sabby on the next flight back to Toronto. Cousin Zubby went to pick her up from the airport and came straight to the hospital.

The love my family has for me is astounding. They are the kind of people who would drop everything in a heartbeat, just to be by my side as I lay unconscious. I didn't know they were there at the time, but I am certain I drew strength from their presence. I think their collective love for me saved my life that night.

Mummy continues to detail the events of that night, and the days to follow. As the medical team prepped me for surgery, Mummy, Daddy, Yassy, Aunty Dhun, Uncle Farokh, Aunty Katy and Aunty Nilufer all waited outside for me in the hall. They formed a circle and joined hands, and recited two sacred prayers, over and over again.

Ashem Vohu Prayer:
Asem vohu vahistem asti
usta asti usta ahmai
hyatt asai vahistai asem

Translation:
"Truth is best (of all that is) good.
As desired, what is being desired
is truth for him who (represents) best truth."

Yatha Ahu Vairyo Prayer:
Yatha ahu vairyo
atha ratush ashat chit hacha,
Vangheush dazda manangho
shyaothananam angheush Mazdai
xshathremcha Ahurai a
yim drigubyo dadat vastarem.

Translation:
Just as the Lord (ahu) is to be chosen (in accordance
with truth), (asha)
So also the judgment (ratush) (is to be chosen) in
accordance with truth (asha).
As a result of this good thinking (vohu mano, the
comprehension and choosing of asha)
establish the rule (xshathra) of actions stemming from
an existence of good thinking
for the (sake of the) Wise One, and for the lord (ahura)
whom they (the divine aspects) established as pastor
for the needy-dependents.

I picture them all there outside the operating room, gripping hands tightly, eyes closed, chanting in this grim hospital hallway, and it brings tears to my eyes. I think they made some kind of magic in the hallway that night.

They were also probably very loud! It makes me laugh a little to imagine people walking by, seeing these Indian people chanting in a circle. It's not really something you see every day in a Toronto hospital!

I can hardly believe everything she is telling me. I'm so *healthy,* why would someone like me need brain surgery?

The surgery itself took over six hours. When Dr. Hodaie came out of the operating room, she said, "Dina did so well! Her heart was very strong throughout the surgery. She is a strong fighter."

Mom tells me that as soon as Yas heard Dr. Hodaie saying "her heart was strong," she *knew* you would be fine.

She tells me that when I woke up, I fought hard with the nurses. "Do you remember you tried to pull out all the tubes?"

I do remember it was terrifying. I'm still trying to comprehend the magnitude of what she is telling me. Only people that are *sick* have brain surgery. I'm *never* sick. I'll fight off a cold in a day!

I simply don't allow myself to get sick. Now you're telling me I was so sick I needed brain surgery?

Apparently, when I woke up, no one knew if I was in a vegetative state or not. They just had to wait and hope for the best. How shocking! I imagine my poor family thinking the worst. What if I was brain-dead? What if I could never speak, or move, ever again? It's all so terrifying I have to put it out of my mind.

Mom tends to notice things other people don't because she was a nurse. She tells me that even though I was smiling and looked happy in the past few weeks, she could see the deep confusion in my eyes. She tells me that I respond to every question I'm asked with the thumbs-up signal, but she sees through my veil of optimism. I guess I'm just eager to please everyone and alleviate their worry, so I smile and give the thumbs up even when it doesn't make any logical sense. I know she's wondering if I can understand and comprehend her right now. I wish I could reassure her in some way, but I still have work to do.

Mom created a few rules for anyone that entered my room after my surgery. First, any family member entering my room had to *immediately* sit on my right side and begin "Passive Range of Motion" exercises on my right limbs to promote blood flow and circulation. You start with the largest limbs and move to the smaller. For example, taking my leg while I'm lying in bed and moving it from a straight to bent position into my chest, and back again.

Secondly, only positive words and smiles were permitted. If a visitor was scared or crying – they had to finish it up before entering. Mom did not want me to see any looks of fear or people feeling sorry for me because that would cause me to worry. Any negative words were banned.

Yassy and Zubin made a plan together for one of them to be there as much as possible—they wanted to ensure there was always some "young blood" in the room with me.

She tells me that after surgery, I could not talk or walk, and explains that all the strangers that come see me every day are trying to help me. They are my therapists and will help me get better.

She reminds me that Toronto is home now. I had moved back from Napa. Ohhhh ... I was wondering where I lived! Then it hits me. I have a job! I was supposed to start a job! Mom tells me that after surgery, she called the company and said she didn't know if or when I'd be able to start.

Tears are streaming down my face. I feel like I've lost everything. And then I remember something else—I had a brand-new apartment! With my left hand I draw a square with a triangle on top to resemble a house and shrug my shoulders to indicate "What happened with that?" Mom tells me she spoke with the landlord and said I would not be moving in.

My tears don't stop and I bury my head in Mom's chest and she rocks me back and forth.

Up until this point, I knew something had happened but I had no memory of my past and was therefore blissfully unaware. Today I was reminded of what I had lost, and how much I needed to regain. I hear a ticking clock in the back of mind ... I'm not sure what it means, but I feel disappointed in myself. I think I had a plan ... I was on track for something ... I'm not sure what. Now that plan is all but lost.

Mom tells me I will have a second brain surgery in a few months to reattach my skull. I will have to learn how to walk and talk again. It hits me like a tons of bricks. My life is on pause. Big time. Only after I move out of the hospital, which will not be for some time, will I be able to resume my normal life. I'll have to look for a new job and a new apartment. I'll have to start all over again.

I don't think I've ever felt this overwhelmed. I feel as if I'm in a deep hole in the ground. It's so dark down here I can barely see any light from the surface. Just thinking about how to climb my way out is exhausting. It doesn't seem possible! I've lost too much. It feels easier to accept defeat.

Mom just holds me and lets me cry. She tells me we will all work together and I will be just fine. I'm not as sure as she is.

• • •

Yesterday felt like the worst day of my life. It was very difficult to learn just how dire my current situation really is, but I guess it's better to know than not know. Hearing the truth about my condition sucked, but it also served as a cold bucket of water to the face. Wake UP, Dina! You have a lot to get done!

I have to get back to *me.* I now know what that ticking sound is in the back of my head. It's a clock telling me there is a timeline, and I have to get back on *track!* I know what has to be done. I *will* work with my therapists. I *will* get feeling on my right side. I *will* get a new job. I *will* get my own apartment. I will work my ass off.

Everything currently sucks, but *fuck it.* I'm going to get back on schedule and back to me before anyone expects. I'm going to show everyone just how quickly I can recover. I'm going to *set a new record* for recovery! I'll be the *world champion* of recovery!

Game ON.

• • •

Ever since I woke up in the hospital, the only thing I look forward to is seeing my family. But now that I know what I have to accomplish, I relish seeing my therapists the most.

These are the people who will help me get back to being ME again. For the past week, my physiotherapists have been coming in around 8 a.m. each morning. I eagerly anticipate their arrival. My feelings of despair and hopelessness have been replaced by feelings of determination and motivation. I don't need hugs to make me feel better, I need a therapist to kick my ass every morning!

I know that feeling sorry for myself will not do me any good. I want to get back to being myself as *soon* as possible, so I make a choice. I shove those frustrated feelings to the back of my mind and replace them with some Tony Robbins mantras:

"If I can't—then I must. If I must—then I will!"

"The Past does not equal the Future!"

"Decision is the ultimate power. Decisions shape destiny!"

I decide now: I'm going to get better! I can't allow any weepy feelings of sorrow prevent me from getting better *fast.*

This morning, my physiotherapists came into my room, got me into my wheelchair and we moved into the hallway. There are four physiotherapists and we have one mission this morning: I am going to get out of my wheelchair and try my best to take *one* step forward.

One single step forward.

I can't speak but I use my left hand to say "Stop!" I then tap my chest as if to say, "Let me try to get myself out of the wheelchair by myself. If I can't—then you can help."

I still get tired very easily so I know this will take a *lot* of energy. I use both my feet to propel myself into the spot in the hallway where there are no people I might topple into. I gather all my energy and take a deep breath. I shift my butt forward and firmly plant my left foot into the floor. It will be my anchor. I hope to God all my years of practising balance in gymnastics finally pays off!

I decide to place my left hand in between my thighs as I try to stand up. I feel this technique will help me distribute my weight.

I'm standing! I have put both feet on the floor! I'm upright! I can hear Oprah's voice inside my head screaming out, "YOU GO GIRL!"

I take a minute to relish this joyful feeling. I'm dying to just bust a move and start dancing! I'm surrounded by the four physiotherapists but still, I am standing on my own.

The next part is going to be tricky. I have to remember the feeling of slightly bending my right knee, placing the weight in my toes, using my left foot as my anchor, lifting my right toes off the floor and then landing on my right heel and then toe.

Since I don't have a part of my skull, the therapists can't risk having me fall. Catherine is behind me, and Tyler is also behind me holding my waist. He's quite cute but I remind myself, "Now is not the time for flirting, Dina," and chuckle to myself. Why do I always see eligible bachelors at the most inopportune times? I also clearly have a "medical personnel" fetish. Wouldn't that just make my parents jump for joy! I never followed through on my own medical career, but that doesn't mean I can't bring home a sweet nurse or doctor!

It takes four therapists to get me to take just one step. I can't stop now! I take my left hand and point all the way down the hallway. One step is just luck. A few steps—*now that* is progress. I want to continue. Half an hour and three more steps forward, I'm finally out of breath so they bring me my wheelchair.

Tyler thinks I'm done but little does he know! I'm fired up. I just need to catch my breath and then I'll be good to go again. Yolanda is behind the nursing station and yells out, "That's my girl! Go Di-na! Go Di-na!" She's shaking her booty and when I see her doing this, I give the thumbs up to my therapists, get myself out of my wheelchair, ground my two feet on the floor, and try to shake my non-existent booty along with her.

I'm starting to understand the rhythm of walking and feel so pumped up! I feel like I'm on a surge of adrenalin. I don't want to stop. I indicate to Tyler that I want to change direction and *walk* back to my room, not ride in the wheelchair. The therapists can see I'm tired but I want to push harder.

I'm not taking no for an answer. My plan is to stand on my left foot and pivot off it so I can land in the opposite direction. I hold out my left hand so Kara can help me. I'm LOVING the feeling of my two feet on solid ground! The thought of going back to my wheelchair is unacceptable. Who knew the act of standing was so pleasurable!

As I take the five steps back to my room, I don't want to stop but I'm physically exhausted and my still recovering brain needs sleep. Tyler lifts me into my bed and I pass out immediately. I dream about waking up and trying it again. I want to try, over and over and over again! It feels like the anticipation before Christmas morning.

I notice that when I face any goal, especially an active or physical goal, I have tunnel vision. I become so excited to achieve these goals that I block out anything or anyone that gets in the way. I can be sad or mad or frustrated for a few minutes but I will always get back to the task at hand. It's not always a good thing, I realize. But right now, tunnel vision is exactly what I need.

• • •

I wake up to Mom's and Dad's smiling faces which is the absolute best. Yolanda comes in to bring my parents up to speed.

My mom shrieks with excitement as Yolanda explains my first steps. I am ridiculously happy and want to try standing again. I take off my blanket covers and point to my feet and my wheelchair. I want to be out of my room, practicing standing and walking.

My parents often wheel me to a big window, which is just off the long hallway on my unit. I shake my head as Daddy starts to push my wheelchair. Nope, I'm going to get to our window by using my right foot. The more I use it, the stronger it will get.

We move very slowly, but 20 minutes later we finally make it to the window. I've never looked outside this window so I point in the upwards direction to tell them that I want to stand and look out. I'm going to try the technique I used earlier by placing weight on my left foot, then pushing myself up by placing my left hand in between my legs and pushing down on the seat of my wheelchair.

Daddy is a bit scared but Mom holds his hand and says calmly but firmly, "Let her try." The smiles and cheers from both of them would lead you to think I'd just crossed the finish line of a marathon. It's just me standing up, but the high I get feels like I just finished Boston.

I place my hands on the ledge of the window and peer outside. There is snow on the ground and snowflakes glitter in the sky on their way down. It's beautiful. How I've missed Canadian winter! This is the first chance I've had to really look at where I am now—and I love it. This is home.

I shift my weight from my left leg to my right leg. Every tiny movement fuels the hopeful feeling in my heart. I *know* I will run again. I have grown to love and cherish every single step I take—literally and figuratively. Each step is a reminder: I am moving forward. I am strong. I am alive.

Eventually, these single steps will add up to something more. I just have to keep taking them, no matter how sad or discouraged I'm feeling. No ifs, ands or buts!

By next week I want to be able to use a walker on my own. After that, I'll master using a cane. I can't wait to see Yas this weekend and show her all of my progress. She will be *so* surprised and happy!

• • •

I'm lying in bed. I've just finished my physical therapy sessions for the day—much to my chagrin. I think that in the back of my head, there is a lingering fear that my right leg will be paralyzed forever if I don't constantly work it. If I'm not moving and trying to walk at all times, I'll lose the small progress I have made and end up back at square one.

I also just hate, hate, *hate* standing still. Stillness, silence—no, thank you! Stillness is just an unwelcome opportunity for negative thoughts to swirl around in my mind. If I'm not doing *something,* I inevitably think of all the things that are wrong with me. I think of all the things I am not accomplishing. I think of that clock ticking in the back of my mind, reminding me that I'm way off schedule and unlikely to ever catch up or get ahead. This is really how it's always been with me.

Daddy arrives and asks me about my session. He massages my arm and my hand as we've been told constant stimulation on the right side of my body will help me to reestablish the connections to my brain.

Daddy is so patient. He will hold my right pinky finger on my left hand, squeeze it and then do the same thing on my right hand. We're learning that we have to help the right side "learn" how to do things by demonstrating with the left side.

I see the paper and point to the business section as I often do with Daddy and he tells me what's happening in the news. We have our special daddy-daughter time.

It's 4 p.m. and that means it's tea time. Mom is in the staff kitchen on our floor where she always makes tea for her and Daddy and a plate of snacks depending on how hungry they are. They are both a tad peckish, so Mom whips out crackers, slices of cheese and some almonds. She is always so prepared! I love it! I am only allowed liquids or "baby food," as my doctors are still concerned about my gag-reflex. Mummy has brought me different flavors of yogurt as well as my favourite, apple sauce! This kind is apple-banana—YUM!

They move the table in my room and Mom lays down the two Styrofoam cups of tea and the large paper plate with snacks for her and Dad.

Mom starts to tell me that one of my aunties dropped off some tasty chicken last night so they had that for dinner. I would actually *kill* for some tasty, spicy Indian food right now! My mouth waters as Mom describes the dish.

Dad continues to press my right hand in between sips of tea and bites of crackers and cheese. I'm listening to Mom's story and out of the blue I say, "TEA."

Mom jumps up, almost knocking the tea and plate of snacks over. HOLY SHIT! My first sound!

"TEA! TEA! TEA! " I can't stop repeating this sound! Mom's arms are flailing with excitement and Dad is standing up and cheering. I'm in a complete daze. I can see them but I'm shocked. Did I really just make a sound?

"*Mari Jaanu*, you want tea? Let's get you tea!" Mom and Dad can't contain their pride and excitement.

Yolanda rushes into my room and hugs me and my parents. "Girrrrl! You are speaking!"

Some of the other nurses hear the commotion and run in. "Dina! You can speak?"

Heather and Lena, two of the speech therapists that happen to be on the floor also run in and I can see how happy they are. They've noticed my fear over the past few weeks. I have been terrified that I might be mute for the rest of my life.

"Dina! We are coming back in one hour to start your first speech therapy session. Get ready!" Heather informs me excitedly.

I see tears of joy, smiles and happy tear-filled twinkling eyes all around me. It's a party with all of my biggest supporters in the room! After weeks of silence, we now have a starting point. I laugh a little. A good Indian girl at heart, of course I would pick "TEA" as my first word!

I feel a huge sense of relief, as if 100 heavy concrete bricks have been lifted off my tiny shoulders. Is it bad that I'd love nothing more than to run out into the hospital hallway and yell out "FUCK YEAH!" at the top of my lungs?

. . .

Heather and Lena walk into my room. I've been waiting for this moment for weeks on end. Our very *first* speech therapy session. Mom and Dad leave the room and we begin.

So far, I'm able to say "T." Heather says "T" with me, over and over. She asks me to look at her mouth, where her tongue is when she is saying this letter. The tip of her tongue is on the roof of her mouth and I can see her mouth is wide and horizontal.

She invites me to watch her mouth and tongue as she says the letter "D." I watch her and try to comprehend this in my mind. She invites me to join in. My first few attempts I just keep saying "T." I don't think my brain knows how to switch to a new letter. After about ten more tries, success! I say my second letter! "D!" Wow, I can say a whole two letters of the alphabet! I'm genuinely proud, but it is pretty funny that this grown woman with a master's degree is ecstatic about learning the alphabet at this point.

I don't want to stop. I want to keep going. We try "Z" (Zee). I want to make sure I can say all the letters with the same enunciation as "T" so that we can move on to letters with a different enunciation tomorrow. I'm feeling revved up and now that we're here at last, I cannot get distracted. I *must* be moving forward.

At the end of the hour, Mom and Dad walk in and Lena informs them I made a lot of progress in just one session. I can say "T, D, Z, B," and surprisingly, "F!" I'm sitting on the edge of my bed, beaming with pride.

I write down my five letters with my left hand and start reciting each of them. Mom insists that first, I have a snack as she wants me to keep my energy up. I gobble up one container of strawberry yogurt and one apple sauce as fast as I can so I can show them what I've accomplished today.

"WOW!" Daddy says. He is so impressed! He shows me the different speech therapy apps he downloaded for me while I was in my session. He shows me how I can use the app to learn new letters and sounds. Bonus! I'm going to be ahead for tomorrow's session.

I'm so proud of my dad. He's never had an iPad and isn't very "tech savvy," so his help finding these apps is particularly special. Yas told me that the day after my surgery, I was unconscious and everyone was very scared. She took out her iPhone and played my favourite classical music piece, "Pachelbel's Canon," and I smiled. Dad left that very day, ran to the Apple Store, bought an iPad, learned how to download music, and made sure there was a long list of my other favourites so he could play them for me. Apparently he would sit with me for hours, listening to music with me, hoping to see me smile and waiting for me to wake up.

And now look at him! My sweet daddy has researched and found the best apps to help me recover my speech. I look at him and smile because he's living proof that "Where there's a will, there's a way."

Mom wants to get some exercise so she goes on a walk while Daddy and I practise saying letters. When she gets back, they help me get into my wheelchair and we head to my new favourite spot—the big window. It's only been a week but I can now walk five steps all by myself. Of course I am not allowed to try on my own; there always has to be one person in front of me and one person behind just in case I fall.

As I get back into my wheelchair and go back to my room, Mom can tell I'm getting tired. I point to my list of letters and insist on doing a little more speech therapy before dinner.

"*Jaanu*, only ten more minutes. I don't want you to exhaust yourself. You need to sleep." I give her the thumbs up to tell her that I'm totally fine.

Just like she does every evening, Mom brushes my teeth, washes my face, and braids my hair so I feel fresh. She then tucks the blanket under my feet and folds the top down just below my chin so I'm all comfy and cozy. She says a special prayer, gives me a huge bear hug, and makes sure the nurses' call button is within reach in case I need it during the night. She then swaps places with Daddy who also says a prayer to me, and gives me a hug. They then wait until I fall asleep, and will only leave once they see I am fully passed out, usually around 6 p.m.

• • •

It's been four days since I said my first words. Heather and Lena are astonished. They tell me that they have to update the speech schedule based on how fast I am progressing, and that they've never seen someone move ahead this quickly. This is music to my ears! My competitive personality, and the encouragement and praise from them is what fuels me. I want to continuously build and be better. I hate the idea of being "average." I want my recovery to be extraordinary!

I flashback to when Mom had cancer and a mastectomy. I remember we wanted her to rest and not push too hard during her recovery, but she just wanted to get back to her normal self. She never had a "woe is me" attitude, and I see now how similar I am. Like mother, like daughter.

I remember two weeks ago, my physiotherapists came into my room and wanted to get me out of bed. I was overwhelmed, feeling blue and having a "my life sucks" moment. I ignored them all and refused to get out of bed, and just started crying uncontrollably. Mom came into the room at this moment and found me like that.

She immediately hugged me and let me cry on her shoulder. After a minute or two of crying, she then whispered to me,

"My sweet *Jaanu*. This all sucks and it's not fair. I know. It's okay to cry. We will cry together for five minutes. But after five minutes, you are going to get up, we are going to wipe the tears away and wash your face, and then you will work with your therapists and do as they ask. You are going to do the work you need to do so you can get back to being *you*. *Okay?* You *know* you can do it *Jaanu*.

"So let's cry it out for a couple minutes more, and then we'll stop and get on with our day. Do we have a deal?"

I stopped crying, took a few deep breaths, and decided to face the day as she asked. That's how I've learned how to deal with less than perfect situations: Cry a bit, because yes—it sucks, and tears are allowed. But at some point, the tears have to stop, and you have to get on with living.

I think I'm finally ready.

. . .

It's family meeting time with my medical team. Dr. Hodaie, Dr. Steiner, the nutritionist, my speech therapists and physiotherapists are all in the room.

Dr. Hodaie explains to us, "The MRI scans are showing Dina's mass is shrinking, which is wonderful news. She is ready to move to an in-patient rehab facility. Under normal circumstances, there is a six to 10 week waiting period, but Dina's recovery is going much better and faster than we've ever seen and we don't want to stall this progress in any way. I have requested that she start at Toronto Rehab Institute on Monday next week."

Dr. Hodaie turns to me and says, "Dina, it will be a very intensive therapy facility. Are you prepared for that?"

If I could speak, I would not hesitate in saying, "Are you *fucking kidding me?* Yes, yes, YES!"

I have a feeling my parents want to scream out something similar. But of course, they are much too polite and proper. I can tell by their smiles, though, they are so excited for all of us to finally get the hell outta here!

. . .

As I leave Toronto Western Hospital, Dr. Hodaie embraces me. I see how proud she is of me. She smiles and tells me, Mummy and Daddy that this is all just a "passing cloud." I see the look of relief almost instantly in Mom's and Dad's eyes. They trusted Dr. Hodaie with my life and she performed a miracle. When she says that things will get better, it must be so.

The doors close behind me and I feel relief, fear, sadness, gratitude, but most of all, I feel more ready than ever to escape from under that "passing cloud" and get on with my life.

The ambulance is waiting to take me to Toronto Rehab Institute (TRI), which is on the "Hospital Row" of University Avenue in downtown Toronto.

We arrive at TRI and take the elevator to the ninth floor. I notice as Mom pushes the button that it is labelled the "Stroke Unit." We get off the elevator and Mom holds my hand even tighter as she can feel me trembling. I look around and all I see are old, frail people. I don't see a single patient who appears to be younger than fifty years old.

I start to panic. I wonder how long these people have been here. Are they going to die here? Do they even get better? They all look so sick and old. I really don't have anything against "senior citizens," especially sweet old granny-looking types, but it's very obvious these people are not well. Many are clearly paralyzed, some seem catatonic, and no one seems to resemble what I would call a "healthy adult."

I don't want to be here. Please let me go home. I feel like I'm in God's waiting room.

The nurse shows me to my room. There are many bright signs posted on my headboard notifying everyone, "REQUIRES SUPERVISION," "ADL ASSISTANCE REQUIRED," (ADL = Activities of Daily Living), "WHEELCHAIR," "HELMET—ALL TIMES," and "BATHROOM SUPERVISION REQUIRED."

Basically, I'm not allowed to be alone at any time, do anything on my own, or apparently, wipe my own ass. I think of friends coming to visit me and seeing these glaring signs. How embarrassing! There is no *way* I am letting anyone other than immediate family visit me here. I cannot let anyone see me or think of me as an "invalid."

The nurse tells me I will meet with all my new therapists and doctor tomorrow morning for our first official "Family Meeting" at TRI.

My brain feels so overwhelmed by my new surroundings that I just start crying. I feel helpless.

Mom holds me and reassures me. *"Jaanu,* it will be fine. We'll be here every day and the other times you'll be in therapy. You won't be alone. You'll get better soon and we'll go home, my angel."

• • •

My nurse, Susan, wakes me up the next day. She congratulates me on being here. She tells me that Toronto Rehab's goal is to get me to function on my own again. This means I will have to learn how to brush my teeth, wash my face, take a shower, go to the bathroom, get dressed each day, move around, cook for myself and all the other activities for daily living.

I'm still scared so I just listen to her. She asks where my clothes are and I point to the closet. She gets me dressed, socks and shoes on and fastens the seatbelt on my wheelchair.

She takes me into the communal dining room and brings me my breakfast tray. My right arm is now in a sling because I can't hold it upright on my own. It's become dead weight and is pulling on the nerves and joints in my shoulder. My nurse opens up everything on the tray because I can't open them with just my left hand—the cereal box, the juice container, the hot entrée ... She also butters my toast, and opens the plastic package containing cutlery. Another few elderly men come into the room and turn on the TV.

I slowly turn my eyes to the TV and after watching it for less than a minute, I start crying. The way the pictures flash and move so rapidly—something about it is overwhelming. It feels like my brain is being assaulted with horribly loud teenagers, punching and kicking it.

Susan sees my tears and me trying to clutch my head and calmly wheels me back to my room. "It's okay, dear," she tells me. "You can eat in your room. Sometimes with all of the action around you will feel like there is too much stimuli—that is normal. Your brain is still healing—it can't take too much at one time."

So on top of my laundry list of basic things to learn, I have to teach my brain to handle multiple stimuli? Are you kidding me with this shit? I feel so far away from the marathon finish line I want to curl up in a ball and disappear.

Mom and Dad arrive early today because we have our family meeting with the TRI team. I thank the Lord they are here! I am not very good at feeding myself with my left hand and am quite hungry. For the past week at Western, I have tried, but a lot of the food just ends up all over me or my bed sheets. I need Mom and Dad to feed me!

Mom helps me to eat and then we go to the Family Meeting. First we meet Dr. Lang. He's maybe 5'8 and thin, and he exudes confidence and compassion. He introduces himself to my family and we all immediately take to him.

The first question he asks me is whether I was on any birth control bills. I say yes and Mom fills him in, saying that I have been taking these pills since about the age of 10 to control my acne.

Next, we meet Audrey, head of the speech therapy team, and Logan, who will be my physical therapist. Lana and Julie are next, they will be working with me on cognitive therapy. There are also many nurses and a tall doctor named Julia who is the medical director at TRI.

After introductions, we all sit down. Julia gets up and gives everyone a recap of who I am. This is the first time I learn that I had a stroke. Strike that: this is the first time learn that I had not one, but *two* strokes. One hemorrhagic (when a vessel or artery bursts or leaks) and one ischemic stroke (when the brain is deprived of oxygen). They can't tell us when exactly they occurred, but one thing they are certain about: it is very, very rare for someone my age to have one stroke, let alone two!

All of us are completely taken aback by this information. We all thought I was in this unit (which was clearly labelled on the elevator "STROKE UNIT") because there was a free bed! Mummy used to be a nurse and even worked with older people who have had strokes, but even she didn't make the connection. I am just 29 years old and so healthy and active! Strokes are something old people get, or so we thought.

I am told that the blood thinners are shrinking the mass in my brain, and that my brain scans are continuously getting better, which is a huge relief. Dr. Lang tells me that once or twice a day, a nurse will take my blood because they need to "titrate" my blood. I don't know what that means which must be evident on my face as he explains. Every day, they will be testing my INR blood levels which need to be between two and three. My blood can't be too thick or too thin, just like Goldilocks and her porridge, which couldn't be too hot or cold.

Every day, they will adjust my warfarin (blood thinners) dose based on my INR levels. It must be in the two to three range for three consecutive days.

The doctors also warn me that my time at Toronto Rehab will be very intense, and for the first week it will be quite hard because it will be tiring. Due to my brain surgery, I still need about 20 hours of sleep every day, and those four hours I'm awake are going to require a lot of effort and focus.

Okay, I think to myself, enough talk. I'll deal with the intense therapy. You just deal with my blood and get me out of this place as soon as possible.

I'm done with all the warnings. I need to start actually *doing* something.

87

MARCH 2013.
FIRST WEEK OF THERAPY.

THE DOCTORS WEREN'T KIDDING—THERAPY IS *exhausting.* I have physical therapy, speech therapy, cognitive therapy, special therapy for my right hand, and group speech therapy—every single day. It takes a huge toll on my body.

For the first week, I'm in a daze. I need to sleep between each therapy session as my brain just shuts down. I get wheeled back to my room and I pretty much pass out on arrival. My therapist or my mom have to put me in bed because I am completely drained. Dr. Lang was right, therapy is more intense than I expected.

My brain is still healing so I need a lot more sleep than I would like. It's frustrating because I have goals I need to accomplish, but it's impossible to accomplish much of anything when you're unconscious! I am so unaccustomed to all of this rest. I'd much rather be waking up at the crack of dawn, hiking a mountain and kicking the day's ass! I feel like I'm sleeping through life right now, and how is that any different than just being dead?

I want to keep pushing myself but physically it's not always possible. I try to make a deal with my brain: If you allow me to stay awake more, I can push myself more and we can get out of this hospital faster! For the first week, my brain wants no part of this deal— it needs sleep!

• • •

It's the end of week two and I'm (thankfully) getting used to therapy and my schedule. I'm quite proud of myself because when I look at my progress from last week to this week, the difference is huge. I can stay awake longer, I'm getting better in all my therapies, and my spirits are up. I always want to do things faster (the fastest!), but I am slowly learning to just be proud of what I accomplish in the present moment and not worry about the end goal as much.

I have mixed feelings about Toronto Rehab. While I *hate* being around sick, old people, I *love* my therapists. First is Logan, my physiotherapist. I feel he actually understands my personality and really "gets me." He, too, is a runner, and when I tell him I'm dying to run again and complete the Scotiabank half-marathon later in the year, he doesn't scoff at me or look at me funny. He is on board and he promises to help me get there. I really don't feel like I'm in therapy when I'm with him. It feels like we're playing fun games! He has found a way to fuel my competitive appetite so our sessions feel more like intense rounds on the basketball or tennis court.

When I'm with Logan, I feel like I'm me *again!* A young vivacious, active and happy person. I don't feel like I'm in the hospital but rather playing games with a friend—a friend who pushes me to do better. As soon as I finish though, I see the drab hospital walls and all the signs on my hospital bed that make me feel like I'm an invalid. The emotional ups and downs every day are a struggle.

It seems like everywhere I turn, there is something to remind me of the fact that I am not a normal 29-year-old woman. When I take a shower, I have to have a student nurse help me. She can't be more than twenty years old, which makes me painfully self-conscious. Here I am, 29 years old, and I'm basically like an old grandma who needs this cute, fresh young woman to help her. I get so embarrassed that I just avert my eyes and look down.

How could I have gone from executive jet-setter travelling the world to this?

The other constant reminder I have of being a stroke victim is my helmet. It is a black, rock-hard helmet with zero cool factor. It feels like I'm wearing a hard hat and I hate it. If people weren't sure already, my big goof-proof helmet certainly screams "Stroke Victim" to anyone who might see it. It makes me feel like a help-less child instead of my normal independent self. It's also just plain ugly!

I'm not allowed to walk around if my helmet is not on my head, but I have this desperate urge to take it off as soon as I get to therapy. Part of it is vanity—I just feel ugly in it. And part of it is the fact that I hate feeling different from other young people around me. My therapists are pretty much all my age, and I feel like they are my only "friends" in the hospital. I want them to see me as one of them, just a cool young chick who likes to work out and can roll with the best of 'em! Kind of impossible to fit in, though, when I've got this lame helmet on my head.

I am so fond of Adrienne, my speech therapist. Much like Logan, I never feel like I'm in therapy when I'm around her. She makes therapy fun by finding interesting articles for me to read out loud, or playing word games that I can actually relate to. She doesn't treat me like a victim. We talk about boys, her studies and school life, our families, where we want to travel next, clothes and shopping. She allows me to feel like I'm talking to a friend and not a therapist.

The more time I spend with my young therapists, the more anxious I become to get out of the hospital. They get to go out for dinners, spend the weekends skiing at the cottage and having fun with their families and friends ... I'm so envious! I *have* to get out of this place ...

I've also started going to group therapy speech sessions every day, where we are given an article to read and we all take turns. I feel like the old people all hate me. I always put my hand in the air to be picked to read the next sentence and after a few sessions, I notice how much faster I am progressing than any of the old people. I've begun to feel self-conscious and guilty that they are not getting better, while I so clearly am. Every time the group session is done I quickly avert my eyes and scoot out of the room as quickly as I can. My parents are usually waiting for me in my room, and I know at least they will appreciate my progress.

• • •

It's been a few weeks and now I am able to handle TV and multiple stimuli. I'm also better at staying awake longer. I try my best to avoid any reminders that I'm in a hospital. I don't eat in the communal dining room because it's depressing to eat with the old people who are drooling and have to be spoon-fed. They will probably never recover. It always leaves me with a feeling of anxiety. What if I end up like that? I choose to keep it out of sight, out of mind.

Since I am able to stay awake a little longer, I have found a new ritual that lets me feel just a little more normal. There is a small room that no one uses in the evenings and it has a TV. Every evening, I watch *Friends* before I go to bed. For half an hour each day, I get taken away to the fun, goofy world of Rachel, Ross, Phoebe, Joey, Monica and Chandler. I get to turn off my mind and forget about my frustrations. For a short while, I don't worry about the fact that I still speak like a robot, in a monotone voice void of any personality. I forget that I still don't have some of my skull attached to my head, and I don't worry about my next brain surgery. I forget that I still need a nurse to help me wake up every day.

I forget for a short time that I sometimes throw temper tantrums and burst out yelling and crying because I can't always handle my emotions. I don't always know why I'm doing these things but my brain still has a lot of healing and learning to do, which is apparently why I have these outbursts. A few days ago, I was in the communal dining room and reached for a dinner tray but a man stepped in front of me. Instead of reaching for the next tray, I began yelling at him. When I put my tray down where Mummy was sitting, I started sobbing. Mom used to work with patients who'd had strokes and she explained to me that it is okay. My brain is still relearning how to control impulsive behaviours. These outbursts really scare me. I would *never* yell so meanly at someone, let alone a helpless old person, but I couldn't help it. I fear I will be like this forever—different from who I was. Maybe this is me now—a grouchy, volatile person who yells at the drop of a hat.

But for half an hour, I can shut down those spinning wheels of worry and just chill out. When I watch *Friends* in my secret little private room at the hospital, I get to laugh, smile and go to bed happy.

88

APRIL 2013

I'VE NOW BEEN AT TORONTO Rehab for about a month and can officially say: I AM DONE. Over it. Finished. Dun-zo. D-O-N-E.

I need to go home and start my life! I can now walk on my own, my speech is going well (not perfect by any means) and I'm even wiping my very own butt! Yay, me! The next step is outpatient rehab, but they will not let me leave the hospital because my warfarin level is still out of whack.

I pester Dr. Lang every single time I see him. "Can I go yet? Is my blood checking out yet? I can go home now? What about now? And today?" I think he might be avoiding me and my family because he knows I'm at my wits' end.

I WANT TO GO HOME!

Two *long* weeks later, I *finally* get to leave. I am able to take care of myself now. What a glorious morning it is! I wake up, take a shower, brush my teeth, get dressed, gobble up breakfast and have everything in my hospital room all packed up and ready. I am just waiting desperately for my parents to arrive so Dr. Lang can give us the "going home talk" before I bolt. I will start outpatient rehab on Monday, so for the next six weeks, Daddy will drive me to rehab and pick me up at lunchtime.

As soon as I'm out of the hospital, that means I'm one step closer to being a normal 29-year-old again. No old sick people, no drab hospital walls, no more hospital food, no one dictating when I have to do therapy and when I have to eat. I can sleep in my own bed, have my mummy's yummy cooking, not wear a helmet … I am *so* very ready to chuck that fucking helmet off the roof and say goodbye to it forever!

Come on, Mummy, can't you get here any sooner?

. . .

I have this nagging fear. I can walk and talk and I'm improving each day, but no one can definitively tell me *why* I had a stroke. That seems kind of important. If I don't know what caused it, how can I prevent it from happening again? I'm always looking over my shoulder in a sense, worrying that I maybe did something wrong today that will set off another stroke. How can I live my life like this, in perpetual fear?

I can't go through this hell again and I certainly cannot put my family through it again. I know—I would die.

Yesterday I went to the thrombosis clinic at Toronto General Hospital and I finally spoke with Dr. Peterson, who helped ease my mind.

"We cannot say with 100% certainty why you had a stroke or what caused your stroke. Regardless of the cause, Dina, being on blood thinners will prevent another stroke from occurring."

I needed to hear that. The constant fear and anxiety finally melts away. I'm still mad as hell that none of these so called "medical experts" can figure out what caused my stroke, but at least I can move on knowing that it is unlikely to happen again.

. . .

Outpatient Rehab is at the Rumsey Centre on Bayview Avenue in North York. I like my physical therapists, my speech therapists and the extra therapy I receive for my right hand, but mentally and emotionally, I'm at my breaking point.

I know I am lucky that I've progressed so quickly and have been accepted into the different therapy programs (normally there is a long wait list), but I'm done. I feel drained. I'm no longer the pink Energizer Bunny that kept going and going just a couple of weeks ago. I want to stop. I need a break.

Therapy is a constant reminder of what I can't do perfectly, and anyone and everyone who knows me (before the stroke, at least) knows—I am a perfectionist! I simply don't do "less than." I have to be number one at everything! I have to prove to everyone that I am extraordinary in everything I do. When I look at myself now, and I see my "average," or more often "below average" performance—it is soul-crushing. It is humiliating. I want to fall off the face of the earth entirely so that no one who knew me before the stroke ever finds me. I cannot let them see me like this! I can barely hold a fork in my hand. My handwriting looks worse than it did in grade one. Siri's voice on my iPhone is more lifelike than my own.

My response to all of this inadequacy is to embrace it. This is the new Dina: rebel who doesn't give a fuck.

I just don't care anymore. So what if my handwriting looks like a cat wrote it. Screw it! So what if I can't always remember how to vocalize my thoughts. I just won't speak! So what if don't have full dexterity in my right hand. Who needs it? I'll make do with my left thank you very much. I'll start eating like a dog, just put a dish in front of me and if you don't like it—you know where you can go.

I'm drained from spending hundreds of hours trying to get my thumb and pinky finger to touch on my right hand. It's too goddamn slow! I want to be back to my go-go-go self and hours and hours of trying to move each finger on my right hand only makes me want to kill myself.

I'm 29 and I've wasted half a year with this stupid stroke. I want to forget this whole thing every happened, go out, have fun and travel. I feel trapped in a therapy bubble. I want to poke a hole in this bubble and get the hell out! I just want to forget about the stroke, brain surgery, the hospital, rehab—all of it.

Every time I think about the past six months and all the valuable time I have lost, I cry.

I hear a clock ticking in my head. Did this clock start before or after my stroke? I'm not quite sure, but it feels very familiar. I feel like this clock has been ticking my whole life, telling me to move faster, be better, go harder ... It's louder than it's ever been.

"TICK-TOCK-TICK-TOCK ..."

"You're going to be thirty years old soon, Dina. Thirty years old, and what can you say for yourself? You can touch your thumb to your forefinger? Mark Zuckerberg was a millionaire at 23. The founder of Google was a *billionaire* by age 30 ..."

Holy shit. I've got to get moving.

I write down the three goals I set for myself back in February and circle the third one a few times: *Finish the Scotiabank marathon in record time.*

89

APRIL 2013.
SISTER'S GRADUATION.

ONE OF THE FIRST GOALS I had set back when I first wiggled my toes was that I wanted to walk into my sister's MBA graduation ceremony. I still have not had my second brain surgery to reattach my skull and so my neurosurgeon flat-out refuses to allow me to go to Yas' MBA graduation. It is simply too dangerous for me to be outside without my skull. Pfft—what does she know! Skull-shmull. I pull out the old sweet-daughter charm and pouty face and lay it on Dad—hopefully he will cave and let me go.

"Absolutely NOT, Dina. This will not work on me!"

Darn it! I used to be so good at that. I don't give up. After a ton of negotiation, they say I can go but only if I wear the helmet. Good fucking grief! *What* do I have to do to make that helmet disappear for good? It follows me around like a bad stink. I will never wear that embarrassing headpiece in public, ever! I would be mortified to have to wear that in a room full of educated, well dressed 25-to-35-year-olds.

I think Dr. Hodaie and Daddy are envisioning the worst possible scenario: some MBA grad is going to knock me to the floor and my head will hit a nail precisely on the area where I don't have my skull.

Yas can see my frustration and argues my case. "Guys, we're not going to a child's playground. This is a room full of sophisticated adults. It's not the rowdy affair that you have in your minds."

Mom also sees the tears in my eyes and gently adds that she will be holding my arm at all times and assures both Dad and Dr. Hodaie that I won't go anywhere alone.

I think in that moment: Daddy and Dr. Hodaie realize how badly I need this. After everything I have lost, I just need to do this one thing so I can feel a tiny bit normal again. I need to be a part of something hopeful and positive—seeing my sister graduate will boost my morale just enough to get me through this next leg of recovery.

They both finally agree and I squeal with excitement and gratitude, hugging them both and thanking them repeatedly.

The day finally arrives and I feel excitement, and also, relief. This is *her* day. These last months, all the focus has been on me, and frankly—I could use a break from all of the constant attention. Also, Yas deserves this. I want this day to be all about her and her amazing accomplishments. Not many sisters could manage to pull off a master's degree while their sister is in the hospital recovering from a stroke. She was there with me whenever she had a spare moment from school. She was strong for me when I couldn't be. She never complained, and she never let me see her sweat—but I *know* it has been tough for her. Now, I am so proud to just be here for *her*, and cheer loudly as she collects the diploma she has rightfully earned.

This is my first time getting dressed up in months! I've been wearing sweats or hospital gowns for almost five months. I don't remember how to straighten my hair or even put makeup on. I don't have the dexterity in my right hand, so I fear I'm going to poke my eye out with the mascara wand or make myself look like a demented clown.

Mom has said from the beginning that it is better if I try and see what I can do on my own. If, *and only if*, I fail, will she help me. I know she wants me to build my confidence up again, and it won't happen if I don't try on my own. First step, opening the powder. I use my left hand and, voila, the little black circular compact pops opens. Things like buttons and clasps are a challenge, so already, I'm feeling optimistic! I clumsily wrap my left hand around the large brush. I fumble a few times as I dab it in my MAC Studio Fix Powder but I finally get enough powder on the brush and sweep it across my face.

Next up is eye shadow. I try to adjust the brush in my left hand and need to reposition my grip a few times before I'm confident that I will in fact *not* get the brush in my eyes. Success! Mom's right there celebrating all these small makeup milestones with me.

Lastly, mascara. How the heck will I pull *this* off? I show Mom the grip I have on the mascara wand and she gently adjusts it. Wow. I'm pretty darn proud! I ignore the fact that normally, makeup takes me all of 45 seconds to do and today it's taken about 45 minutes ... This is victory!

I'm very self-conscious because the dent on the left side of my head seems obvious. Mom keeps telling me I look beautiful and no one will even notice, but it doesn't matter. I notice. I may be vain but I don't care. Mom is understanding, at least, and actually took me to a hair boutique last week. We bought clip on extensions that I can discretely put where my hair is shaved to help my head look more round and give me some volume.

I'm going to wear a black knit top with leggings and tall boots. I'm able to get my left hand to assist my right hand with bigger things like getting dressed. It's only with tasks that require precise movements and dexterity that I run into problems.

I can't fasten my bra in the back as that requires two hands and a great deal of precision. So, I lay my bra flat on my bed, line up the hooks in the back and use my left hand to hook them. Then, I take the bra, put it over my head and since it's already hooked up, all I have to do is shift the bra so it's actually where it is supposed to be.

I feel pretty darn clever right now, I must say!

Over an hour and a half later, I'm finally ready. Daddy tells me how beautiful I look and I eagerly tell him how Mom and I figured out different ways to do my hair and makeup.

Daddy is an amazing photographer and loves capturing memories of our family. He can't stop taking pictures of his three girls! He's beaming with pride and I see the twinkle in his eyes—I love it. There is really nothing more heartwarming than my dad's sweet, loving smile. I have to remind him he has to actually *be* in some of the pictures, too!

As we approach the hall where the graduation ceremony is taking place, I start to think about how robotic my voice still is. Mom, Dad, Yas, my family, nurses and doctors are all used to hearing my choppy, inarticulate, monotone voice, but I've only emailed or texted friends to this point. I suddenly realize that I may sound dumb or silly. I don't want to frighten anyone off!

Every single day, from my very first sound until now, Yas has cheered me on. If she sees me embarrassed to speak or lowering my eyes, she gets stern, puts her hands on her hips and tells me to talk my heart out as often as I can.

"NO ONE is going to think you sound stupid, D. You *must* keep talking. Everyone around you loves you for *you, not* your voice."

I'm trying to feel confident but admittedly, I have a pit in my stomach and feel very self-conscious.

All her friends will think I'm just Yas' dumb older sister. They'll feel sorry for me and I'll see those stares of pity, which I despise. I think I'll just keep my mouth closed.

I see Yas hug her friends, happily introducing us. She can see I'm nervous to speak and wondering if anyone notices my skull and weirdly shaped head. She squeezes my hand, gives me a huge smile and leans in, then clenches her fist in a way we have come to secretly tell each other, "Go for it! You've got this."

It takes only a few minutes to realize I had nothing to be afraid of. Her friends give me hugs and all tell me how happy they are to finally meet me and how remarkable my journey and recovery has been. I may have lost a lot of confidence, but I see that I should be proud of myself and how far I have come.

I finally lose the jitters and start to enjoy myself. Mom and I are in our seats but Dad has his eye on Yas. He steps out of his seat and makes his way to the very front of the aisle and starts snapping pictures, regardless of whose way he might be in. He's a proud papa! Mom and I just look at each other: "Classic Daddy."

When Yas gets on stage, I stand up and cheer with no thought of how I am sounding at all. She has her cap and gown on and I know she also has some super high heels on underneath the gown. Mom and I just pray she gets to the top of the stairs and stage without tripping!

After we took about 1000 other pictures, we had a celebratory dinner. Glasses of champagne, spectacular food and, of course, lots of dessert. It was such a wonderful event for Yas and I think Dad could see that it not only meant a lot to me to be there for Yas, but it meant a lot to Yas to have me there.

Part one of my recovery plan—seeing my sister graduate—complete. Next up: celebrating my parents' anniversary!

90

APRIL 15, 2013

AFTER OUR WONDERFUL CELEBRATION FOR Yas' graduation, I'm back at outpatient rehab which I now loathe with every fibre of my being. It feels so tedious and mundane. Stupid movements like trying to get my thumb and index finger to touch. It's this movement that allows you to pick up a pen, or turn the page of a newspaper. It's this teeny tiny movement that allows me to pick up a cup of tea and not spill it. I have tried hundreds and hundreds of times.

When the young therapists tell me about the anniversary dates they have with their wonderful boyfriends or their spa weekends planned in Montreal, I feel like a total dork in comparison.

"Oh hey, Dina! We had a fa-a-a-bulous weekend drinking champagne and dancing and being f-a-a-abulous. What did you do?"

"Well ... let me see. I tried about one hundred times to use my index finger and did NOT succeed. Hoo-fucking-rah for me!"

There is one good thing about therapy: I despise it so much, it's reanimated the Type-A, go-go-go, "Get the FUCK outta my way" woman inside of me. I should clarify—its' really good for me, not so great for anyone who happens to be in my path when I happen to let my rage-flag fly free. The slow pace of therapy makes me incredibly edgy and I snap at everything. My parents let a lot of my irritation and anger go because they are happy to see me motivated and active. At the same time, they see that I often set an unrealistic pace for myself, and those around me.

I honestly have no idea how they put up with me a lot of the time. Their patience is limitless!

I have cut myself off from my computer and don't really care to have a cell phone. After I came back from Napa, I was supposed to get a company phone when I started my new job. Dad has repeatedly told me he will give me his phone or buy me a new one, but I decline his offers. I really don't care to hear about everyone's fun life, or scroll through pictures of Saturday nights and fun events on Facebook. I don't need yet another reminder of how much time I've lost, or the fun things I cannot do, or how happy everyone else is.

I have my second brain surgery next week. I know I have to be careful, but I'm also desperate for a little fun. A little mindless, twenty-something, stupid, let-loose time sounds absolutely amazing. My friend Anthony offers to take me out one night— nothing crazy. Just dinner out somewhere and a couple of hours where I don't have to think about connecting my forefinger to my thumb. My parents can see how much I want this "normal" experience, so they give me the green light.

Getting ready for my night out once again takes over an hour, and that's not including getting dressed! I want to wear black pantyhose and a skirt. I grab both sides of the pantyhose, but since I have more of a barbaric grip with my right "claw" hand, I rip the tights straight through. Mom sees the dejected look on my face and pipes up, "Never mind, Dina. It doesn't matter that those tights are gone! At least you tried! There is another pair in your drawer—don't you worry at all!"

I manage to get my black skirt on but can't figure out how to pull up the zip and fasten the button using only my left hand. The great thing is that Mom treats every small task like a game. When I can't do it, it becomes a game to try to learn a new way of doing something. Eventually, we manage to get me fully clothed and presentable.

Anthony assures Mom and Dad that we are just going to a restaurant 10 minutes away. When I get tired (which is often by 8 p.m.), I start to get painful headaches and need to go to bed, so they want to make sure I'm not too far. It's my brain basically telling me that I need to rest.

We arrive at the restaurant and I'm feeling great! I've got this—no problemo. I'm starving by this point and I tell Anthony to just order a bunch of dishes and we'll split everything. Big mistake! When our food comes, one of the dishes is calamari, and I realize, I don't know how to place a knife in my right hand in order to cut food. What was I thinking? After months of baby food and being spoon-fed, I'm only just learning how to properly use cutlery again on my own. I stare at the calamari in horror.

I'm lucky to have friends who can read my mind without having to explain. Before I have a chance to say anything, Anthony grabs the dish, cuts up the calamari without even blinking and carries on talking like it's no big deal. I'm so grateful for this small gesture.

It's not long before I get tired. Anthony notices my eyes drooping and that I'm having trouble getting the words out. He swiftly tells me he is full, pays the bill, takes my hand and leads me to his car.

He drops me off and I promptly fall into bed and go straight to sleep. As I nod off, I forget when or where I am—it just feels like any other regular night I've had over the last few years. Tonight, I got to be a regular 29-year-old woman. I got a little break from my stroke and recovery. I got to have fun with a friend, and it felt wonderful.

91

APRIL 20, 2013

I HAVE ONE MORE MAJOR hurdle to jump over: my second brain surgery. The piece of my skull that was removed during my emergency surgery has been sitting in a freezer at Western for months, just waiting to be reunited with my head. There is a chance that the frozen piece was infected, in which case they will have to use metal plates instead. Surgeons will reattach the piece of skull, and I will have to spend four to seven days in recovery at Western Hospital.

Up until this day, I've put on this front that it's really no big deal. Second brain surgery? Totally no biggie! I'll be out of this hospital in less than a week. This is nothing. I've been through worse!

While that may be true, as we drive to the hospital, I start tensing up. When the nurses direct us to the area where I will change into a hospital gown, it hits me. Holy shit! Who was I trying to kid? I'm having brain surgery! It's a big, fucking scary deal! I am terrified. One wrong move during surgery could cripple me. I've worked *so* hard to learn how to walk and talk, and what if all of it was for nothing? What if they can't use my frozen skull and I need to get metal plates? Will alarms go off every time I walk through an airport? And that's assuming I can even walk again ... What if I have to get a blood transfusion? I don't want one. What if I get infected blood and I'm paralyzed? No, no, no. I don't want brain surgery. Maybe I'm fine and can just go on living life with a piece of my skull missing? I dodged a huge bullet with my first brain surgery. Who on earth dodges two? I'm just tempting fate. What if something goes terribly, terribly wrong?

I feel paralyzed with fear. I do not want to go through with this. For my first surgery, I had no clue what was happening because I was in a coma. I was blissfully unaware. Now I know everything. I am aware of all the things that could go wrong and it scares the shit out of me.

"*Jaanu,* do you need me to tie the dressing gown?" Mom asks.

She takes one look at me and can tell that I'm too scared to move. She hugs me tightly and tells me:

"My Jaanu, everything will be fine. Dr. Hodaie is the *best.* You are in safe, good hands. We will all be waiting for you and will see you as soon as the surgery is done. You have one last obstacle. In just a few hours you will be done. It will be over soon. We're so close, *Jaanu!* Just one last push. Let's say a prayer together and we will walk slowly to the room ... okay?"

She continues to hold me until she sees that I'm willing to get up and walk to the surgical prep area.

I feel like I'm so close to experiencing life again and yet—I'm still so far. I just want this crappy chapter of my life to end. I never want to step foot in a hospital or rehab facility again.

I tightly hold Mom's hand until we get to the operating room doors. The nurse says they will hook me up to the IV and prepare me for surgery. Mom has to leave. I start to cry.

I try to remind myself over and over, "This will be over soon. This will be over soon ..."

My arms are black and blue as three different nurses try to find a vein for the IV but are unable to. They've tried both my left and right arm with no success. I try to stay calm but I can see their frustration. After four months of having my blood taken daily, this is a normal occurrence and it's rare to have a nurse find a "good" vein on the first attempt. Finally, on the seventh attempt, they find a good vein.

They tell me they will be shaving part of my hair off (again). I guess I'm just not meant to have hair on part of my head. The shaved area of my head was finally getting small strands of hair growing back but all that will be removed again. Maybe I should just go back to my preschool hairstyle—where my Mom would trim my hair herself into a super short "bowl cut" style. A return to my tomboy roots!

I'm not sure why they are being so stingy with the drugs. Why don't they put me under already? I need DRUGS. Give me drugs so I can be blissfully naïve again! Seriously, the drugs cannot come soon enough!

The room feels sterile and cold. The skimpy hospital gown is not helping. The nurse sees I'm shivering and wraps me in a few blankets. I watch them as they hook me up to more machines than I can count.

I close my eyes again and tell myself, "It will all be over soon."

. . .

When I open my eyes, I see my family all around me. I want to smile, but the pain hits me like a ton of bricks. All I feel is pain. I can't open my left eye because of the surgery. The muscles on each side of the brain actually connect to the facial muscles so it looks (and feels) like someone has punched me in the face. Every single movement hurts. It's hard to blow my nose, smile or even open an eye.

Damn, the pain!

The hospital is undergoing some sort of renovations or repair so I am now sharing a "makeshift" room. My neighbour's family brings him McDonald's and I can smell all the yummy junk food which is annoying. There is NO way I would eat that salty, fatty fried food! It does smell delicious, though ...

My family brings me food everyday so I'm not forced to eat hospital food. Yesterday Uncle Farokh brought me the most delicious potato-and-leek soup. Mummy brought me quiche today and a lovely fruit bowl with raspberries, orange segments and grapes.

I spend five days at Western before I get to go home. It's a pretty mundane, boring visit. Most of my time is spent going back and forth between MRI and CT scans, visits from my doctors and of course lots of sleep. I try my hardest not to snap at the nurses. I'm a lot less edgy because I get updates all the time on how well my brain surgery went, so I know that I'm going to go home soon.

As I am getting ready to leave, a young nurse (whom I've never met before) walks into my room and says to me, "Wow! What do you do to have such radiant skin?"

I know there is no one else in the room except the older man who is my neighbour, but she can't be talking to me. Can she? I've always been so self-conscious of my skin, now more than ever since I'm not allowed to be on the birth control pills that would control my out of whack hormones. I turn around to catch a glimpse of this chick with the "radiant skin" and I realize the nurse is talking about ME!

Talk about a complete boost of confidence! I've *never* thought of myself as having nice skin, let alone "radiant skin." I have no clue who that nurse was but she completely made my day. As we walk out of the hospital, I'm walking on air!

I'm holding Mom's hand and skipping along. "Radiant skin" and I have my skull back? It's a good day. Scratch that. It's a GREAT day!

92

END OF APRIL 2013

WE ARRIVE HOME AND I breathe a sigh of relief. I feel like I've cleared the highest of the hurdles now that my surgery is *done.* No more hospital visits (God willing!) for a good long while!

I head up to my room to decompress and maybe nap for a bit. As I remove my sweater, I catch a glimpse of myself in the mirror.

I can hardly believe what I'm seeing. I look amazing! I have never seen my body looking so svelte. I lift up my shirt and—miracle of miracles—I actually have a six-pack! I think of all the hours I've put in at the gym over the years in the hope of getting this kind of definition in my abs. In the end, it isn't the thousands of sit ups that got me here—it was my stroke! I guess months in the hospital, then a gruelling daily schedule of rehab and a diet of mostly mush is the secret to success.

I have to know the number ... How many pounds have I actually lost? It's been a while since I dared to pull out my old friend from under my parents' bed. I casually head to their room and, just as I thought, it looks like it hasn't been moved or touched in over ten years.

I step onto it and watch the arm pivot back and forth from 100 to 120 pounds until it finally lands.

Holy shit! 110 pounds. It's my dream weight! I could kiss the scale right now—thank you, old friend!

I head downstairs where my mom is preparing afternoon tea and snacks. I can't keep this news to myself, so I (half-jokingly) tell her, "Apparently there is an upside to all of this. I lost over 10 pounds without even trying! Total silver lining, eh?"

She just glares at me disapprovingly. She does know how much I love to eat and sees how huge my appetite is, so she doesn't seem alarmed and doesn't outright condemn my words. But I know this is a road she does not want to see me go down again.

She'll never really get it, though. How could she? After the stroke, I need to prove to myself that I am still the travelling, healthy, active person I once was. Being slim is a part of that. Despite all the setbacks, losing 10 pounds is a victory I cling to, because it is visible proof to the world that I am strong, sensational, exceptional, Dina! I may talk like a robot, but I'm skinny! I may not be able to use a knife and fork properly, but I've got six-pack abs! I am finally at my "goal" weight and love it!

I am lucky. Imagine if I had gotten fat on top of everything else? I think I honestly would have wanted to kill myself. I can't mess up this gift—it's a gift I have been waiting for about 15 years. I don't just tolerate or like my body now, I LOVE it!

• • •

The happiness of yesterday fades as I get back to my everyday routine. Wake up, have breakfast, go to outpatient therapy, come home and have lunch, do mundane at home therapy exercises, take a nap, do more therapy exercises, go to the gym with Dad, do more therapy exercises, have dinner, more therapy exercises and go to bed. Every day, over and over—the same.

Daddy is so patient and does the hundreds of different hand therapy exercises we have, but I'm tired and frustrated. Each day, I get up and am mainly excited because I look forward to having breakfast, but by the end of the evening I'm mentally and emotionally exhausted. Each day, Mom tucks me into bed and she lets me cry. We have our "cry it out" sessions, which allow me to alleviate my frustration so I can get up and do it all over again.

I have stitches on my head which look like huge black staples. I try not to look—it's so grotesque! I look like Frankenstein's monster. Mom checks each night to see how the stitches are healing and we have a small celebration each day as we see one of them dissolve. We feel through the ridge on my skull, checking to see if there are any new or strange sensations or pain. Since none of us know anyone who has had brain surgery, we take it day by day. Dr. Hodaie calls often to check up on me.

There is a small area where my hair won't grow back and it really disturbs me. I pray to God that this is temporary and that I won't need to resort to wigs or a hair transplant to hide my weird bald spot!

My therapists and doctors tell me most of my progress will take place in the first six months, which terrifies me. Now I have a new countdown clock ticking away. I only have a couple of months left! What if don't get full dexterity back in my right hand? What if I don't get the pitch, tone and personality back in my voice?

My favourite therapist at outpatient rehab is Nadia, who has just recently become engaged. She gushes to me about her "partner in life" and all of the lovey-dovey things they do together. I hear the stories about her exciting new life, and I try to feel happy for her. Truthfully, I have to use every ounce of restraint to keep from rolling my eyes and making fake barf sounds. Give me a break! Do I *have* to listen to her gush for the whole session? I long for the days when the only sound at the gym came from my headphones, blaring loud music to me and me alone!

I'm jealous beyond belief. It hurts. I want love! I want adventure with a "partner in life"! I want everything she has. Will I ever get them, though? I'm not very encouraged these days.

. . .

In Ontario, our government health program (OHIP) only covers one six-week block of physiotherapy and we are now approaching the end of it. If I want to continue, we have to pay for it. I don't have a job or any private health insurance plan, but my parents have told me repeatedly, "Dina, we will pay for therapy if you want to continue. Don't even worry about it. It's a non-issue."

I am grateful for their offer, but I think I'm done. I sit down for a long talk with Mom and Dad to explain where I'm at.

"Therapy is taking a huge toll on me emotionally and mentally. I need to stop. I want to start living and being young again. I want my life back."

They understand and agree. In just a couple of weeks, I'll be free! The light at the end of the tunnel is getting brighter and brighter as each day goes by.

93

MAY 2013

HARD TO BELIEVE IT'S BEEN five months since I had my emergency brain surgery. I visit with my doctors to make a plan for the future.

"While we can't definitively say that your stroke was caused by taking a birth control pill, it's the only reason we can come up with," Dr. Lang explains. "Moving forward, you will not be able to take any birth control pills or medication containing hormones of any sort. We have to take every precaution to ensure you never have a stroke again. Make sense, Dina?"

I know why we are having this conversation, and I am completely fine with it. No more birth control means there is a chance that my acne will return. I am *way* too scared to take the pills again anyway. If my acne comes back, so be it. It's better than the alternative, which is the possibility of another stroke, paralysis, even death.

They tell me that it will take some time for my hormones to rebalance, and on top of this, my body will require some time to recover from the trauma of the stroke. It is normal that I haven't had a period in months, and it is possible my menstrual cycle won't return to normal for quite some time. I am a little nervous about all of this—I picture my hormones suddenly going berserk and manifesting themselves in some brutally painful zits, but I accept it. If in fact my acne returns, I will deal with it at that time. All I can do is hope and pray that doesn't happen.

A few days later, I get my period. Hooray! This is my body getting back to normal! I rejoice for a minute until I am reminded of what I've been missing all these months: cramps! Ugh. The return of my monthly visitor is bittersweet. I take a Tylenol and hope that my skin doesn't go berserk.

In any case—I know I'll be okay. A pimple or two seems a lot less dire once you've had a stroke, been in a coma, had your skull cut out and reattached, and come back from partial paralysis ...

• • •

My time at outpatient therapy is almost ending, and today I get a break from it so I can meet with my neurosurgeon and neurologist, and have a few tests done.

So far, it's going well. The MRI reveals that my brain looks healthy. The mass is pretty much gone, the craniotomy is healing well and there are no signs of infection. All this is lovely news but I'm dying to finish all of the tests so I can ask my neurologist the one question I've been dying to ask him for months.

As we wait for our appointment I can barely sit still. Dr. Steiner arrives, hugs Mom and me, and invites us into his office. He's seen all my scans and the latest test results and tells me he's very happy with everything. He does some reflex action tests and is once again impressed with my responses.

I'm ready to pounce but I hold back until I hear him say with certainty that everything is fine and dandy.

"You're doing well, Dina. I would say you've made a full recovery."

The words have barely left his mouth when I pounce. "Great. Can I fly? Can I be on a plane?"

He smiles. "Yes. You're good to fly."

The second we get home, I jump on the computer and book a trip. I'll be taking Yas to New York for a girls' weekend! It's *my* time to *live,* dammit! I want to be normal and forget about the past six months! I have a lot of time to make up for and cannot wait to get this party started!

I also decide I'm going to take a big trip. I search on G Adventures and find the perfect trip: I will be hiking the Amalfi Coast in Italy and staying in a villa where they cook us local food each day.

Booked, and booked. These trips represent my comeback. It's my little way of saying, "Screw you, stroke! I'm back, and I'm ready to *kick ass* in life!"

I do a little jig and start thinking of what I will pack for my trips, when I suddenly remember there is something else I have to do first.

Back in the hospital, I set three goals for myself. I've only crossed one off the list! My parents' anniversary is in July, and falls just one week before I leave for my trip to Italy. I want this night to be one for the books, so I better start looking for great restaurants now ...

94

JULY 2, 2013

YAS AND I DECIDE TO take Mom and Dad to one of our favourite restaurants in Toronto called Note Bene. It's downtown on Queen Street West, right where the chic business district meets the cool, "bohemian" west end. We've made sure to tell the management in advance: this is a special night! We want a great table with a good view, we want champagne on arrival, and we want a special dessert to cap off the night. Tonight, I want to celebrate my parents and treat them to an amazing meal. I really want to show them how much they mean to me.

As we walk into the restaurant, I silently congratulate myself on checking this second goal off of my list. Six months ago, I was lying in hospital bed. When I woke up, I was so lost. The thought of living my life paralyzed, or mute, was too much to bear. Thinking of this moment was one of the things that kept me going. And now, here we finally are! I feel good, I think I look good, and most important, my parents are smiling and happy.

We enjoy a wonderful dinner with lots of wine, delicious gourmet food, love and laughter. As we walk out, I feel so grateful that I was able to celebrate this moment my family. It almost didn't happen. I get chills when I think of how close I came ... How quickly things can change ... How such a simple thing— dinner with my family—would become more precious than gold to me.

Whoever is up there, thank you, thank you, thank you!

95

MIDDLE OF JULY 2013

IN LONDON, I RUN AROUND seeing as many old friends as possible for the few days I am there before I fly to Sicily. I've always wanted to see southern Italy, so I figure I may as well do it now before I meet the tour group on the Amalfi Coast.

I'm up super early and exploring every day. In Taormina, I come across a beach called Isola Bella. It is breathtaking. I stop to take in my surroundings. I sit down, soak in the scenery and just breathe. I start sobbing, but these are not like the dispirited tears of sadness, frustration or anger which I've become accustomed to these last few months.

These are tears of gratitude, pride and happiness. I realize that for the past six months, I have rushed everything in a desperate attempt to get better and to leave the hospital. No accomplishment was ever enough. There was always something more that I had to achieve. More that I had to check off my list. More to do before the countdown clock reached zero. I was never satisfied. I was never convinced that what I was doing was ever good enough.

I never really stopped to process what happened to me and take stock in my achievements. Look at what I fought my way back from! From almost dead, to this moment right here, right now. I look at the sea, and sun, and feel the wind against my skin, and reflect upon my life.

I *made it*. I *survived*. Holy shit—look at everything I've survived! I'm not even thirty years old and I've had more brushes with death than I care to remember.

I survived adolescence! Which really was a miracle considering how much I hated myself at that time. Enough to attempt suicide? How the hell did I come back from that? What got me out of the bathroom that night? I'll never truly know or comprehend what saved me that night. But whatever it was, I know for sure it was *strong,* and it was deep inside me, and it's still *there.* It's a strength that is bigger than me, and smarter than me—because it gets me to the next goalpost even when I'm sabotaging myself (which I'm starting to see, I do quite a bit).

I survived a car crash and lived to tell the tale! I think of all the people who are not so lucky. Every night on the news there is a story of a car wreck on the highway. Every night, a story about someone who didn't get to walk away. They died, they were left injured, they lost loved ones ... but I *made it.* That strength inside me found its way to the surface just as I was about to crash. It helped give me the presence of mind to make a split second decision that would save my life. It pushed me to admit to myself that I was unhappy in California—that I needed to move home and be with my family. It's not easy admitting you *need* people when you're super independent like me! But the strong part of me knew what was right, and helped me get past my foolish pride so I could start to be truly *happy.*

I survived a massive stroke. A stroke! My brain was bleeding out and deprived of oxygen. They cut my head open. They took a piece of my skull and left it unattached for months. Months! They weren't sure if I was brain dead. I couldn't walk, or talk. I was like a slobbering, inept, helpless infant, trapped in a woman's body. I had to fight every day, *hard,* just to make it through to the next. I had to fight feelings of hopelessness, fear, despair and shame, every single day. But those feelings were no match for the strong part of me. That part kicked and punched and endured every torturous minute of forefinger-to-thumb exercises and I *made it.* Against all odds!

I survived.

I feel a sense of peace and calm I have never felt. I have no desire to be anywhere else. I could care less about the countdown clock ticking incessantly in my head since ... birth, really. All I hear is the wind, and the waves of the sea. My mind is blissfully quiet.

I see a nearby café and decide to get lunch and sit by myself and just enjoy this sweet feeling for a little while longer. I think it's a feeling that I have needed for a long time, but never gave myself permission to feel.

96

AUGUST 2013

I RETURN HOME AFTER MY trip to Italy feeling re-energized, rejuvenated and proud. I'm ready to tackle the third goal I set for myself back in the hospital. I do the math and realize that the Scotiabank half-marathon is about three months away, which means I'd better start training ASAP!

I have not actually tried to run at all since the stroke. I don't know if my head can handle the pounding of my feet on the pavement—I'm still quite sensitive after my second surgery. I don't know if I will get headaches. I don't know if this third goal is realistic at all! The first two goals were pretty tame: all I had to do was show up! Running a marathon requires major athletic ability, focus and stamina. I might not be able to pull this off ...

There is a part of me that is furious at my body. I'm so mad that it has let me down—after everything I do for it! I eat fresh healthy food. I exercise daily. I have never smoked or done drugs. I have only a small amount of wine with dinners when I'm out with friends. Damn you, body! I treat you so well, and this is the bullshit I get in return? *Not. Cool.*

In a way, I want to punish my body. More accurately, I want to "get back" at the stroke. I do some research and discover that in just over a month, there is a duathlon. It seems like a good opportunity to get in a "trial run" before the big half-marathon. I have no idea if I can even get on a bike again, but there is a fire in me. I want that to show the stroke that it has messed with the *wrong* chick!

I register for the duathlon and my training begins. My good friend Chandra's dad is a cycling pro and she has arranged for me to get some pointers and also have him tune up my bike, my ol' pal Roxy. I am not sure if my right hand will have the strength to hold the drop handlebars, but Chandra and her dad assure me that there is a way to do it and we will figure it out together. They show me different ways I can grip the handle if my right hand starts to feel any pain or aches.

When I get home, the moment of truth comes: Can I actually run? Since the stroke, I have these images of a cartoon bobblehead where my soft, mushy brain bounces around in my skull. I'm scared I won't be able to handle the impact of my feet hitting the pavement.

I am still not able to put my hair up in a ponytail or tie my shoelaces, so Mom helps me. I've gotten very accustomed to asking for help with these two tasks each day. When Yas and I went to New York, she'd help me. When I went to the Sicily, the bed and breakfast owner would help me, and later my room-mate for the G Adventures part of my trip would help me. If it's someone I just meet, I just say I "hurt my hand." Simple and easy. If I have to ask for help in order to be able to exercise, walk and run, so be it! I'll do whatever it takes.

Mom, Dad and Yas are all with me for my first attempt at running around the block.

"You can do it, D! You can do it, *Jaanu!* We are so proud of you!" they all cheer.

I start with a light jog, one step at a time. I make a point of landing each step gingerly—balls of the foot first then heel. I want to minimize the impact against the concrete as much as possible.

I jog a few steps, then a few more … and I feel fine! Oh my God! Oh my God! Mummy! Daddy! Yassy! I can jog! I see them behind me jumping for joy. Any passersby must be wondering what all the fuss is about. I imagine they are thinking, "This funny Indian family—they are cheering on their daughter for ... what exactly? She's only moved a few steps. Very peculiar."

I pick up the pace. I feel great! I run around the block give them the thumbs up as I return and decide to go for a second lap! The runner's high I feel is like nothing I've ever experienced before. I could go all day!

My normal route is what we call "The Longo's Run." I run from my house to Don Mills, and then go south on Don Mills until I reach York Mills. I then turn west, passing the Westin Hotel and all the new restaurants that are being built until I get to Leslie Street, which is where the Longo's grocery store is. I turn right, running past the community tennis courts, past the Keg restaurant, past the North York General Hospital and then at the corner of Sheppard and Leslie, make my final right turn eastward and run until I reach home.

Forty minutes later I'm in shock! I did it! Six months of fear ... It's all vanished! I had built up this crippling fear that I might not be able to run. I was so afraid I would *lose* this part of me. Running has been a huge part of my daily life for such a long time—I was terrified I wouldn't be able to do it anymore.

Running allows me to de-stress from ANY worry. Running gives me a sense of accomplishment. I ALWAYS feel better after I run. Running also allows me a freedom to eat what I want. I couldn't lose that. I run into the house and collapse in my mom's arms and start crying. I am in total shock that I could actually run. The joy and sense of accomplishment was palpable.

I see the finish line in my mind's eye. I see myself running past it. I see myself on the other side.

97

SUNDAY,
SEPTEMBER 19, 2013.
RACE DAY.

MY HEART IS BEATING LOUDLY inside my chest. I've been staring at the ceiling for hours. Today is finally the day I check off the third and final thing on my recovery to-do list: Today I will run the Scotiabank half-marathon.

Nine months later and here I am. Just twenty-one kilometres to go until I reach the finish line I've been picturing in my mind since I first wiggled my toes in the hospital.

While I was tucked into bed by 9 p.m., I couldn't sleep a wink. Adrenalin is pumping through my body and I've been up long before my alarm went off. The excitement and anticipation and nerves are just too much. I can't wait to get to the start line and begin!

It's still dark out as I leave the house. I start the drive downtown and notice the roads are eerily quiet. It almost feels as though the city is clearing a path, just for me. I park quite far from the starting line as all the roads are blocked off for the actual race. There are at least 25,000 runners participating so every hotel, coffee shop and warm area by the start line is packed. Everyone is just trying to stay warm on this chilly October day.

I find a spot in one of the hotels and try my hardest to remain calm. "I can do it. I will do it," I keep telling myself. I had a lot of tea for breakfast (as I always do each morning) so I run to the washroom one last time before I head to the start line.

I look for the purple corral—which is the section designated for my category of runners—and wait. I'm in the second last corral, way behind the semiprofessional and elite runners who line up first. There are probably 15,000 runners ahead of me, which means I'll be waiting to get to the start line even after the start gun fires. All of the waiting is killing me! I've done what seems like an eternity of waiting this year. I'm ready to *start,* dammit!

I'm pumped. It's race day; I'm about to *do this. At last.* I can't believe this moment is actually here. Months and months of slow recovery, gruelling training over the summer and fall, and many nights of lying awake wondering: Am I actually going to be able to *do* this?

The butterflies in my stomach are fluttering so furiously that my impulse is to just bolt when I hear the start gun. I have to remind myself, if I do that and run very fast right at the start, I'll expend all of my energy and won't be able to finish the long haul. I have to pace myself so I can finish strong.

Funny—this is maybe a pattern in my life. Pacing myself and taking my time does not come naturally. I want everything right here, right *now.* I silently wonder why I chose a half-marathon as my third recovery goal. Maybe I should have chosen sprinting! The irony of it all is not lost on me. Dina in a marathon? This is a girl who moves so fast through life, she barely gives herself the opportunity to actually live it. The fact that I'm participating in an event that requires patience is a complete oxymoron.

The starting gun fires. My heart skips a beat and I jump. As I suspected, I'll have to wait for the runners in front of me to get going, so the starting line is still a good five or ten minutes away.

I hear the din of the spectator crowd getting louder as I move forward. I must be getting close to the starting line. Suddenly, I hear someone call out my name.

"Go, Dina! You can do it, Dina! Go, go, go!" they cheer.

Wait ... Do they mean me? No, it can't be.

It dawns on me: these people must have read about me in the newspaper or heard me on the radio. A couple of weeks ago, I was approached by the *Toronto Star* (a major newspaper in Toronto). They wanted to write a story about me, my stroke, my road to recovery, and also my experience training for the marathon.

On Thursday, October 17, 2013, the *Toronto Star* article came out and I made the front page! I really don't understand all the fuss but I will admit, it's pretty cool to see an article about yourself in a well-regarded newspaper.

That same day, I got a call from a producer for a popular radio show. Apparently, the host read the *Toronto Star* article and wanted to have me on his show as well as wish me good luck before the big day. Again, I'm quite baffled as to why someone would want to have me on their show, but I think I may have been bitten by the attention bug, so I agreed. I'm kinda loving this!

Now, I have complete strangers cheering me on from the sidelines. It occurs to me—all of these people have read about me, or heard me talk about my three post-stroke goals. I swallow a pang of fear: now they *all* expect me to finish this race. I'm still not 100% positive I can do this! What if I fail? Everyone will be watching me. They'll be so disappointed. More important, I will be so fucking humiliated.

I recognize a girlfriend from high school in the crowd and she is holding a huge purple sign that reads, "You've GOT this, Dina! We love you!"

As I continue to run, I spot a few more signs. "See you at the finish line, Dina!" "One step at a time Dina—you can DO IT!" All of this love and support makes me forget about my fears. I just want to keep running! My legs are exhausted but they keep on going; it's like the positive energy from the crowd is carrying me.

I *have* to finish. I just *have to.*

I see the marker that indicates only one more kilometre to go and hear the faint sound of drums and cheering ahead of me. I'm almost there!

The sounds get louder and I see Nathan Phillips Square and City Hall. There are hundreds and hundreds of people surrounding the barricades cheering and whistling. I can't feel my legs at this point. I think I'm running faster than I ever have. My legs have a mind of their own, and they have decided they are not going to let me down. *I am going to make it.*

I feel myself speeding up. This is it: now I can finally sprint. I'm allowed. I've taken my time, I've been patient, I've been slow and steady—but now I'm ready to fly. With every step, I feel myself getting farther and farther away from the stroke. It's like I see my life ahead of me, and I want to start really *living it,* as soon as possible!

Before I realize it, I cross the finish line and collapse into the arms of a stranger. I don't even bother to look up at this person as I just let loose crying. I can barely catch my breath between sobs. I've never cried so hard. I've held back for months, trying to be strong, trying not to show anyone how absolutely fucking terrified I am. I didn't want anyone to think I was a fraud: pretending to be fierce and driven, but really just a scared little girl on this inside.

My eyes are hazy and clouded with tears, and when I finally look up, I see that the person who is holding me is a guy I dated briefly over the summer, Greg. My legs are shaking and wobbly, but Greg holds me firmly. I know he won't let me fall. It's truly amazing who will show up for you when you least expect it. I went on a few dates with this guy and thought nothing of it. In fact, I was always too embarrassed to talk to him about my stroke. I thought it would make me look unattractive and guys would be scared of all the "baggage" that comes with me. But here he is, and he's here just for me, and he's proud of me. I hug him and thank him, and I mean it from the bottom of my heart.

The crowds are mind-boggling and I desperately search the sea of people for my family. Where are they? This is the moment I've been waiting for! The moment when I cross the finish line and see them all there waiting for me! When I imagine my future, I still have no idea what I want, or what my life should, or will look like. But I know one thing for certain: my family is there with me. Always, and forever.

I finally spot Mom, Dad, Yas, Aunty Latha and Aunty Katy. The pride on all their faces is overwhelming. They've all seen me complete many half-marathons, but this one is different. Mom is crying, Dad has his camera out (and I suspect he is hiding his tears behind the lens), and Yas is just whooping it up and clapping for me. I find one last hidden reserve of strength and run over to them as fast as I can.

We all hug. I'm the happiest I've ever been, in my life. I love these people so damn much! I think I'm the luckiest person on face of the earth.

As we huddle there in an embrace, I picture my checklist in my head, and mark off my third post-stroke goal. Done. I did it. I proved to myself that I am the same person I was before the stroke. I haven't *lost* anything. In fact, I'm probably stronger. I realize how remarkable and resilient our minds and bodies can be, and for the first time ever: I know that no matter what happens to me, I *will* be *okay*. Even if that countdown clock keeps ticking in my mind and I never, *ever* catch up, at least I'm alive.

And I'm ready, more than ever, *to really live.*

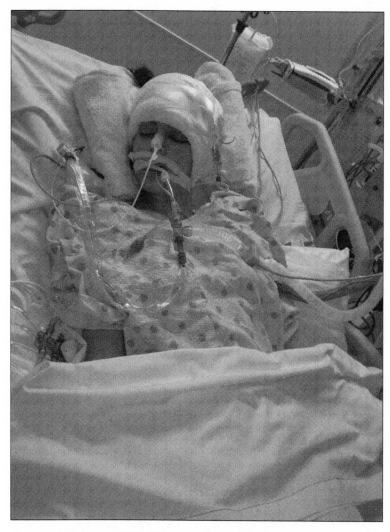

January 2013: After emergency brain surgery

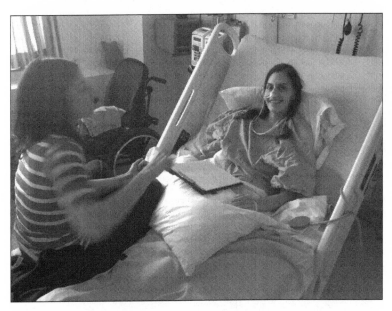

January 2013: Me and Yas at Toronto Western Hospital

**April 2013: Goal 1—Attending Yasmin's
MBA Graduation Ceremony**

July 2, 2013: Goal 2—Celebrating my parents' 35th wedding anniversary

**October 20, 2013: Goal 3—Scotiabank
half-marathon (Toronto)**

EPILOGUE

OCTOBER 2017

WHEN I FIRST SAT DOWN to write this book, I thought it would be all about inspiring others to conquer any challenge they faced. I thought it would be all about my successful and "against all odds" survival from a stroke and brain surgery. I'd look like superwoman AND be helping others, total bonus!

I scoffed when people told me that it would be an emotional experience and I'd have to share moments of my life that were private. Pish-posh, I thought.

I've never really done "emotional," and while it is true that during the stroke I was reduced to an adult with childlike functionality, that didn't seem to matter. I did a duathlon seven months after my stroke and my seventh half-marathon 10 months after my stroke! This makes me look good so puhleeze ... no emotional crap here! I'll gloss over those moments with ease and panache!

I quickly had to face facts: I was naïve and "those people" were right. The past year of writing this memoir has been the most uncomfortable, emotionally painful experience for me because I was forced to be brutally honest with myself. I had to stop doing what I always did which was to brush anything that didn't paint me in a strong, perfect light, under the rug.

On one of our first "book unravelling" sessions, Erin asked me "Dina, do you love yourself?" As I squirmed in my chair, I hesitated for a few seconds while my eyes darted around the room as I wasn't sure what to say. I quickly said, "Yeah ... sure I do. I've done many cool things and accomplished a lot. Yeah, sure I love myself ... Yeah, sure."

I tried to sound confident but I had NO idea of not only why she was asking me this question but what it really meant. "Self-love" seemed like some airy-fairy concept to me. Utter nonsense.

I always thought I was this strong invincible woman. All that mattered was checking off goals and accomplishments. I had heard the words "vulnerable," "self-love," "being open," "raw," but that's all they were – just words. It was all foreign language mumbo-jumbo talk as far as I was concerned, and someone as strong as I was didn't have any time for it.

I didn't realize this "strong" front I always put on was actually masking the shame I felt for being anorexic and the hatred I had for myself.

It never dawned on me that for the past dozen or so years, I was in a battle with myself. The stupid weakling who allowed herself to be anorexic and the new strong Dina—the one who would kick ass at anything that stood in her way.

I fell in love with anything that gave me the opportunity to challenge myself so I could give one extra point to strong Dina. The more difficult the better!

It's as if weak anorexic Dina and strong Dina were in a boxing ring and each activity (training for a half-marathon), move (doing grad school in London and Paris), or event (getting a job and negotiating a higher than expected salary) was as if I was sucker-punching weak Dina.

It became apparent that much of the anger, shame, and lack of love for myself resulted from not acknowledging and sharing the areas of my life I was embarrassed about. I chose to brush everything that wasn't perfect under the rug and never speak about it.

I realize now that was a mistake. I never realized how much healing happens when you share and allow yourself to be vulnerable.

Writing this book was the hardest thing I have ever done. Harder than running a half-marathon or moving across the world by myself. It's been harder than any of the things I've done to prove to myself that I was strong.

The process of uncovering all of my past that I have kept hidden for so long forced me to acknowledge and actually understand my behaviours today and what is not working. It's never easy to admit to being wrong and see the need for change. Even though I have been doing the same thing for 15 years, it doesn't make it right or a healthy way to be living.

It's uncomfortable to expose the parts of myself that I did not love. I am now slowly understanding the concept of loving myself and letting go of my need to control everything. However, I've just barely grasped them. It requires constant reinforcement every single day.

There is a lot of work I need to do. Trying to undo the way I have thought of myself and treated myself over 20 years is not miraculously cured overnight. These things do not come naturally to me and therefore require a lot of work on a daily basis. There are sticky notes all over my desk and walls, reminding me to "Trust your gut," "Believe in yourself," and "You've got this!" I have notes in my Google calendar to remind me of the daily progress I am making with regards to binge eating. Yesterday's note said "Day 221—Woohoo! Be SO PROUD!"

It takes SO much energy each day to not revert to my "normal" tendencies. It is easy to want to do what I've always done. I feel like I'm on this emotional rollercoaster where I have no clue (or control) of how I will feel each day. Some days I am so frustrated at not learning these things 15 years ago and how I should have known better. I have to resist the urge to beat myself up.

There are days where I'm so grateful and feel like I'm on a high. There are others when I burst into tears because I realize I do actually want to live. There are often times I am so exhausted by all these new "learnings" that have come about. And there are others where I become sad and sombre because one small thing will trigger so many painful memories I hid. I don't know when this emotional roller coaster will stop and I will be able to get off this ride, and feel I have fully healed and forgiven myself.

I may have survived three brushes with death, but that seems easy in comparison to what I face now. I started off wanting to be superwoman. Now, I'd just love to continue building the emotional strength required to continue on this new path of loving myself, being kind to myself, and being human.